D1187098

GRANDMA'S RECIPES

Compiled by
Ray and Elsie Hoover and family

Stratford, WI

1st Printing January, 2003
2nd Printing October, 2003

LITTLE MOUNTAIN PRINTING
4A Bordner Road
Richland, PA 17087

ISBN 0-9718456-1-1

We dedicate this book
to our parents
and all our aunts and uncles
who learned the art of cooking from
Grandma and passed it on to
their children and
grandchildren.

Introduction and Acknowledgments

Ray and I bought my Grandma Horst's collection of recipes at her disbursement sale. At the time we toyed with the idea of making a cookbook of older recipes. Six years later, at Ray's Grandpa and Grandma Hoover's sale, we bought Grandma Hoover's recipe collection. With recipes from both Grandmas we had a good selection of recipes from the 20's, 30's and 40's and decided to make a cookbook. Both Grandma Horst and Grandma Hoover had a few larger cookbooks, but many of the recipes came from recipe booklets printed by companies selling staples like flour, yeast, or baking powder. Each grandma also had a notebook or two filled with handwritten recipes gleaned from family and friends. Unfortunately many of their recipes were not written down.

Although the majority of the recipes come from Grandma Horst and Grandma Hoover we did find some of Ray's Grandma Martin's and my Grandma Kulp's recipes still in circulation. We are grateful to our many aunts and uncles who so freely contributed recipes and memories for this cookbook. A special thanks to my parents, Isaac and Florence Kulp and Ray's parents, David and Miriam Hoover, for their patience in answering questions and their diligence in ferreting out information.

The picture on the cover is Grandma Hoover. The old recipes on the divider pages come from two very old, yellowed, coverless cookbooks Grandma Horst had in her possession. Many of the longer quotes used throughout the book come from these old cookbooks. We found the remaining quotes in their various other cookbooks and booklets.

In the back of the book you will find histories of all four grandmas. Though we recorded events only in their lives, its a story common to thousands of depression era farm women. Like many women, they labored constantly to feed a house-full of growing children. Along with their regular cooking, they made bread, butter and cottage cheese. Some of them made their own noodles, some made cheese.

They sewed dresses out of floral feed bags, cared for large gardens and canned hundreds of jars of fruits, vegetables and meat. They also cooked for threshing crews, helped butcher when the weather turned cold and made their own soap.

Our Grandmas not only taught their children to work, but to enjoy life and, I believe, to love the Lord. Though unknown to them their influence continues today. We are happy to present to you this basic but practical cookbook of Grandma's recipes.

Elsie Hoover
2002

GENERAL INFORMATION
FROM GRANDMA'S COOKBOOKS

I. Oven Temperatures

Slow Oven	250-325°
Moderately Slow Oven	326-349°
Moderate Oven	350-375°
Moderately Hot Oven	376-399°
Hot Oven	400-449°
Quick Oven	450-500°
Very Hot Oven	501-575°

II. Equivalents and Measures

1. Equivalents of Capacity

3	Teaspoons	=1 Tablespoon
1/2	Fluid Ounce	=1 Tablespoon
16	Tablespoons	=1 Cup
2	Gills	=1 Cup
1/2	Liquid Pint	=1 Cup
8	Fluid Ounces	=1 Cup
16	Fluid Ounces	=2 Cups
1	Liquid Pint	=2 Cups

2. Dry Measure Equivalents

2	Pints	=1 Quart
8	Quarts	=1 Peck
4	Pecks	=1 Bushel
36	Bushels	=1 Chaldron

3. Liquid Measure Equivalents

4	Gills	=1 Pint
2	Pints	=1 Quart
4	Quarts	=1 Gallon
31 1/2	Gallons	=1 Barrel
2	Barrels	=1 Hogshead

4. Long Measure Equivalents

12	Inches	=1 Foot
3	Feet	=1 Yard
5 1/2	Yards	=1 Rod
40	Rods	=1 Furlong
8	Furlongs	=1 Mile
3	Miles	=1 League

5. Square Measure Equivalents

144	Square Inches	=1 Sq. Ft.
9	Square Feet	=1 Sq. Yd.
30 1/4	Square Yards	=1 Sq. Rod
40	Square Rods	=1 Rood
4	Roods	=1 Acre
640	Acres	=1 Sq. Mile

6. Cloth Measure Equivalents

2 1/4	Inches	=1 Nail
4	Nails	=1 Quarter
4	Quarters	=1 Yard

7. Miscellaneous Equivalents

2	T. butter	=1 oz.
2	c. butter	=1 lb.
1/4	c. flour	=1 oz.
4	c. flour	=1 lb.
2	c. white sugar	=1 lb.
3 1/2	c. powdered sugar	=1 lb.
2	c. lard	=1 lb.
2 2/3	c. cornmeal	=1 lb.
2 1/2	c. dry navy beans	=1 lb.
2	c. rice	=1 lb.
2 2/3	c. brown sugar	=1 lb.
	butter the size of an egg	=1/4 c.

SLIPPERY-ELM BARK TEA

Break the bark into bits, pour
boiling water over it, cover and let
it infuse until cold. Sweeten, ice and
take for summer disorders, or add lemon
juice and drink for a bad cold.

BEEF TEA

One pound of lean beef, cut into small pieces.
Put into a jar without a drop of water; cover
tightly, and set in a pot of cold water. Heat
gradually to a boil, and continue this steadily
for three or four hours, until the meat is like
white rags, and the juice is all drawn out.
Season with salt to taste, and, when
cold, skim.

COCOA

Our grandmas used unpasteurized milk so they heated their cocoa to scald. This is not necessary if you use pasteurized milk.

1/4 c. cocoa	1/2 c. water
1/3 c. sugar	5 1/2 c. milk
1/8 tsp. salt	1/2 tsp. vanilla

Mix cocoa, sugar and salt in a heavy saucepan. Add water and stir until smooth. Cook 3 minutes. Add milk. Heat thoroughly. Add vanilla and beat with egg beater. Serve hot. Top each serving with a marshmallow or a teaspoon of whipped cream.

HOT COCOA FOR FIFTY

3 c. cocoa	2 qt. boiling water
2 1/2 c. sugar	2 1/2 gal. milk
1 tsp. salt	1 T. vanilla

Mix cocoa, sugar and salt. Add to boiling water and bring to a boil, stirring occasionally. Add milk and heat to desired temperature. Do not boil. Add vanilla.

COFFEE COCOA

1/2 c. hot coffee	1/4 tsp. vanilla
1/2 c. hot cocoa	

Mix. Garnish with whipped cream if desired.

CAFÉ AU LAIT

1/2 c. hot coffee	1/2 c. hot milk

Stir. Serve hot.

COFFEE CREAM PUNCH

1 qt. coffee	1 qt. whipping cream
1 qt. chocolate ice cream	1/4 tsp. almond flavoring

Chill coffee and pour into punch bowl. Add ice cream and stir until partially melted. Whip cream and almond flavoring until stiff. Place cream on coffee punch. Sprinkle lightly with nutmeg if desired.

CREAM FLOAT

1 qt. ginger ale   1 pt. pineapple ice cream

Pour ginger ale into six tall glasses. Add several spoonfuls of ice cream to each one.

LEMONADE

2 qt. water	1 c. lemon juice
1 1/2 c. sugar	

Boil sugar and water until sugar dissolves. Add lemon juice. Cool and serve with ice.

ORANGEADE

1 qt. hot water	4 oranges, juiced or 1 1/2 c.
1/2 c. sugar	orange juice
	1 lemon or 3 T. lemon juice

Dissolve sugar in hot water. Add juice and stir well. Chill.

GRAPEADE

1 qt. grape juice	2 c. water
1 c. grapefruit juice	1/3 c. sugar or to taste

Combine ingredients, stirring well. Chill.

GRAPE PINEAPPLE DRINK

1 qt. grape juice

1 qt. unsweetened pineapple juice

Fill tall glasses with crushed ice. Fill each glass to the top with grape juice and pineapple juice by pouring juices simultaneously—one on each side of the glass—over the ice. The juices should be cold. Serve at once with a long spoon before juices blend. Other light and dark juices can be used to accomplish a two-tone effect.

GRAPE GINGER

1 c. grape juice

1 qt. ginger ale

Blend well and serve at once.

WHITE GRAPE PUNCH

1 large grapefruit
1 orange
1 qt. white grape juice

2 c. water
1/3 c. sugar or to taste
1 qt. ginger ale

Rub pulp of grapefruit and orange through a sieve. Mix with grape juice and water. Add sugar and stir well. Chill. When ready to serve add ginger ale.

Variation for **PLAIN WHITE GRAPE PUNCH:** Use only white grape juice and ginger ale. Chill and serve with ice.

LIGHT PUNCH

2 c. water
1/2 c. sugar
1 c. pineapple juice

3/4 c. lemon juice
1 qt. ginger ale

Boil water and sugar for several minutes. Cool. Add juices. Stir and chill thoroughly. Add ginger ale just before serving.

CHERRY PUNCH

6 oz. cherry gelatin
1 qt. hot water
1/2 c. sugar
1/8 tsp. salt

6 c. water
3/4 c. lemon juice
1 qt. ginger ale

Dissolve gelatin in hot water. Add sugar and salt and stir until dissolved
Add water and lemon juice. Chill. Add ginger ale.

*Sugar syrup used as a base for fruit drinks is made by boiling equal amounts of sugar
and water for five minutes. Refrigerate until needed. If thicker, sweeter syrup is
desired use twice as much sugar as water.*

RUBY FRUIT PUNCH

1 1/2 c. sugar
2 c. boiling water
3 c. cranberry juice
1/3 c. lemon juice

2 c. orange juice
1 qt. ginger ale
thin lemon slices
thin orange slices

Dissolve sugar in boiling water. Add juices. Chill. Just before serving
pour in a punch bowl and add ginger ale and citrus slices.

SPICED CIDER PUNCH

3 c. water
1 c. sugar
1/2 tsp. nutmeg
2 c. grape juice

3 c. cider
4 c. ginger ale
3 thinly-sliced lemons

Boil water, sugar and nutmeg for 5 minutes. Cool. Add other
ingredients. Put in a punch bowl with ice cubes.

SPICED PINEAPPLE DRINK

2 c. water
3 c. sugar
3 cinnamon sticks

1 tsp. whole cloves
2 qt. pineapple juice

Combine water, sugar, cinnamon sticks and cloves. Boil 10 minutes.
Strain and mix with pineapple juice. Chill and pour over ice cubes.

PINEAPPLE ORANGE DRINK

3 c. sugar
1 qt. water
1 qt. pineapple juice
2 c. orange juice

2 c. crushed pineapple
1/2 c. maraschino cherries
4 oranges

Mix sugar and water and boil 5 minutes. Cool. Add juices, pineapple
and cherries. Slice oranges very thin. Remove seeds but not rinds. Cut
circular slices in half and add to punch. When ready to serve, pour over
a block of ice in a punch bowl.

FRUIT NECTAR

1 1/4 c. sugar
2 c. water
1 1/2 c. orange juice
1 c. pineapple juice

1 c. grapefruit juice
1/4 c. lemon juice
1 qt. ice water

Boil sugar and 2 c. water for 5 minutes. Cool and add fruit juices and
ice water. Serve cold.

"The best of all beverages is water. Nothing approaches water as a beverage."

NOTES

GRANDMA'S

BROWN CHEESE CRACKERS

Split common crackers; spread with
cheese; place in oven and brown. Serve hot.

PUFFED CRACKERS

Split common crackers; cover with cold
water and let stand five minutes. Sprinkle
with grated cheese, dot with butter; place in
hot oven until puffed and brown.

APPETIZERS

Appetizers, according to one source, are the small touch that turn an ordinary meal into a party affair. If the lack of appetizer recipes found in their cookbook collections is any indication, our Grandmas didn't care much about turning meals into parties. They spent their energy getting a lot of food on the table rather than spending time making attractive little bits that only teased the appetites. Though our Grandmas probably never served appetizers, we are including a few of the more practical ones from their recipe books.

STUFFED CUCUMBER

1 cucumber	2 T. chopped onion
salt	pepper
1/2 c. cream cheese	1 tsp. Worcestershire sauce
1/4 c. green pepper	

Peel cucumber. Cut in half lengthwise. Dig out seeds and some pulp. Sprinkle with salt. Mix cream cheese, green pepper and onion. Season with Worcestershire sauce and pepper. Pack mixture into cucumber. Chill. Cut into 3/4-inch pieces.

STUFFED CELERY I

chopped, hard-cooked eggs	chopped celery
chopped olives	mayonnaise
chopped pimiento	celery stalks

Combine eggs, olives, pimiento and chopped celery. Add enough mayonnaise to hold it together. Fill celery stalks. Cut stalks into 2-inch lengths. Chill.

"Some appetizers are served almost entirely as an introduction to meals. Others, however, are widely used as snacks late at night or as an accompaniment to beverages."

STUFFED CELERY II

cream cheese
chopped nuts

celery stalks

Combine cream cheese and chopped nuts. Fill celery stalks and cut int
2-inch lengths. Chill.

CELERY AND CHEESE BALLS

chopped celery
cream cheese
salt

pepper
chopped parsley

Mix equal parts of chopped celery and cream cheese. Season with sa
and pepper. Mold into small balls and roll in chopped parsley.

STUFFED TOMATOES

small tomatoes
chopped ham

chopped celery
mayonnaise

Cut stem end off tomatoes. Scoop out centers and turn upside dowr
Drain thoroughly. Combine chopped ham, chopped celery an
mayonnaise. Stuff tomatoes. Flaked tuna may be used in place of han

ONIONS IN BLANKETS

sliced, uncooked bacon

small pickled onions

Wrap bacon slices around onions. Fasten with toothpicks. Broil at hig
heat, turning occasionally, until bacon is crisp.

Hors-d'euvres (ôr'durv') is the French term for relish.

CHEESE STUFFED OLIVES

olives   sliced, uncooked bacon
cheese

Remove pimiento from olives. Fill with cheese. Wrap a slice of bacon around each olive. Bake at 425° until bacon is crisp. Serve on cracker or toast rounds.

CHEESE AND BEEF ROLLS

thinly sliced bread   cheese slices
mayonnaise   dried beef

Spread small squares of bread with mayonnaise. Add a slice of cheese. Top with dried beef. Roll. Fasten with toothpicks. Broil until bread is well-browned on both sides.

CANAPÉS

Cut thin slices of white, wheat or rye bread. Cut into small rounds, triangles, diamonds, squares, half-moons or oblongs. Toast or fry in butter until delicately browned on one side. Spread the other side. Garnish with peppers, radishes, cucumbers, olives, pickles, bacon, etc.

JELLY CANAPÉS

Place tiny mounds of brightly colored jellies on each piece of bread. Use two or more flavors and colors for each canapé. Jelly can also be mixed with cream cheese.

CHEESE AND OLIVE CANAPÉS

grated cheese   olives
butter   toast or crackers

Place grated cheese that has been creamed with butter on pieces of toast or crackers. Garnish with a narrow border of chopped olives or pickles.

CHEESE AND ONION CANAPÉS

grated cheese
minced onion

mustard
bread or crackers

Combine grated cheese, minced onion and mustard. Spread on toasted bread shapes or crackers.

BACON AND EGG CANAPÉS

crisp bacon
hard cooked eggs

mayonnaise
bread or crackers

Combine crisp bacon pieces and hard-cooked egg with enough mayonnaise to moisten. Place on bread shapes or crackers.

HAM AND CELERY CANAPÉS

minced ham
chopped celery

mayonnaise
bread or crackers

Combine minced ham and chopped celery with enough mayonnaise to moisten. Spoon onto toasted bread rounds or crackers.

DRIED BEEF AND CREAM CHEESE CANAPÉS

dried beef
cream cheese

bread or toast

Mix chopped dried beef with cream cheese. Place on toasted bread or crackers.

GRANDMA'S

TO KEEP EGGS

To four quarts air-slacked
lime, put two tablespoonfuls cream
tartar, two of salt, and four quarts
cold water. Put fresh eggs into a stone
jar, and pour this mixture over them. This
will keep nine dozen, and if fresh when laid
down, they will keep many months. If the
water settles away, so as to leave the upper
layer uncovered, add more water. Cover
close, and keep in a cool place.

EGGS

SCRAMBLED EGGS

6 eggs
1/4 c. milk
3/4 tsp. salt

1/8 tsp. pepper
1 T. butter

Beat eggs slightly. Add milk, salt and pepper. Heat butter in frying pan and add eggs. Cook slowly, stirring constantly, until creamy. Serve at once. Add 1/4 c. dried beef, cooked chopped ham or crisp bacon along with eggs if desired. Sautéed mushrooms may be added.

SCRAMBLED EGGS WITH ONIONS

2 T. butter
1/4 c. finely-chopped onions
2 T. finely-chopped green
    pepper

6 eggs
1/4 c. milk
1 tsp. salt
1/8 tsp. pepper

Heat butter. Add onions and pepper. Cook about 5 minutes. Combine remaining ingredients and add. Stir and cook until done.

FRIED EGGS WITH ONIONS

2 T. butter
small onion, finely chopped

5 or 6 eggs
salt and pepper

Melt butter in frying pan. Sauté onions until light brown. Remove onions and fry eggs in same fat. Sprinkle eggs with salt and pepper. Fry until whites are set. For a harder yolk fry on both sides. Serve with onions.

"There are many wonderful things in the world to think about—and if we would fill our minds with these instead of the trash that is accumulated, we would be much happier."
-a saying Grandma Kulp copied into her note book

POACHED EGGS

Fill frying pan 2/3 full of water. Add 1/2 tsp. salt to every quart c water used. Bring to a boil. Break eggs onto a saucer and carefully sli into water. There should be sufficient water to cover eggs. Remov from heat and cover. Let stand about 5 minutes or until whites of egg are firm and yolks covered with a thin white film. Serve at once o buttered toast. If desired, use milk instead of water and pour milk and little butter over eggs when serving.

BAKED EGGS

6 slices toasted bread	1/8 tsp. pepper
6 eggs	1 T. butter
3/4 tsp. salt	1/2 c. milk

Cut a small circle out of each piece of bread. Place in a greased cak pan. Break eggs into the center of the bread. Sprinkle with salt an pepper. Dot with butter. Pour milk over eggs. Bake at 350° for 2 minutes or until eggs have set.

OMELET

6 large eggs	1/8 tsp. pepper
1/3 c. milk	1 T. butter
3/4 tsp. salt	

Beat eggs. Add milk, salt and pepper and mix well. Melt butter in frying pan and pour in egg mixture. Cover. Cook over low heat withou turning until firm to the touch and brown on the bottom. Crease, bu don't cut, omelet. Fold and turn out on platter. If desired, sprinkle hal of the omelet with 1/3 c. cooked, chopped ham or bacon, or grate cheese.

"If no paste is available, the white of an egg makes an excellent adhesive."

FLUFFY OMELET

6 eggs, separated
6 T. milk or water
3/4 tsp. salt

1/8 tsp. pepper
1 T. butter

Beat egg yolks until thick. Add milk or water, salt and pepper. Mix well. Beat egg whites until stiff. Fold lightly into yolks. Melt butter in an iron frying pan or an omelet pan. Pour in egg mixture and spread evenly. Cook over a slow fire (low heat) until well puffed and slightly brown on the bottom. Put pan under a low broiler flame 2-3 minutes or complete the cooking process by placing in a 375° oven approximately 8 minutes. Or, if preferred, steam top of eggs by covering the pan while cooking. Crease omelet and fold. Serve at once.

SPANISH OMELET

2 T. butter
3 T. chopped green peppers
3 T. chopped onion
1/4 c. chopped mushrooms
1 tomato, peeled and chopped

1/4 tsp. salt
6 eggs
1/4 c. milk
3/4 tsp. salt
1/8 tsp. red pepper

Melt 1 T. butter in frying pan. Add green pepper and onion; cook until soft. Add mushrooms and tomato and 1/4 tsp. salt and heat through. Melt remaining butter in another pan and pour in well mixed eggs, milk and seasoning. Cover. Fry slowly, without turning, until eggs are set and slightly brown on the bottom. Pour vegetable mixture over half of omelet. Add 1/2 c. shredded cheese if desired. Fold omelet. Serve.

ROLLED EGGS

12 eggs
1 c. milk
1 T. flour

1 1/2 tsp. salt
1/2 tsp. pepper
1 T. butter

Beat together all but butter. Melt butter in a 13x9 pan. Add eggs. Bake until set. Roll and slice. Cheese may be added before rolling.

HAM AND EGG SANDWICHES

3 beaten eggs
1 c. chopped, cooked ham
1 T. chopped onion

1/4 tsp. salt
1/8 tsp. pepper
buttered toast

Combine ingredients. Pour as pancakes, the proper size for sandwiches, onto a hot, greased griddle. Brown well on both sides. Place between slices of buttered toast.

BREAKFAST HAM AND CHEESE SANDWICHES

12 slices buttered bread
6 slices cooked ham
6 slices cheese

3/4 c. milk
1 beaten egg
1/4 tsp. salt

Arrange one slice ham and cheese on one slice of buttered bread. Top with another slice of buttered bread. Make six sandwiches. Mix milk, egg and salt. Briefly dip each sandwich into milk mixture. Cook on a hot, greased griddle, browning both sides. Serve hot.

HAM AND CHEESE SOUFFLÉ

1/4 c. butter
1 onion, finely-chopped
1/4 c. flour
1/2 tsp. salt
1/8 tsp. pepper

1 1/2 c. milk
1 c. grated cheese
3/4 c. chopped, cooked ham
4 eggs, separated

Melt butter and fry onion until tender, not brown. Add flour, salt and pepper and mix well. Slowly add milk. Bring to a boil, stirring constantly. Stir in cheese. Remove from heat. Add ham and well-beaten egg yolks. Fold in stiffly beaten egg whites. Pour in a buttered baking dish. Bake at 350° for 40 minutes. Serve at once from baking dish.

"Allow 1/8 tsp. salt for each egg used."

BOILED EGGS

SOFT-BOILED...................... Boil—3 minutes

MEDIUM-BOILED................ Boil—5 minutes

HARD-BOILED.................... Boil Over Low Heat—20 minutes (Ten minutes at a full boil will hard cook eggs but whites are tougher.)

CREAMED EGGS WITH ONION

2 T. butter
2 T. chopped onion
1 T. fresh parsley, chopped
1/4 c. flour
1 tsp. salt

1/8 tsp. pepper
2 c. milk
4 hard-cooked eggs, sliced or chopped

Melt butter in pan. Sauté onion and parsley. Stir in flour, salt and pepper. Add milk; bring to a boil, stirring constantly. Add eggs and heat through. Serve on buttered toast.

SCALLOPED EGGS AU GRATIN

1/4 c. butter
1/4 c. flour
1 tsp. salt
1/8 tsp. pepper
2 c. milk

1/2 c. grated cheese
6 hard-cooked eggs
1 1/2 c. buttered bread or cracker crumbs

Melt butter. Mix in flour, salt and pepper until smooth. Slowly add milk. Bring to a boil, stirring constantly. Stir in cheese. Slice eggs, sprinkle with salt. Put 1/3 of crumbs in a greased baking dish. Add half of eggs then half of sauce. Repeat. Sprinkle remaining crumbs on top. Bake at 350° approximately 20 minutes. Layers of chopped cooked ham or other cooked meat can be added.

STUFFED EGGS

6 hard-cooked eggs	1 tsp. mustard
2 T. mayonnaise	1/2 tsp. salt
2 tsp. vinegar	1/8 tsp. pepper

Cut eggs in half lengthwise. Remove and mash yolks. Add remaining ingredients and mix thoroughly. Pile lightly into egg whites. If desired sprinkle with paprika or garnish with fresh parsley.

Variation for **OLIVE STUFFED EGGS:** Add 2 T. finely chopped olives.

Variation for **GREEN PEPPER STUFFED EGGS:** Add 2 T finely-chopped green peppers.

BACON STUFFED EGGS

6 hard-cooked eggs	1 tsp. Worcestershire sauce
2 T. diced, crisp bacon	1 tsp. mustard
2 T. mayonnaise	1/8 tsp. pepper

Cut eggs in half length-wise. Remove and mash yolks. Add remaining ingredients. Refill egg whites with mixture.

ONION MUSHROOM STUFFED EGGS

6 hard-cooked eggs	1/2 tsp. salt
1 T. butter	1/8 tsp. pepper
1/4 c. chopped mushrooms	catsup
2 T. finely chopped ham	

Cut eggs in half lengthwise and remove and mash yolks. Saute mushrooms and onions in butter. Add to yolks. Add salt, pepper and enough catsup to moisten.

GRANDMA'S

CORN MEAL

Put four quarts fresh water in a
kettle to boil, salt to taste; when it
begins to boil stir in one and a half quarts
meal, letting it sift through the fingers
slowly to prevent lumps, adding it a little
faster at the last, until as thick as can be
conveniently stirred with one hand; set in the
oven in the kettle, (or take out into a pan), bake
an hour, and it will be thoroughly cooked. It
takes corn meal so long to cook thoroughly that it
is very difficult to boil it until done without
burning. Excellent for frying when cold. Use a
hard wood paddle, two feet long, with a blade
two inches long, to stir with. The thorough
cooking and baking in oven afterwards takes
away all the raw taste that mush is apt
to have, and adds much to its
sweetness and delicious
flavor.

CEREALS

GRAPE NUTS

This was a common breakfast cereal probably all the grandmas made.

8 c. whole wheat flour   2 tsp. soda
2 c. brown sugar   4 c. buttermilk or sour milk
2 tsp. salt

Combine dry ingredients. Mix well. Add milk. Beat until smooth. Spread in two greased 13x9-inch cake pans. Bake at 350° approximately 45 minutes. Cool thoroughly. Crumble by hand or cut into strips and put through a food chopper or grinder. Place crumbs on cookie sheets, cake pans or in a big bowl. Put in the oven at 250°. Stir occasionally. Bake until grape nuts are completely dry and crisp.

OATMEAL

4 c. water   2 c. oatmeal
1 tsp. salt

Add oatmeal to boiling salted water, stirring constantly. Boil five minutes. Cover and let stand five minutes. If using quick oatmeal boil one minute. One cup cooked raisins may be added with the oatmeal.

FRIED OATMEAL

Press cooked oatmeal into a cake pan 1/2-inch thick. Cool until firm. Cut into squares. Fry in butter until browned, turning once. Serve with syrup.

GRANDMA MARTIN'S
OATMEAL GRAVY

3 c. milk   1/2 c. sugar
1/2-3/4 c. dry oatmeal   1 tsp. salt

Combine ingredients and bring to a boil. Simmer three minutes. Serve on fried potatoes or fried cornmeal mush.

CORNMEAL MUSH

*Our Grandmas often served cornmeal mush for supper in the evening makin
enough so they could have fried cornmeal mush for breakfast the next morning*

3 c. water
1 c. cornmeal

1 c. cold water or milk
1 tsp. salt

Bring water to a boil. Combine remaining ingredients and pour int
boiling water, stirring constantly. Bring to a boil. Reduce heat. Coo
approximately five minutes, stirring frequently. Eat warm with suga
and milk. Makes approximately three cups. Slices of cornmeal mus
can also be put into a well-buttered pan and baked at 350° approximatel
20 minutes. Brush tops with melted butter.

FRIED CORNMEAL MUSH

Prepare cornmeal mush. Pour hot mush into a greased bread pan
Smooth surface of the mush. Cool overnight or until firm. Slice 1/4 t
1/2-inch thick. Fry in butter, turning once. Serve with syrup.

CRACKED WHEAT

3 c. water
3/4 tsp. salt

1 c. cracked wheat

Bring salted water to a boil. Add cracked wheat. Simmer 30 minutes
Makes approximately three cups.

*"As a rule whole or cracked cereals require four cups water to one cup cerea
flaked cereals require two cups water to one cup cereal, and the granula
cereals require four to five cups water to one cup cereal."*

CREAM OF WHEAT

4 c. water   3/4 c. cream of wheat
1 tsp. salt

Bring salted water to a boil. Stir in cream of wheat. Simmer one minute. Add raisins if desired. Let stand several minutes. Serve with milk or cream or fruit. Juice from canned fruit may be used as part of the water. Makes approximately four cups.

"Do not waste uneaten remainders of cooked cereals. Sometimes they can be used in place of some of the flour called for in bread recipes. They add bulk to meat and vegetable hashes and mixtures and can often be turned into delicious puddings."

FRIED CREAM OF WHEAT

Pour hot cooked cream of wheat into a greased bread or cake pan. Cool overnight or until firm then slice 1/4 to 1/2-inch thick. Fry in butter, turning once. Serve with butter and syrup.

BARLEY

2 1/2 c. water   1 c. barley
1/2 tsp. salt

Combine and bring to a boil. Simmer 30-40 minutes.

HOMINY GRITS

3 c. boiling water   3/4 c. hominy grits
3/4 tsp. salt

Bring water and salt to a boil. Add grits. Stir, then simmer for five minutes or to desired thickness. Makes approximately three cups.

GRANDMA MARTIN'S
HOMINY

1 gal. water	1/2 gal. dry, shelled field corn
1 T. lye	(yellow or white corn can be used)

Using caution, dissolve lye in water in a stainless steel (do not use aluminum) kettle. Add dry corn and heat to boiling. Cook until the hulls and germ easily slip away from the corn kernels. Remove from heat and drain water. Wash corn with cold water rubbing the kernels to remove germ. Rinse. Repeat the washing process until all the hulls and germ are removed and rinse water is clear. To use, boil hominy until kernels are soft. To can, fill quart jars with boiled, soft hominy, leaving two inches of headspace. Hominy can also be canned right after the washing and rinsing process; however, jars should be filled to just past half full since the kernels will expand while canning if they were not cooked and softened first. Fill jars with water, leaving 1-inch headspace. Add 1 tsp. canning salt to each quart jar. Process quarts at 10 lb. of pressure for 85 minutes; pints at 10 lb. pressure for 55 minutes.

HOMINY CAKES

2 c. cooked whole grain hominy	2 c. milk
	1 c. flour
2 eggs	3/4 tsp. salt

Beat eggs in milk and add to hominy. Stir in flour and salt. Fry in butter, turning once. Serve with syrup.

GRANDMA'S

MRS. BLEEKER'S WAFFLES

One quart of milk, a little sour if
possible; a piece of butter the size
of an egg; a piece of lard the same
size; four eggs. Mix well with flour enough
to make a stiff batter. If the milk is a little
sour, enough soda to cover a five-cent
piece will be sufficient to raise the waffles;
but if it is fresh a teaspoonful of soda must
be used; a teaspoonful of salt. Bake as
quickly as possible.

GRIDDLE CAKES AND WAFFLES

GRIDDLE CAKES

Though known today as pancakes, most cookbooks in Grandma's day called them griddle cakes.

2 c. flour	1 egg
4 tsp. baking powder	2 c. milk
1 tsp. salt	1/3 c. melted shortening

Combine dry ingredients. Beat egg, add milk and shortening then pour into dry ingredients; beat quickly. Using about 1/4 cup, pour batter on a hot lightly greased griddle and cook over medium heat until golden brown on the underside and bubbles appear on the topside. Turn cakes and brown on the other side. Makes eighteen, 4-inch griddle cakes.

Variation for **CINNAMON GRIDDLE CAKES:** Add 1 tsp. cinnamon.

WHEAT GRIDDLE CAKES

1 c. flour	2 T. sugar
1 c. whole wheat flour	1 egg
4 tsp. baking powder	1 3/4 c. milk
1 tsp. salt	3 T. melted shortening

Combine dry ingredients. Beat egg. Add milk and shortening, then add to dry ingredients. Mix. Bake on hot griddle. For whole wheat griddle cakes use all whole wheat flour.

RAISED WHEAT GRIDDLE CAKES

1 pkg. or 1 T. yeast	1 tsp. salt
1 c. lukewarm water	2 T. melted shortening
1 c. milk	2 eggs, well beaten
2 T. brown sugar	2 1/2 c. whole wheat flour

Dissolve yeast in water. Add milk, sugar, salt, shortening and eggs. Mix in flour, beating thoroughly to make smooth batter. Cover and let rise until light—about one hour. Stir well and fry on a hot, greased griddle. Can be mixed the night before. Cover and refrigerate.

BUCKWHEAT GRIDDLE CAKES

2 c. buckwheat flour	1 egg
5 tsp. baking powder	2 3/4 c. milk
1 tsp. salt	1/3 c. melted shortening or
2 T. sugar	cooking oil

Combine dry ingredients. Beat egg, add milk and shortening. Pour into dry ingredients. Beat quickly. Using about 1/4 cup, pour batter on lightly greased medium hot griddle. Makes approximately twenty, 4 inch griddle cakes.

RAISED BUCKWHEAT GRIDDLE CAKES

1 pkg. or 1 T. yeast	1 1/2 tsp. salt
3 T. molasses	2 c. buckwheat flour
2 1/4 c. warm water	1 c. flour
1 c. milk	

Dissolve yeast and molasses in warm water. Add milk and salt. Mix in buckwheat and white flour gradually, beating until smooth. Cover and let rise in warm place, free from draft, until light—about one hour. Stir well and fry on hot, greased griddle. Can be made the night before, if covered and refrigerated.

CORNMEAL GRIDDLE CAKES

1 c. cornmeal	1 egg
1 c. flour	2 c. milk
2 tsp. baking powder	2 T. melted shortening or
1 tsp. salt	cooking oil

Combine dry ingredients. Beat egg thoroughly and add milk and shortening. Mix liquid and dry ingredients. Bake on a hot, greased griddle.

BRAN GRIDDLE CAKES

1 c. flour	1 c. bran
1 T. sugar	1 1/2 c. milk
1/2 tsp. salt	1 egg
2 tsp. baking powder	1 T. melted shortening

Mix together flour, sugar, salt and baking powder. Add bran and milk into which egg has been beaten. Add shortening last. Beat well. Bake on hot griddle in small cakes.

OATMEAL GRIDDLE CAKES

2 1/2 c. buttermilk or sour milk	1 1/2 c. flour
2 eggs	1 T. sugar
2 T. melted butter or cooking oil	1 tsp. baking powder
2 c. oatmeal	1 tsp. soda
	1 tsp. salt

Beat eggs in milk. Add butter and oatmeal. Mix together remaining dry ingredients and add to first mixture. Don't over mix. Bake on a hot, greased griddle.

SOUR MILK GRIDDLE CAKES

2 c. flour	2 c. sour milk
1 tsp. salt	1 egg, well-beaten
1 tsp. soda	1 T. melted butter

Mix flour and salt. Dissolve soda in sour milk and add to flour. Mix in beaten-egg and melted butter. Drop onto well-greased, hot griddle; brown on both sides. Serve hot with maple syrup or jam. Sour milk can be made by putting 1 T. vinegar in a cup then filling it up with milk. Let stand several minutes.

APPLE GRIDDLE CAKES

2 c. flour	1 egg
1 T. baking powder	1 c. milk
2 T. sugar	2 T. melted butter
3/4 tsp. salt	3 tart apples, finely chopped

Combine flour, baking powder, sugar and salt. Beat egg thoroughly, then add milk and melted butter. Combine liquid and dry ingredients. Add peeled, finely-chopped apples. Bake on a hot, greased griddle. Cinnamon may be added.

BLUEBERRY GRIDDLE CAKES

1 egg	2 c. flour
2 c. milk	2 T. sugar
1/2 tsp. salt	4 tsp. baking powder
1 T. melted shortening	1 c. blueberries

Beat egg until light. Add milk, salt and shortening. Combine flour, sugar and baking powder and stir into first mixture. Add blueberries. Drop onto hot, well-greased griddle and brown on both sides.

Variation for **RAISIN GRIDDLE CAKES:** Substitute 3/4 cup raisins for blueberries.

FRENCH TOAST

1 c. milk	1/2 tsp. salt
2 eggs, slightly-beaten	6 slices bread

Combine milk, eggs and salt. Dip bread into egg mixture. Place slices of bread on a well-greased griddle. Brown on one side. Turn and brown on the other side. Serve with maple syrup or jelly.

SYRUP

4 c. sugar
2 c. water

1 tsp. maple flavor

Bring sugar and water to a boil. Stir to dissolve sugar. Remove from heat and add maple flavor.

PLAIN WAFFLES

2 c. flour
2 T. baking powder
1 tsp. salt
1 T. sugar

2 eggs
1 1/2 c. milk
1/4 c. melted butter

Combine dry ingredients. Beat eggs, add milk and butter and pour onto dry ingredients. Beat until smooth. Bake in a hot waffle iron.

Variation for **WHEAT WAFFLES:** Use 1 c. wheat flour instead of white flour.

Variation for **WHOLE WHEAT WAFFLES:** Use all whole wheat flour.

Variation for **CORNMEAL WAFFLES:** Substitute 1 cup cornmeal for one cup of flour.

CHOCOLATE WAFFLES

2 c. flour
5 tsp. baking powder
1 tsp. salt
3/4 c. sugar
1/3 c. cocoa

2 eggs
1 1/2 c. milk
1/4 c. melted shortening
1 tsp. vanilla

Combine dry ingredients. Beat eggs. Add milk, shortening and vanilla to eggs, then mix into dry ingredients. Bake in a hot waffle iron. Serve with hot syrup, whipped cream or ice cream.

GINGERBREAD WAFFLES

1 c. molasses	1 egg, well-beaten
1/3 c. butter	2 c. flour
2 tsp. soda	2 tsp. ginger
1/2 c. sour milk	1/2 tsp. salt

Bring molasses and butter to a boil. Remove from heat and mix in soda. Stir in milk then add beaten egg. Combine flour, ginger and salt, then add to molasses mixture. Mix well. Bake in a hot waffle iron. Serve hot with syrup or whipped cream.

SOUR CREAM WAFFLES

1 1/3 c. flour	1/4 c. melted shortening
1/2 tsp. salt	1 T. sugar
1 tsp. soda	1 c. sour cream
2 eggs, separated	

Combine dry ingredients. Beat egg yolks until light and foamy. Add shortening and sugar. Mix well. Add sour cream alternately with dry ingredients to egg mixture. Beat egg whites until stiff; fold in. Bake in a hot waffle iron.

APPLE CORNMEAL WAFFLES

1 1/4 c. flour	3 T. sugar
3/4 c. cornmeal	1 c. peeled, diced apples
1 T. baking powder	1 egg
1 tsp. cinnamon	1 3/4 c. milk
1/2 tsp. salt	1/4 c. butter, melted

Combine dry ingredients. Add finely chopped apples. Beat egg, add milk and butter and pour into dry ingredients. Mix until well blended. Bake in a hot waffle iron. Serve with butter and maple syrup. Can be made with all white flour if desired.

BLUEBERRY WAFFLES

2 c. flour	1 1/4 c. milk
4 tsp. baking powder	2 eggs, separated
1 tsp. salt	2 T. melted shortening
1 T. sugar	3/4 c. blueberries

Combine dry ingredients. Add milk. Beat egg yolks and add to mixture. Mix well. Beat egg whites until stiff and fold into the mixture. Add shortening and berries. Bake in a hot waffle iron. Serve with maple syrup or honey.

Variation for **BLACKBERRY WAFFLES:** Substitute blackberries for blueberries.

"Muffins, waffles and griddle cakes may be good foods or very poor ones. It depends on the way in which they are used. If they are well baked, thoroughly masticated and eaten with butter they are good foods. If they are poorly baked, hurriedly gulped down and served with much syrup or sugar, they are poor foods. The products made with whole grain flours are far superior to the white flour ones"

GENERAL RULES ON TABLE ETIQUETTE

"When you are at the table do not show restlessness do not play with th table utensils or crumble your bread; do not put your elbows on th table, nor sit too far back in your chair, nor lounge; do not talk loud o boisterously; be cheerful in conduct and conversation; never, if possible cough or sneeze while at the table; do not bend the head down to th plate, as the food should go to the mouth and not the mouth to the food never tilt back your chair at the table or elsewhere; do not talk when th mouth is full; never make a noise while eating; keep the lips closed, as i is unnecessary to show persons how you masticate your food; neve indicate that you notice anything unpleasant in the fare; chew you victuals well, but quietly, and slowly. Break your bread when no buttered; do not bite it. Never leave the table in advance of the rest o the family or guests without asking to be excused. Eat soup from th side of the spoon, and without noise. The fork is used to convey food t the mouth, except when a spoon is necessary, as is the case with sauces puddings and liquids. Raw oysters are eaten with a fork. If you wish t be served with tea or coffee a second time place your spoon in you saucer. Tea or coffee should not be poured into the saucer, but sippe from the cup. If a dish is passed to you, help yourself and then pass i on. Avoid all gross heaping up of plates. At a large dinner party it i better to confine your conversation to your immediate neighbor. Ther is one good rule which, if followed, will make you acceptabl everywhere. 'Be not obtrusive; do everything smoothly and quietly; tal in a low tone of voice; handle your knife, fork and dishes withou clatter, and eat without smacking your lips.'"

GRANDMA'S

MUFFINS

Three cups of milk, one
tablespoonful of melted butter, two
eggs, beaten stiff, three tablespoonfuls
of yeast, one tablespoonful of white sugar,
one teaspoonful of salt and one-quarter
teaspoonful of soda; flour to make a pretty
stiff batter. Make all the ingredients,
except the eggs, into a sponge, and set it
to rise over night; half an hour before
breakfast add the eggs and the soda
(dissolved in hot water), beaten all
together hard; part into muffin rings;
let them stand on the hearth ten
minutes, and bake about
twenty minutes in a brisk oven.

BISCUITS AND MUFFINS

BAKING POWDER BISCUITS

2 c. flour
1 T. baking powder
1/2 tsp. salt

1/3 c. shortening
3/4 c. milk

Combine flour, baking powder and salt. Cut in shortening, using a pastry blender, or two knives, or rub in with fingertips. Add milk, stirring just until dough stiffens. Turn out onto a floured board. Roll or pat 1/2-inch thick. Cut out with a floured biscuit cutter or cut into squares with a knife. Transfer to buttered baking sheet. Top of biscuits may be brushed with melted butter if desired. Bake at 450° approximately 15 minutes. Makes sixteen, 2-inch biscuits.

Variation for **DROP BISCUITS:** Use 1 1/4 c. milk. Drop onto a buttered baking pan, leaving at least 1-inch between biscuits.

SOUR MILK BISCUITS

2 c. flour
1 T. baking powder
1/2 tsp. salt

3 T. shortening
1/2 tsp. soda
3/4 c. sour milk

Combine flour, baking powder and salt. Rub in shortening. Mix soda and milk and add to dry ingredients. Stir just until dough stiffens. Roll out on a slightly floured board to 1/2-inch thickness. Cut with a biscuit cutter or cut into squares. Bake at 450° approximately 15 minutes.

"Who learns and learns—
But acts not what he knows,
Is one who plows and plows
But never sows."

-a verse Grandma Kulp copied into her notebook

WHEAT BISCUITS

2 c. whole wheat flour
1 c. flour
4 tsp. baking powder
3/4 tsp. salt

2 T. sugar
1/3 c. shortening
1 c. milk

Combine flour, baking powder, salt and sugar. Cut in shortening. Stir just until dough stiffens. Roll out on a floured board 1/2-inch thick. Cut with a floured cutter or cut into squares with a knife. Place on a buttered baking sheet. Bake at 450° approximately 15 minutes. Makes twenty-four, 2-inch biscuits.

Variation for **WHOLE WHEAT BISCUITS:** Use all whole wheat flour.

OATMEAL BISCUITS

1 1/2 c. flour
1 T. sugar
4 tsp. baking powder
1 tsp. salt

1 1/2 c. oatmeal
1/3 c. shortening
3/4 c. milk

Combine flour, sugar, baking powder and salt. Add oatmeal. Rub in shortening. Add milk slowly and mix to a soft dough. Roll out on a floured board 1/4 to 1/2-inch thick. Cut. Brush tops with milk. Bake at 450° approximately 15 minutes.

"This bread [whole wheat] is excellent for growing children and for brain workers. None of its nutritive qualities are diminished by fermentation, and eaten with good cow's milk and some sub-acid fruit it forms perfect food."

CHEESE BISCUITS

2 c. flour	1/4 c. butter
4 tsp. baking powder	3/4 c. grated cheese
1/2 tsp. salt	3/4 c. milk

Combine dry ingredients. Work in butter. Mix in cheese. Add milk, stirring just until dough stiffens. Roll out on a floured board to 1/2-inch thickness. Cut with a biscuit cutter or into squares. Bake at 450° approximately 15 minutes.

CINNAMON RAISIN BISCUITS

2 c. flour	1 tsp. cinnamon
1 T. baking powder	1/4 c. butter
1/2 tsp. salt	3/4 c. milk
2 T. sugar	1/2 c. raisins

Combine dry ingredients. Rub in butter. Add milk and raisins, stirring just until dough stiffens. Turn onto a lightly floured board. Pat into a sheet 1/2-inch thick. Cut with a floured cutter or into squares. Bake at 450° approximately 15 minutes. Ice if desired.

CINNAMON ROLL BISCUITS

2 c. flour	3/4 c. milk, scant
2 tsp. baking powder	3 T. butter, melted
1/2 tsp. salt	1/2 c. brown sugar
1/3 c. shortening	1 1/2 tsp. cinnamon

Combine dry ingredients. Cut in shortening. Add milk and stir just until dough stiffens. Roll out into a thin sheet 18x9x1/4-inches. Brush with melted butter. Sprinkle with combined sugar and cinnamon. Roll up loosely like a jelly roll; press edges down. Cut into 1-inch slices and place in an 8-inch, greased pan. Brush with remaining butter. Bake at 400° approximately 15 minutes. Ice if desired.

HONEY DATE BISCUITS

2 c. flour	1/4 c. butter
1 T. baking powder	2 T. honey
1/2 tsp. salt	1/2 c. chopped dates
1/3 c. shortening	1/4 c. chopped nuts
3/4 c. milk	

Combine dry ingredients. Rub in shortening. Add milk. Mix quickly and lightly. Roll or pat into a 1/2-inch thick rectangle. Cream butter. Add honey gradually. Add nuts and dates. Mix well. Spread mixture on dough. Roll as a jelly roll. Cut into 1-inch slices. Bake at 425° approximately 20 minutes. Raisins may be used instead of dates.

"When using honey in a recipe, oil or wet your measuring cup for easier pouring."

ORANGE TEA BISCUITS

1/4 c. butter	2 c. flour
1/2 c. sugar	2 tsp. baking powder
2 T. light corn syrup	3/4 tsp. salt
1/4 c. orange juice	1/3 c. shortening
1 tsp. orange rind	3/4 c. milk

Heat butter, sugar, corn syrup and orange juice until butter melts. Add rind. Pour into an 8-inch square pan. Make biscuits by combining flour, baking powder and salt. Cut in shortening. Add milk, stirring just until dough stiffens. Knead 12-15 times. Roll out 1/2-inch thick on a floured board. Cut with a 2-inch cutter, rerolling scraps of dough. Place in syrup. Bake at 450° approximately 15 minutes. When done, turn out on a plate so syrup is on top. Serve hot with butter for luncheon or afternoon tea. Makes sixteen, 2-inch biscuits.

PLAIN MUFFINS

2 c. flour
2 T. sugar
1 T. baking powder
3/4 tsp. salt

1 c. milk
1 egg, well-beaten
1/4 c. melted shortening

Combine dry ingredients. Mix together remaining ingredients and add. Beat only until smooth. Fill well-greased muffin tins 2/3 full. Bake at 425° approximately 20 minutes.

Variation for **CORN MEAL MUFFINS:** Substitute 1 c. cornmeal for 1 c. flour.

Variation for **WHEAT MUFFINS:** Substitute 1 c. whole wheat flour for 1 c. flour.

WHOLE WHEAT MUFFINS

1 3/4 c. whole wheat flour
1 T. baking powder
1/2 tsp. salt
2 T. brown sugar

1 egg, beaten
1 c. milk
1/4 c. melted butter

Mix dry ingredients. Combine remaining ingredients and add. Stir until dry ingredients are just dampened; then give 4 or 5 more stirs. The whole mixing process should not take more than 30 seconds. Dip quickly into buttered muffin pans. Bake at 425° approximately 20 minutes. Makes one dozen.

"Remember that smooth batter never makes good muffins. Stir only enough to wet the dry ingredients. Overmixing causes peaks and tunnels."

RAISED WHEAT MUFFINS

1 pkg. or 1 T. yeast	1 egg, well beaten
5 T. baking molasses	1 1/2 tsp. salt
2 c. warm milk	2 c. whole wheat flour
1/4 T. melted shortening	1 3/4 c. flour

Dissolve yeast and molasses in milk. Add shortening, egg and salt. Add flour gradually. Beat until smooth. Cover and let rise in a warm place free from draft until light—about 1 1/2 hours. Fill well greased muffin pans about 2/3 full. Cover and let rise again, about 1/2 hour. Bake at 400° approximately 25 minutes. Makes 1 1/2 dozen muffins.

OATMEAL MUFFINS

1 1/2 c. oatmeal	1 T. baking powder
3/4 c. hot water	3/4 tsp. salt
1/4 c. milk	1 egg, well-beaten
3/4 c. flour	3 T. cooking oil
2 T. sugar	

Pour hot water over oatmeal. Add milk and let stand. Combine dry ingredients. Add egg and cooking oil to oatmeal mixture. Add oatmeal mixture to dry ingredients, mixing lightly. Fill well-greased muffin tins. Bake at 425° approximately 25 minutes.

GRANDMA HORST'S
SOY MUFFINS

1 1/2 c. soy flour	4 eggs
1/2 c. whole wheat flour	2 c. milk
1/2 c. sugar	2 tsp. vanilla
2 tsp. baking powder	1/2 tsp. lemon flavor
1/2 tsp. salt	

Combine dry ingredients. Beat eggs. Add milk and flavoring to eggs then add to dry ingredients. Mix only until moistened. Bake at 400° approximately 25 minutes.

RAISIN BRAN MUFFINS

l c. flour
l c. bran
3 T. brown sugar
4 tsp. baking powder
3/4 tsp. salt

1 egg, well-beaten
1 c. milk
3 T. melted shortening
3/4 c. raisins

Combine dry ingredients. Mix together egg, milk, shortening and raisins, then add to dry ingredients. Stir only until mixed. Drop into well-greased muffin tins. Bake at 425° for 20-25 minutes.

SPICE MUFFINS

2 c. flour
1/2 c. sugar
1 T. baking powder
1 tsp. salt
1 tsp. cinnamon

1 tsp. ginger
1/4 tsp. nutmeg
1 egg, well-beaten
1 c. milk
1/4 c. melted shortening

Mix dry ingredients. Combine remaining ingredients and add to first mixture. Beat only until mixed. Fill well-greased muffin tins 2/3 full. Bake at 425° approximately 25 minutes. Makes 12 muffins.

BLUEBERRY MUFFINS

2 c. flour
1 T. baking powder
1/3 c. sugar
1 tsp. salt

1 egg, well-beaten
1 c. milk
1/4 c. melted butter
1 c. blueberries

Combine 1 1/2 c. flour with baking powder, sugar and salt. Beat egg, add milk and butter and add to dry ingredients. Mix blueberries with remaining 1/2 c. of flour and stir in lightly. Fill well-greased muffin tins. Bake at 400° for 20-25 minutes.

Variation for **HUCKLEBERRY MUFFINS:** Substitute huckleberries for blueberries.

CRANBERRY MUFFINS

1 1/2 c. coarsely chopped cranberries	1 tsp. salt
1/2 c. sugar	2 tsp. sugar
1 3/4 c. flour	1 beaten egg
1 T. baking powder	1 c. milk
	1/4 c. melted shortening

Mix cranberries and sugar and let stand while mixing muffins. Combine dry ingredients. Beat egg. Stir milk, shortening and cranberries into egg then add to dry ingredients. Bake in well-buttered muffin tins at 425° for approximately 25 minutes.

PUMPKIN MUFFINS

2 c. flour	1 egg
1/3 c. sugar	1 c. milk
2 tsp. baking powder	2/3 c. mashed pumpkin or squash
1 tsp. soda	
1/2 tsp. salt	1/4 c. melted shortening
1/2 tsp. cinnamon	

Combine dry ingredients. Beat egg and add milk, pumpkin and shortening. Add to dry ingredients, stirring only until mixed. Dip batter into greased muffin tins. Bake at 425° approximately 20 minutes.

HAM AND CHEESE MUFFINS

2 c. flour	1/2 c. grated cheese
1 T. baking powder	1 egg
3/4 tsp. salt	1 c. milk
1/2 c. minced, cooked ham	2 T. melted butter

Combine dry ingredients. Mix in ham and cheese. Beat egg and add milk and butter. Add to first mixture and mix lightly. Drop into well-greased muffin tins. Bake at 425° approximately 20 minutes.

APPLE CORNMEAL MUFFINS

1 c. cornmeal
1 1/2 c. flour
4 tsp. baking powder
1 tsp. salt
1/4 c. sugar

1 tsp. cinnamon
1 1/2 c. finely-chopped apples
1 egg
1 c. milk
1/4 c. melted butter

Combine dry ingredients. Mix in apples. Beat egg. Add milk and butter, then add to dry ingredients. Stir only until mixed. Put into well-greased muffin tins. Bake at 375° for 25-30 minutes.

GRANDMA HOOVER'S
DATE MUFFINS

2 c. flour
1/4 c. sugar
1 T. baking powder
1 tsp. salt
1/2 tsp. soda

1/4 c. shortening
1 c. chopped dates
2 tsp. grated orange rind
1 egg
1 c. buttermilk

Combine dry ingredients. Work in shortening. Add dates and rind. Beat egg and combine with milk. Blend into first mixture, mixing only until moistened. Spoon into greased muffin tins. Bake at 425° approximately 20 minutes.

PRUNE MUFFINS

3 c. flour
1/2 c. brown sugar
1 T. baking powder
1/2 tsp. salt
1/4 tsp. nutmeg

1 1/2 c. milk
2 eggs
1/2 c. melted shortening
1 1/2 c. chopped prunes

Combine dry ingredients. Add beaten eggs, melted shortening and prunes to milk. Combine mixtures. Do not over mix. Spoon into well-greased muffin tins. Bake at 400° approximately 25 minutes.

DOUGHNUT MUFFINS

1/4 c. shortening	2 tsp. baking powder
1/2 c. sugar	1/2 tsp. salt
1 egg	1/4 tsp. nutmeg
1 3/4 c. flour	1/2 c. milk

Cream shortening and sugar. Beat in egg. Mix together dry ingredients and add alternately with milk. Put in small, well-greased muffin tins. Bake at 400° for 15-20 minutes. Dip in melted butter. Roll in powdered sugar, or into a sugar cinnamon mixture.

GINGERBREAD MUFFINS

1/2 c. butter	2 c. flour
1/3 c. sugar	1 1/2 tsp. ginger
2/3 c. molasses	1/2 tsp. salt
1 egg	1 tsp. soda
2/3 c. milk	1 1/2 tsp. baking powder

Cream butter and sugar. Add molasses, egg and milk. Mix dry ingredients and fold in. Bake at 400° for 20-25 minutes.

ENGLISH MUFFINS

1 pkg. or 1 T. yeast	1 tsp. salt
1 c. lukewarm water	6 c. flour
1 c. milk	4 T. melted shortening
2 T. sugar	

Dissolve yeast in water and add milk, sugar and salt. Add half of the flour; beat until smooth. Add shortening and remaining flour. Knead until smooth and elastic (about 10 minutes). Place in a well greased bowl. Cover and let rise in a warm place free from draft, until double in bulk—about 2 hours. Divide into 18 portions and shape into round biscuits. Cover and let rise on lightly floured board about 1/2 hour. Roll each biscuit about 1/4-inch thick, keeping round shape. Bake on hot ungreased griddle for 10 minutes. As they brown, reduce heat and bake more slowly. Serve warm with marmalade or honey or slit and toast.

POPOVERS

Popovers depend on air for leavening. Unlike muffins, popovers should be thoroughly beaten.

1 c. flour	**2 eggs**
1/2 tsp. salt	**1 T. melted butter**
1 c. milk	

Mix flour and salt. Add milk gradually. Add beaten eggs and shortening. Beat batter 5 minutes with an egg beater or until batter is smooth and bubbly. Pour into hot, greased muffin tins. Bake at 425° approximately 30 minutes. Serve warm with butter and jam.

Variation for **WHOLE WHEAT POPOVERS:** Use whole wheat flour instead of white flour.

Variation for **CHEESE POPOVERS:** Add 2 T. grated cheese along with eggs and shortening.

SOME BISCUIT MAKING HINTS

·*Cut in the shortening with one or two knives.*

·*Although water may be used, the biscuit is better when made with milk.*

·*If fresh milk is too blue, thin and poverty-stricken, diluted evaporated milk will serve nicely.*

·*Toss the biscuit dough onto the floured board and roll quickly and gently or lightly—we mean to use no heavy-handedness.*

MISCELLANEOUS OBSERVATIONS TO HOUSEKEEPERS

"Instances may be found of women in the highest walks of life, who examine the accounts of their house stewards, and, by overlooking and wisely directing the expenditures of their husband's income, save much financial embarrassment. How necessary, then, is domestic knowledge to those whose limited incomes compel them to consider even the slightest expense. The management of the table is no inconsiderable part of a woman's education; it involves judgment in outlay, respectability of appearance, the comfort of her family and those who partake of her hospitality. There are few incidents in which the honest pride of a man is more immediately felt than in the style of the dinner to which he may bring a friend. If but two or three dishes are well served with the usual sauces, the table linen clean, the table neatly laid, and all that is necessary at hand, the husband and friend are gratified because no irregularity of domestic arrangement will disturb the social intercourse."

GRANDMA'S

DOUGHNUTS

Twelve eggs, three-fourths
of a pound of butter, two pounds
of sugar, one pint of sour cream, one
teaspoonful of saleratus; season flour
sufficient to roll them out. Fry in lard.

BUNS

Break one egg into a cup and fill with sweet
milk; mix with it half cup yeast, half cup butter,
one cup sugar, enough flour to make a soft
dough; flavor with nutmeg. Let it rise till
very light, then mold into biscuits with
a few currants. Let rise a second
time in pan; bake, and when nearly
done, glaze with a little molasses
and milk. Use the same
cup, no matter what the
size for each
measure.

DOUGHNUTS
AND ROLLS

DOUGHNUTS

3/4 c. sugar
1/4 T. shortening
2 eggs, well-beaten
3/4 c. milk
4 c. flour

4 tsp. baking powder
1/2 tsp. cinnamon
1/4 tsp. nutmeg
1 tsp. salt

Cream sugar and shortening. Add eggs and milk. Mix well. Combine dry ingredients. Add to liquid mixture and mix thoroughly. Turn out on a slightly floured board and roll to 1/2-inch thickness. Cut with a doughnut cutter. Fry in deep, hot fat (375°) about 2 minutes on each side or until golden brown. Drain on unglazed paper. Sprinkle with powdered sugar or ice with plain, brown sugar or chocolate icing. Makes approximately 48 doughnuts.

RAISED DOUGHNUTS

1 pkg. or 1 T. yeast
1 1/4 c. warm milk
5 c. flour
3 T. butter

2/3 c. sugar
1 tsp. salt
1 egg, well-beaten
1/2 tsp. nutmeg

Dissolve yeast in warm milk. Add 1 1/2 c. flour and beat well. Cream butter, sugar and salt. Add eggs and nutmeg, then add to yeast mixture. Add remaining flour to make moderately soft dough. Knead lightly, then place in a well-greased bowl. Cover and let rise until doubled in bulk— about 1 1/2 hours. Punch down and roll out 1/2-inch thick on floured board. Cut with a 3-inch doughnut cutter. Place on floured board and cover with a cloth. Let rise until doubled in bulk—about 1 hour. Fry them top side down in deep fat hot enough to brown a 1-inch cube of bread in 60 seconds or 375°. Fry on both sides, turning only once. Drain, cool and roll in sugar or powdered sugar. Makes 2 1/2-3 dozen.

"Life is a mixture of sunshine and rain, good things and bad things, pleasure and pain"

-a saying Grandma Kulp copied into her notebook

CHOCOLATE DOUGHNUTS

3/4 c. sugar	3 1/2 c. flour
1/4 c. shortening	1/2 c. cocoa
2 eggs, well-beaten	4 tsp. baking powder
1 c. milk	1 tsp. salt

Cream sugar and shortening. Add eggs, milk and add dry ingredients. Roll 1/2-inch thick on a floured board. Cut with a doughnut cutter. Fry in deep hot fat (375°) about 2 minutes on each side. Drain on crumpled absorbent paper. Sprinkle with powdered sugar or ice.

GINGERBREAD DOUGHNUTS

1/4 c. sugar	1 T. baking powder
2 T. shortening	1 tsp. ginger
1 c. molasses	1/2 tsp. cinnamon
1 egg, well-beaten	1/8 tsp. cloves
1/3 c. milk	3/4 tsp. salt
3 c. flour	

Cream sugar and shortening. Add molasses, egg and milk. Beat well. Combine and add dry ingredients. Mix. Turn out on a floured board and roll to 1/2-inch thickness. Cut with a doughnut cutter. Fry in deep hot fat (375°) approximately 2 minutes on each side. Drain on crumpled absorbent paper. Sprinkle with powdered sugar or ice with plain icing.

APPLE FRITTERS

2 c. flour	1 1/3 c. milk
3 tsp. baking powder	3 apples, chopped and peeled
1/2 tsp. salt	1/2 c. sugar
2 eggs	1/2 tsp. cinnamon

Combine dry ingredients. Beat eggs, add milk, then add to dry ingredients. Combine apples, sugar and cinnamon; stir into batter. Drop a spoonful at a time into deep fat (375°). Fry until evenly browned. Drain on crumpled absorbent paper. Roll in sugar or powdered sugar.

PUMPKIN DOUGHNUTS

1 1/4 c. sugar
2 T. shortening
2 eggs, well-beaten
1 c. mashed pumpkin
1 tsp. vanilla
3 c. flour

1 T. baking powder
1 tsp. salt
1/2 tsp. cinnamon
1/2 tsp. nutmeg
1 c. milk

Cream sugar and shortening. Beat in eggs, pumpkin and vanilla. Combine dry ingredients and add alternately with milk to first mixture. Turn onto a floured board. Roll out 1/4 to 1/2-inch thick. Cut with a floured cutter. Fry in deep hot fat (375°) on each side until brown. Drain. Sprinkle with powdered sugar or ice if desired. Any kind of winter squash can be substituted for pumpkin.

POTATO DROP DOUGHNUTS

2 c. flour
2 tsp. baking powder
1/2 tsp. salt
1/2 tsp. nutmeg
2 T. shortening

1/2 c. sugar
1 egg
2/3 c. mashed potatoes
1/3 c. milk
shortening for frying

Combine flour, baking powder, salt and nutmeg. Cream shortening and sugar. Add egg and beat until fluffy. Beat in potatoes. Add dry ingredients and milk alternately. Mix only enough to combine well. Lightly roll into small balls with floured hands. Fry in deep hot fat (375°) for 4 minutes or until brown. Batter may also be dropped from a spoon. Drain on crumpled absorbent paper.

CRULLERS

Roll out any doughnut mixture 1/2-inch thick. Cut in strips 1x3-inches. Twist and roll each strip. Fry same as doughnuts.

DINNER ROLLS

2 pkg. or 2 T. yeast	1 T. salt
1 c. lukewarm water	6 c. flour
1 c. warm milk	1/3 c. melted butter
1/4 c. sugar	

Dissolve yeast in water. Add milk, sugar and salt. Add 3 c. flour an
beat until perfectly smooth. Add melted butter and remaining flou
Knead well. Place in a greased bowl. Cover and set in a warm place
free from draft. Let rise until double in bulk, approximately 1 hou
Punch down and divide dough into four equal portions. Form nine ball
from each portion. Place in well-greased pans 1/2-inch apart. Cover an
let rise until double in bulk. Bake at 375° approximately 20 minutes
Makes 36 rolls. Can be refrigerated after first rising. Punch dough dow
and cover well. When you get it out punch down again and shape int
rolls. Place rolls into greased pans and let rise until double in bul
before baking. Dough can be kept in refrigerator four or five days.

Variation for **CRESCENT ROLLS:** After dough has risen divid
into 3 equal balls. Roll each ball of dough into a round shape about 3/8
inch thick. Cut into 12 pie shaped pieces. Brush with melted butte
Roll up each piece beginning with the outside of the circle and rollin
toward the middle. Shape into crescents (half-moon shapes) and plac
on well-greased baking sheet. Cover and let set in a warm place unti
light, about one hour.

Variation for **PARKER HOUSE ROLLS:** After dough has rise
roll out 3/8-inch thick and cut with a 2 1/2-inch biscuit cutter. Creas
heavily through the center with the dull edge of a knife and brush lightl
with melted butter. Fold together in a pocket book shape pressing edge
together at ends of crease. Place one inch apart in well-greased pans
Cover and let rise until double in bulk. Bake at 375° approximately 2
minutes.

*"Too much heat kills yeast. When dissolving it for baking, be sure th
temperature is lukewarm."*

Variation for **CLOVERLEAF ROLLS:** After dough has risen, divide into six equal portions. Divide each portion into twelve small balls. Brush sides with butter and place 3 balls in each section of a muffin pan. Cover and let rise until double in bulk—about one hour. Bake at 400° approximately 15 minutes. Makes 24 rolls.

Variation for **FAN TANS:** After dough has risen, roll out into a rectangle 1/8-inch thick. Brush with melted butter and cut into strips 1 1/2-inches wide. Pile 7 strips together. Cut stack into pieces 1-inch long. Place into greased muffin pans with strips upright. Cover and let rise about one hour. Bake at 400° approximately 15 minutes.

Whole wheat flour has all the nutrients of Graham flour and includes the inner bran but not the outer husk included in graham flour.

WHEAT ROLLS

1 pkg. or 1 T. yeast	3 T. shortening
1/2 c. lukewarm water	1 egg, well-beaten
1/2 c. warm milk	2 c. whole wheat flour
2 T. sugar	1 1/2 c. flour
1 1/2 tsp. salt	

Dissolve yeast in water. Add milk, sugar, salt, shortening and egg. Mix well. Add flour, enough to make a soft dough. Turn out on a lightly-floured board and knead until smooth. Place in a greased bowl. Cover and let set in a warm place and let rise until double in bulk, approximately one hour. Punch down. Divide dough into 4 equal parts. Shape each part into five rolls. Place in well-greased pans about 1/2-inch apart. Cover and set in a warm place until double in bulk. Bake at 375° approximately 20 minutes. Makes 20 rolls.

Variation for **WHOLE WHEAT ROLLS:** Use all whole wheat flour.

BUTTERMILK ROLLS

Our Grandmas made butter on a regular basis. This was a handy recipe to use up buttermilk, a byproduct of butter making.

1 pkg. or 1 T. yeast	2 tsp. salt
1/4 c. lukewarm water	1/4 tsp. soda
2 c. buttermilk	1/4 c. melted shortening
1/4 c. sugar	5 c. flour

Soften yeast in water. Add slightly-warmed buttermilk, sugar, salt, soda and melted shortening. Add half of the flour and beat until smooth. Add remaining flour. Mix. Turn out on a floured board and knead until smooth and elastic. Divide dough into four equal portions then divide each portion into 8 balls. Place in a greased pan. Cover and let rise until double in bulk. Bake at 375° approximately 20 minutes.

Variation for **SOUR CREAM ROLLS:** Substitute 2 c. thick sour cream for buttermilk.

POTATO ROLLS

1/4 c. melted shortening	2 eggs, well-beaten
2 T. sugar	2 pkg. or 2 T. yeast
1 T. salt	2 c. warm milk
1 c. hot, mashed potatoes	6 c. flour

Add shortening, sugar and salt to mashed potatoes. Cool and add eggs. Soften yeast in milk and add potato mixture. Add flour gradually. Turn out onto a floured board and knead until smooth and elastic. Cover and put in a warm place until double in bulk. Punch down. Form dough into buns. Place in well-greased pans. Cover and let rise until double in bulk. Bake at 400° approximately 25 minutes.

"All doughs should be thoroughly mixed. . . The dough should be just stiff enough to knead on a lightly floured board."

RAISIN ROLLS

2 pkg. or 2 T. yeast	1 1/2 tsp. salt
1/4 c. warm water	2 eggs, beaten
1 c. warm milk	5 c. flour
1/4 c. soft butter	1 c. raisins
1/2 c. sugar	

Soften yeast in water. Add milk, butter, sugar, salt and beaten eggs. Mix in 2 c. flour and beat well. Add remaining flour and raisins. Turn out on a lightly floured board and knead until smooth and elastic. Place in a greased bowl, cover and let rise until double in bulk. When light, punch down and shape into rolls. Let rise until double in bulk. Bake at 375° approximately 25 minutes. Ice with confectioners' icing.

CINNAMON ROLLS

2 pkg. or 2 T. yeast	2 tsp. salt
1 T. sugar	7 c. flour
1 c. lukewarm water	3 eggs, beaten
1 c. warm milk	6 T. melted butter
6 T. shortening	1 1/2 c. brown sugar
1/2 c. sugar	1 T. cinnamon

Dissolve yeast and 1 T. sugar in water. Add milk, shortening, sugar and salt. Add 2 c. flour and eggs; beat well. Add remaining flour, or enough to make a soft dough. Knead lightly and place in a greased bowl. Cover and set in a warm place. Let rise until double in bulk—about 2 hours. Punch down and divide into two equal portions. Roll out into oblong pieces 1/4-inch thick. Brush with melted butter and sprinkle with brown sugar and cinnamon. Roll up as for jelly roll and cut into 1-inch slices. Place cut side up about 1-inch apart in large shallow greased baking pans. Cover and let rise in a warm place, about one hour. Bake at 350° for 15-20 minutes. Makes 4 dozen. Ice while still warm.

Variation for **RAISIN CINNAMON ROLLS:** Sprinkle one cup raisins over brown sugar and cinnamon.

BUTTERSCOTCH ROLLS

2 pkg. or 2 T. yeast	1 c. milk
1 c. lukewarm water	9 c. flour
3/4 c. shortening	6 T. butter
3/4 c. sugar	2 1/2 c. brown sugar
1 tsp. salt	1/3 c. melted butter
2 eggs, well-beaten	

Dissolve yeast in water. Cream shortening, sugar and salt. Add eggs and milk and add to yeast. Add 3 c. flour and beat well. Add remaining flour and turn out on a floured board. Knead lightly. Place in a well greased bowl. Cover and set in a warm place until doubled in bulk. Thickly grease three 8-inch square baking pans with 1 T. butter in each pan. Sprinkle the bottoms and sides of the pans with 1 cup of the brown sugar and dot with remaining 3 T. of butter. Punch down dough and divide into 3 equal portions. Roll into oblong sheets 1/4-inch thick and about 18-inches wide. Brush each sheet with melted butter, sprinkle with remaining brown sugar. Roll up as for jelly roll. Cut into 1 1/2 inch slices and set close together in prepared pans. Cover and let rise about 45 minutes. Bake at 375° approximately 20 minutes. Turn out of pans immediately, bottom side up. Makes 3 dozen.

Variation for **PECAN BUTTERSCOTCH ROLLS:** Sprinkle 1 1/2 c. chopped pecans over melted butter on oblong sheets before rolling.

"A clean, tidy kitchen can only be secured by having a place for everything and everything in its place, and by frequent scourings of the room and utensils. A hand-towel and basin are needed in every kitchen for the use of the cook or house worker. Unless dish-towels are washed, scalded and thoroughly dried daily, they become musty and unfit for use as also the dish-cloth."

FILLED BUNS

2 pkg. or 2 T. yeast	2 eggs, well-beaten
1 c. lukewarm water	1/3 tsp. nutmeg
3/4 c. shortening	few drops lemon extract
3/4 c. sugar	1 c. milk
1 tsp. salt	9 c. flour

Dissolve yeast in water. Cream shortening, sugar and salt; add eggs, nutmeg, flavoring and milk. Add to yeast mixture. Add 3 c. flour and beat well. Add remaining flour. Turn out on a floured board and knead lightly until smooth and elastic. Place in greased bowl. Cover and set in a warm place, free from draft, until doubled in bulk—about 2 hours. Turn out on floured board and shape into 48 round rolls. Dip in sugar and set on a well-greased baking pan 1/2-inch apart. Cover and let rise until doubled in bulk—about 45 minutes. Make an indentation in the center of the roll and fill with jam or jelly. Let rise again, about 15 minutes. Bake at 400° approximately 20 minutes. Makes 4 dozen.

HOT CROSS BUNS

2 pkg. or 2 T. yeast	2/3 c. sugar
2 T. sugar	1/2 tsp. salt
2 c. warm milk	2 eggs, well-beaten
7 1/2 c. flour	1/2 c. raisins or currants
1/2 c. shortening	

Dissolve yeast and 2 T. sugar in warm milk. Add 3 c. flour. Beat until smooth; cream shortening and sugar; add salt. Add to yeast mixture. Add eggs, raisins or currants, which have been floured and remaining flour. Turn out on a floured board and knead lightly. Place in a greased bowl; cover and let rise again until doubled in bulk—about 2 hours. Shape into 48 round buns and place into well-greased pans. Cover and let rise again, about 1 hour. Brush tops with one egg beaten with 2 T. cold water. With a sharp knife cut a cross on the top of each bun being careful not to flatten the bun. Bake at 400° approximately 15 minutes. While hot, fill cross with plain icing. (See icings.) Makes 4 dozen.

RAISED SCONES

1 pkg. or 1 T. yeast	1 tsp. salt
1/2 c. lukewarm water	3 1/2 c. flour
1/2 c. milk	2 T. melted shortening
1 T. sugar	

Dissolve yeast in water. Add milk, sugar and salt. Add 1/2 of the flour and beat well. Add melted shortening and remaining flour. Knead until smooth and elastic—approximately 10 minutes. Cover and set in warm place free from draft. Let rise about 1 1/2 hours. Punch down and turn out on a floured board. Form into 6 round cakes. Cover and let rise about 15 minutes. Roll 1/4-inch thick. Cut each of the rounds into fourths. Place on well-greased, shallow pans. Dust with flour and let rise until doubled in bulk—about 1 hour. Bake at 400° approximately 15 minutes. Makes 2 dozen.

SCONES

3 c. flour	1/2 c. shortening
1 T. baking powder	1/2 c. raisins
1/2 tsp. salt	1 c. milk
3 T. sugar	

Combine flour, baking powder, salt and sugar. Cut in shortening and add raisins, mixing lightly. Add milk. Stir just until dough stiffens up. Turn onto floured board and knead lightly, 6-8 times. Divide into 3 equal portions and roll out each portion 1/2-inch thick in a circular shape. Cut into 6 pie-shaped wedges and transfer to a greased baking sheet. Bake at 400° for 15 minutes or until golden brown. Split open with a sharp knife, leaving connected by hinge at back. Spread with butter and jam and close. Serve hot. Makes 18 scones.

BAGELS

1 pkg. or 1 T. yeast	1/2 tsp. salt
1 c. warm milk	1 egg separated
1/4 c. soft butter	3 3/4 c. flour
1 1/2 T. sugar	

Dissolve yeast in milk. Add butter, sugar, salt, white of egg well beaten and flour. Knead and let rise approximately one hour. Roll in small pieces width of finger and twice the length, tapering at the ends. Shape into rings, pinching ends together. Let stand on floured board only until they begin to rise. Fill large, shallow pan half full of water. Heat to very hot (just below boiling) and then carefully drop rings into water, one at a time. Cook on one side, then turn. They must be light, keep their shape and not break apart when handled. Place on a baking sheet and brush with slightly beaten egg yolk. Bake in a hot oven, 400°, until crisp and golden brown—approximately 25 minutes. Makes three dozen.

"Dough made from hard-wheat flour requires more kneading than that made from soft-wheat flour."

"Soft-wheat flours, because of the smaller quantity or poorer quality of the gluten, require less moisture than hard-wheat flours to make dough of the right consistency."

GIRLS, LEARN TO COOK

"Yes, yes, learn how to cook, girls; and learn how to cook well. Wha
right has a girl to marry and go into a house of her own unless she
knows how to superintend every branch of housekeeping, and she canno
properly superintend unless she has some practical knowledge herself
It is sometimes asked, sneeringly, "What kind of a man is he who would
marry a cook?" The fact is, that men do not think enough of this
indeed, most men marry without thinking whether the woman of his
choice is capable of cooking him a meal, and it is a pity he is so
shortsighted, as his health, his cheerfulness, and, indeed, his success in
life, depend in a very great degree on the kind of food he eats; in fact
the whole household is influenced by the diet. Feed them on fried cakes
fried meats, hot bread and other indigestible viands, day after day, and
they will need medicine to make them well.

Let all girls have a share in housekeeping at home before they marry; le
each superintend some department by turns. It need not occupy half the
time to see that the house has been properly swept, dusted, and put in
order, to prepare puddings and make dishes, that many young ladies
spend in reading novels which enervate both mind and body and unfi
them for everyday life. Women do not, as a general rule, get pale face.
doing housework. Their sedentary habits, in overheated rooms
combined with ill-chosen food, are to blame for bad health. Ou
mothers used to pride themselves on their housekeeping and fine
needlework. Let the present generation add to its list of rea
accomplishments the arts of properly preparing food for the human
body."

GRANDMA'S

PLAIN
WHITE FAMILY BREAD

Take one pint of flour and half a pint
of good hop yeast and stir it together
about five o'clock in the afternoon; about nine
put one-half gallon of flour in a tray, put
the sponge in the middle of the flour with a
piece of lard as large as a walnut. Knead it all
up with tepid water made salt with two teaspoonfuls
or more to taste; work it well, and put it in
a jar to rise. Next morning knead it over with
a little flour; make it into two loaves; and set
it in a warm place or oven until ready; then put
it to bake, and when done, wrap it in a nice
coarse towel. If you have no sugar in the
yeast you use, stir a large teaspoonful
in it before putting it in the flour.

BREADS AND
QUICK BREADS

Our grandmothers baked bread out of necessity; today it's often a hobby. Other things changed too. Older recipes called for cake yeast; today we most often use dry yeast. Houses were cooler and more drafty so it took bread doughs longer to rise. Recipes reflect that with instructions to put the dough "in a warm place, free from draft." Even today rising time can be shortened by finding a warm place. A gas stove with a constant pilot makes a good place for dough to rise. You can turn the stove on for five minutes to speed it up even more, but don't forget to turn the stove off! Grandmother's recipes called for scalded milk; today with pasteurization that step isn't necessary. Warm milk, however, will shorten rising time. Today we have shorter baking times, usually 35 minutes at 350°; in our grandmothers' day recipes gave baking times of one hour with oven temperatures of 400°. Some things never change. Home baked bread is as delicious and wholesome today as the bread Grandmother baked.

WHITE BREAD

3 pkg. or 3 T. yeast	2 T. salt
2 c. lukewarm water	5 T. melted shortening
2 c. milk	12-13 c. flour
5 T. sugar	

Dissolve yeast in water. Add milk, sugar, salt and melted shortening. Add half of the flour and beat until smooth. Add remaining flour or enough to make easily handled dough. Knead dough 10-15 minutes, until smooth and elastic. Place dough in a greased bowl, cover and set in a warm place, free from draft. Let rise until double in bulk—about 1 hour. Punch down. Divide into four equal portions and shape into loaves. Place in greased bread pans. Cover and let rise again until double in bulk. Bake at 350° approximately 35 minutes. Makes four loaves.

"For all types of breads, use bread flour. It contains the right amount of gluten. An all-purpose flour may also be used. Pastry or cake flours are not advisable."

WHEAT BREAD

3 pkg. or 3 T. yeast
2 c. lukewarm water
2 c. milk
1/3 c. honey

4 tsp. salt
1/3 c. melted shortening
5 c. flour
5 c. whole wheat flour

Dissolve yeast in water. Add milk, honey, salt, shortening and half o
the flour, mixing well. Add remaining flour. Knead 10-15 minutes
Cover and set in a warm place, free from draft. Let rise until double in
bulk—about one hour. Punch down. Shape into loaves and place into
greased bread pans. Let rise until double in bulk—about 30 minutes
Bake at 350° approximately 35 minutes. Makes three large or four smal
loaves.

Variation for **WHOLE WHEAT BREAD:** Use all whole wheat
flour.

CRACKED WHEAT BREAD

2 pkg. or 2 T. yeast
3/4 c. lukewarm water
3 c. cooked cracked wheat
3 T. melted shortening

3 T. sugar
1 T. salt
6 c. flour

Dissolve yeast in water. Mix lukewarm cracked wheat, shortening, sugar
and salt together; add yeast, mix well. Add flour. Turn out on floured
board and knead 10-15 minutes. Place dough in greased bowl, cover and
set in warm place, free from draft. Let rise until doubled in bulk—about
one hour and 15 minutes. Punch down. Divide into two equal portions
and shape into loaves. Place in greased bread pans. Cover and let rise
about 55 minutes. Bake at 350° approximately 35 minutes. Makes two
loaves. To cook cracked wheat, add 1 c. cracked wheat to 3 c. water
and cook approximately 30 minutes.

Best results are obtained if bread is removed from pans to cool.

BRAN BREAD

2 pkg. or 2 T. yeast
1 c. lukewarm water
2 c. milk
1/2 c. molasses

2 T. salt
8 c. flour
5 c. wheat bran
1/4 c. melted shortening

Dissolve yeast in water. Add milk, molasses and salt. Add half of the flour and beat until smooth. Add bran, shortening and remaining flour. Knead dough until smooth and elastic—10-15 minutes. Place dough in a greased bowl, cover and set in a warm place. Let rise until doubled in bulk—about two hours. Punch down. Divide into three equal portions and shape into loaves. Place in well greased pans. Cover and let rise again until doubled in bulk—about 45 minutes. Bake at 350° approximately 35 minutes. Makes three loaves.

RYE BREAD

1 pkg. or 1 T. yeast
3/4 c. lukewarm water
1 c. milk
1 T. molasses
1 T. salt

4 c. rye flour
2 c. flour
1 T. melted shortening
1 T. caraway seed, if desired

Dissolve yeast in water. Add milk, molasses and salt. Add half of the flour and beat until smooth. Add shortening and remaining flour, or enough to make easily handled dough. Knead dough until smooth—about five minutes. Place dough in a greased bowl, cover and set in a warm place. Let rise until doubled in bulk—about 2 1/2 hours. Punch down. Divide into two equal portions. Shape into long loaves. Place on shallow, greased pans which have been sprinkled with corn meal. Cover and let rise again, about 70 minutes. Brush with white of an egg diluted with 1 T. of water. With a sharp knife, lightly cut three strokes diagonally across the top. Bake at 350° approximately 35 minutes.

Variation: To obtain an acid flavor dilute 1 1/2 T. white vinegar with 1/4 c. water. Add to dough after part of flour has been mixed in.

GRANDMA HOOVER'S
OATMEAL BREAD

2 c. boiling water
1 c. oatmeal
1/2 c. whole wheat flour
1/2 c. brown sugar
1 T. salt

1/4 c. butter or cooking oil
1 pkg. or 1 T. yeast
1/2 c. lukewarm water
5 c. bread flour

Pour boiling water over oatmeal, whole wheat flour, sugar, salt and butter. Cool until lukewarm. Dissolve yeast in lukewarm water. Add to batter. Add flour and knead until dough is smooth and elastic. Put in a greased bowl, cover, and let rise in a warm place until double in bulk—about one hour. Shape into two loaves and put into greased 9x5x3-inch bread pans. Cover and let rise one hour. Bake at 350° approximately 30 minutes. Remove from pans and butter tops of loaves.

CHEESE BREAD

2 pkg. or 2 T. yeast
2 c. lukewarm water
3 T. sugar
1 T. salt

2 eggs, well-beaten
4 c. (1 lb.) grated cheese
7-8 c. flour

Dissolve yeast in water. Add sugar, salt, eggs, cheese and half of the flour. Beat well. Add enough of remaining flour to make an easily handled dough. Knead dough until smooth and elastic. Divide into three loaves and put in greased bread pans. Cover and let rise in a warm place until double in bulk. Bake at 350° approximately 35 minutes.

"A good way to whiten bread or meat boards which have become discolored is to rub them with lemon rinds turned inside out"

POTATO BREAD

1 pkg. or 1 T. yeast	2 T. melted butter
2 c. warm milk	1 1/2 c. warm mashed
1 T. sugar	potatoes
1 T. salt	6 c. flour

Dissolve yeast in warm milk. Add sugar, salt, butter and mashed potatoes. Add half of the flour and beat until smooth. Add remaining flour and knead on a floured board until smooth and elastic—about 10 minutes. Put in a bowl, cover, and let rise until double in bulk. Punch down and shape into two loaves. Place in greased bread pans. Let rise until double in bulk. Bake at 350° approximately 35 minutes.

RAISIN BREAD

1 pkg. or 1 T. yeast	3/4 c. sugar
1 c. lukewarm water	1 tsp. salt
1 c. warm milk	6 1/2 c. flour
1/4 c. soft butter	1 1/2 c. raisins, floured

Dissolve yeast in water. Add milk, butter, sugar and salt. Stir in 3 c. flour and beat until smooth. Add raisins and remaining flour or enough to make soft dough. Knead approximately 10 minutes. Place dough in a greased bowl, cover and let rise until double in bulk. Punch down and shape into two loaves. Place in well-greased bread pans. Cover and let rise again until double in bulk. Bake at 350° approximately 35 minutes.

"Sufficient kneading is the imperative. Ten minutes of uninterrupted kneading is the minimum length of time necessary. Knead quickly and lightly until dough is smooth and elastic and the surface blisters. It should not stick to the fingers or board. Push the dough with palms of the hands, with fingers curved to prevent dough from flattening too much. With every push it should be turned one-quarter way round and folded over."

CINNAMON BREAD

2 pkg. or 2 T. yeast	5-6 c. flour
1/4 c. lukewarm water	2 eggs, beaten
1 c. milk	2 tsp. melted butter
1/4 c. soft butter	1 T. cinnamon
1/2 c. sugar	1/3 c. sugar
1 1/2 tsp. salt	

Soften yeast in water. Add milk, butter, 1/2 c. sugar, and salt. Stir in two cups of flour and beat until smooth. Add eggs, mixing thoroughly. Add enough flour to make a soft dough (about 3 cups). Toss onto a floured board and knead approximately 10 minutes. Place in a greased bowl; cover and let rise in a warm place until double in bulk—about two hours. Punch down. Divide dough in half and roll each half into a rectangle about 1/2-inch thick, 6-inches wide and 16-inches long. Spread very lightly with melted butter. Combine cinnamon and sugar and sprinkle on dough. Roll up lengthwise, jelly roll fashion. Pull and smooth out roll to make it even, then pinch ends together tightly to get a smooth loaf. Place in two greased loaf pans (9 1/2 x 5 1/2 x 2 1/2), smooth side up. Let rise in a warm place (80-85°) until double in bulk—about 1 1/2 hours. Bake at 350° approximately 35 minutes.

SUGARPLUM LOAF

1 pkg. or 1 T. yeast	1 tsp. salt
2 T. lukewarm water	1/2 c. raisins
1/2 c. shortening	1/2 c. walnuts
1/2 c. sugar	1/2 c. citron
2 eggs	1/2 c. chopped candied
3/4 c. milk	cherries
5 c. flour	

Dissolve yeast in water. Cream shortening and sugar. Beat eggs; add to creamed mixture. Add milk and yeast. Add 1 c. flour; mix well. Cover; let rise in warm place one hour. Add salt, raisins, walnuts, citron and cherries. Add remaining flour. Knead thoroughly (about 10 minutes). Put into a greased 8-inch round pan. Cover; let rise in a warm place until double in bulk. Bake at 350° approximately 1 1/4 hours. Remove from pan. Cool slightly and ice with plain icing. (See icings.)

CORNBREAD

Grandma Hoover's handwritten cornbread recipe is called Johnnycake. Grandma Kulp's family called it corn pone.

1 c. cornmeal	1/2 tsp. salt
1 c. flour	1 egg, well-beaten
1 T. baking powder	1 c. milk
2 T. sugar	1/4 c. melted shortening

Combine dry ingredients. Beat egg and add milk and shortening. Add to dry ingredients and stir only until mixed. Pour in a greased 9x9 pan. Bake at 425° approx. 20 minutes. If desired, all cornmeal can be used.

Variation for **BACON CORNBREAD:** Add 1/4 c. diced crisp bacon along with egg, milk and shortening.

Variation for **WHEAT CORNBREAD:** Substitute 1 c. whole wheat flour for flour.

NEW ENGLAND BROWN BREAD

2 T. butter	1 tsp. salt
1/2 c. sugar	1 tsp. soda
1 egg	1 tsp. baking powder
1/2 c. molasses	2 c. buttermilk
3 c. whole wheat flour	

Cream butter and sugar. Beat in egg and molasses. Combine dry ingredients and add alternately with buttermilk. Pour into a greased bread pan. Bake at 350° approximately one hour. If desired, one cup of white flour may be used.

"Handle baking powder doughs as little as possible."

BANANA BREAD

1/3 c. shortening	2 tsp. baking powder
2/3 c. sugar	1/2 tsp. salt
2 eggs	1 c. mashed bananas
1 3/4 c. flour	

Cream shortening and sugar. Beat in eggs. Combine dry ingredients and add alternately with bananas. Mix lightly but thoroughly. Pour into a well-greased bread pan. Bake at 350° approximately one hour. Makes one small loaf.

NUT BREAD

1 c. brown sugar	1 T. baking powder
1/4 c. butter	1 tsp. salt
1 egg	1 c. milk
2 1/2 c. flour	1 c. pecans or walnuts

Cream sugar and butter. Beat in egg. Combine dry ingredients and add to creamed mixture, alternately with milk. Add coarsely chopped nuts. Mix lightly but well. Pour into a greased bread pan. Bake at 350 approximately one hour. Makes one loaf.

Variation for **WHOLE WHEAT NUT BREAD:** Use all whole wheat flour instead of white flour.

RAISIN NUT BREAD

3 c. flour	1 egg, well-beaten
1 T. baking powder	1 1/2 c. milk
1 c. sugar	1 c. chopped nuts
1 tsp. cinnamon	1 c. raisins
1 tsp. salt	1/4 c. melted shortening

Combine dry ingredients. Mix egg and milk and add to dry ingredients. Mix. Stir in remaining ingredients. Pour into a greased bread pan. Bake at 350° approximately 1 hour. Serve plain with butter or slice thin and make sandwiches with pineapple cheese and nut filling (see fillings).

Variation for **DATE NUT BREAD:** Substitute 1 c. chopped dates for raisins.

PEANUT BUTTER BREAD

2 c. flour	1/2 c. sugar
4 tsp. baking powder	2/3 c. peanut butter
1 tsp. salt	1 c. milk

Combine dry ingredients. Work peanut butter in with finger tips. Add milk. Mix lightly. Pour into greased loaf pan. Bake at 350° approximately one hour. Makes one small loaf.

ORANGE BREAD

rind from 2 large oranges	1 c. milk
water	2 T. melted shortening
1/2 c. sugar	3 c. flour
1/3 c. boiling water	1 T. baking powder
1 egg	1 tsp. salt

Cut rind in short, narrow strips or grate coarsely. Cover with water and boil until tender. Drain. Add sugar and 1/3 c. boiling water to rind. Boil approximately 20 minutes, stirring constantly. Remove from heat. Cool. Beat egg. Add milk and shortening. Add cooled orange mixture. Combine dry ingredients and add to liquid ingredients. Mix lightly but thoroughly. Pour into a well-greased bread pan. Bake at 375° for 45-50 minutes. Makes one loaf.

"Shortening gives tenderness to baked products. Butter is the most flavorful shortening, but is expensive and has less shortening power than other fat. It is used most for the flavor it adds. Any sweet white fat, lard or vegetable, may be used instead of butter."

PRUNE BREAD

2 T. shortening
1/2 c. sugar
1 egg, well-beaten
1 c. milk
2 1/2 c. flour

1 T. baking powder
1 tsp. salt
1 tsp. cinnamon
1 1/2 c. chopped prunes

Cream shortening and sugar. Beat in egg. Add milk. Combine dry ingredients and add to first mixture. Add prunes and mix lightly but thoroughly. Pour into a well-greased bread pan. Bake at 375° approximately 50 minutes. Part whole wheat flour may be used. Makes one small loaf.

"One teaspoon of baking powder for each cup of flour gives the best results in most recipes. More is needed if bran, whole wheat flour or cornmeal is used, and in very thin batters such as for waffles or pancakes."

GRANDMA'S

SHIN OF BEEF SOUP

Get a shin bone of beef weighing four or five pounds; let the butcher saw it in pieces two inches long, that the marrow may become the better incorporated with the soup, and so give it greater richness. Wash the meat in cold water, mix together of salt and pepper each a tablespoonful, rub this well into the meat, then put into a soup-pot; put to it as many quarts of water as there are pounds of meat, and set it over a moderate fire, until it comes to a boil, then take off whatever scum may have risen, after which cover it close, and set it where it will boil very gently for two hours longer, then skim it again, and add to it the proper vegetables, which are these-one large carrot grated, one large turnip cut in slices, one leek cut in slices, one bunch of parsley cut small, six small potatoes peeled and cut in half, and a teacupful pearl barley well washed, then cover and let it boil gently for one hour, at which time add another tablespoonful of salt and a thickening made of a tablespoonful of wheat flour and a gill of water, stir it in by the tablespoonful; cover it for fifteen minutes and it is done. Three hours and a half is required to make this soup; it is the best for cold weather. Should any remain over the first day, it may be heated with the addition of a little boiling water, and served again.

SOUPS

POTATO SOUP

3 medium potatoes	1 onion, finely-chopped
1 tsp. salt	1 stalk celery, sliced
3 c. water	2 c. milk or cream

Peel and dice potatoes. Put in salted water along with onion and celery. Bring to a boil. Simmer until potatoes are tender. Add milk and heat thoroughly. Sprinkle with fresh, chopped parsley if desired.

Variation for **CREAMED POTATO SOUP:** Melt 1/4 c. butter and stir in 1/4 c. flour. Gradually add the milk and stir until thickened. Mix into cooked potatoes.

SPLIT PEA SOUP

1 1/2 c. dried split peas	2 c. milk
3 qt. water	2 T. butter
ham bone	1 tsp. salt or to taste
1 onion, chopped	1/8 tsp. pepper

Wash and pick over peas and soak overnight. Drain. Add water, ham bone and onion. Cover and cook slowly 1 1/2 hours or until peas are soft. Remove ham bone. Add milk, butter, salt and pepper.

NAVY BEAN SOUP

In Michigan, Grandpa Kulps raised navy beans to sell. After moving to Indiana they bought a 100 lb. bag of navy beans each winter.

1 c. dry navy beans	1 T. butter
2 qt. water	1/2 c. sliced carrots
1 tsp. salt	1/2 c. chopped onion
1/8 tsp. pepper	

Wash beans thoroughly. Drain; put in a saucepan and add water. Bring to a boil. Reduce heat. Cover and let simmer 3-3 1/2 hours or until tender. Add salt, pepper, butter, carrots and onions after beans are nearly tender. Milk or cream may be added just before serving. If beans are soaked overnight they don't have to be cooked quite as long.

CREAM OF TOMATO SOUP

1 qt. canned or fresh tomatoes	1/2 c. water
	1/4 tsp. soda
1 small onion, finely-chopped	1/2 c. butter
1 T. sugar	1/2 c. flour
1 tsp. salt (unless salted	1 tsp. salt
tomatoes are used)	1 qt. milk
1/8 tsp. pepper	

Simmer tomatoes, onions, sugar, salt, pepper and water approximately 15 minutes. Rub tomatoes through a sieve. Add soda. While tomatoes are cooking make a white sauce. Melt butter. Blend in flour and salt, stirring until smooth. Gradually add milk, stirring constantly. Pour hot tomato purée into hot white sauce. Mix well.

TOMATO OKRA SOUP

1/4 c. rice	1 onion, diced
4 T. butter	3 c. canned or fresh peeled
5 c. water	tomatoes
1/2 c. celery	1 1/2 tsp. salt
1 green pepper, diced	2 c. sliced okra pods

Brown rice in 2 T. butter. Add water; bring to a boil. Sauté celery, peppers and onion in another pan in remaining butter. Add tomatoes and bring to a boil. Pour onto rice. Add salt. Simmer, covered, until rice is tender. Add okra and simmer 10-15 minutes more.

"We would give the housewife an idea in regard to spices and herbs for soups. In the early fall buy all the herbs you think sufficient for the coming year; dry, pound, and sift them and keep in well corked bottles. Sage, thyme, bay leaves, marjoram, rosemary, sweet basil, parsley, and, when you are using lemons, where the rind is not required, as in lemonade, grate, dry, and bottle it in the same way. You will find all of the above very desirable in soups."

ONION SOUP

1 lb. onions (3 medium)	6 c. chicken broth
2 T. butter	1/2 tsp. salt or to taste
1 T. flour	1/8 tsp. pepper

Slice and sauté onions in butter until brown. Sprinkle with flour and stir. Add broth slowly, stirring until smooth. Season to taste. Serve with fresh bread sprinkled with parmesan cheese and toasted in the oven. If desired, sprinkle parmesan cheese on soup.

MOCK OYSTER SOUP

12 root oysters (salsify)	1 tsp. salt
4 c. cream or milk	1/8 tsp. pepper
2 T. butter	

Scrape the roots and cut into small rings. Cover with water. Simmer until tender. Add cream or milk and butter. Season to taste. Heat thoroughly. Serve with salted crackers.

MUSHROOM SOUP

1/2 lb. fresh mushrooms or 7 oz. canned mushrooms	1/4 c. flour
	2 c. milk
2 c. chicken broth	1/2 tsp. salt or to taste
2 T. minced onion	1/8 tsp. pepper
1/4 c. butter	

Chop mushrooms. Add to broth along with onion. Melt butter. Add flour and stir until smooth. Add milk, stirring constantly. Pour into boiling broth while stirring. Season to taste. Serve hot.

Note: Broth can be made by dissolving 2 bouillon cubes in two cups boiling water.

VEGETABLE SOUP

5 c. water or beef broth	1/2 c. shredded cabbage
1 c. diced potatoes	1/2 c. diced turnips
1 c. diced tomatoes	1 tsp. salt
1/2 c. chopped onion	1/8 tsp. celery salt
1/2 c. diced carrots	1/8 tsp. pepper

Combine ingredients. Use less salt if broth is salty. Bring to a boil the simmer until vegetables are tender. If desired, cook with a beef bon and simmer one hour.

CHEESE VEGETABLE SOUP

1/2 c. butter	4 c. milk
1/2 c. chopped celery	2 c. grated cheese
1/2 c. chopped green pepper	2 c. chicken broth
1/2 c. chopped onion	1 tsp. salt or to taste
1/2 c. chopped carrot	1/8 tsp. pepper
6 T. flour	

Sauté vegetables in butter. Add flour and stir until smooth. Slowly mi in milk, stirring constantly. When bubbling add cheese, stirring unti melted. Mix in chicken broth. Season to taste. Heat thoroughly.

BEEF BARLEY VEGETABLE SOUP

1 lb. hamburger	1 onion, chopped
2 c. canned or fresh peeled tomatoes	1/4 c. barley
2 c. diced potatoes	2 tsp. salt
2 medium carrots, diced	1/8 tsp. pepper
1/2 c. chopped celery	1 1/2 qt. water

Combine all ingredients in a large kettle. Bring to a boil then simme slowly for one hour. Serve hot with crackers.

GRANDMA HORST'S
CHICKEN CORN SOUP

1 chicken
2 c. corn
1 onion, chopped

1/2 c. celery, chopped
salt and pepper

Cook chicken. Debone and chop meat. Put meat back in broth along with vegetables. Cook until vegetables are tender. Season to taste.

Variation for **CHICKEN CORN NOODLE SOUP:** Add noodles to broth and cook until tender.

Variation for **CHICKEN CORN RIVEL SOUP:** Rub together 1 c. flour, 2 T. milk and one egg until the size of peas. Drop rivels into boiling broth. Boil about five minutes.

CHICKEN RICE SOUP

6 c. chicken broth
1/2 c. rice
1 onion, chopped
1/2 c. diced carrots

1/2 c. diced celery
1 c. cooked, diced chicken
1/2 tsp. salt or to taste
1/8 tsp. pepper

Combine all ingredients. Bring to a boil. Simmer 20 minutes or until rice is tender. Part water can be used for chicken broth.

"Be careful to proportion the quantity of water to that of the meat. Somewhat less than a quart of water to a pound of meat is a good rule for common soups. Rich soups intended for company, may have a still smaller allowance of water."

CHICKEN NOODLE SOUP
"Make your own noodles!"

2 lb. chicken, cut up	1 c. flour
4 c. water	1/4 tsp. salt
1 tsp. salt	1 slightly beaten egg

Cover chicken with water. Add 1 tsp. salt. Simmer until meat is tender—about three hours. Add water if needed to keep at the same level. Remove chicken pieces. Skim fat. Pick chicken off bones and put back into broth. Combine flour and 1/4 tsp. salt. Add gradually to egg until a stiff dough is formed. Knead a few minutes on a floured board. Roll out to a 1/16-inch thickness. Dust with flour. Cut into 1/4-inch wide strips. Drop strips into boiling chicken broth. Boil rapidly approximately five minutes.

CHILI

1 lb. hamburger	2 1/2 c. cooked kidney beans
1 onion, chopped	2 c. canned tomatoes
1 T. chili powder	1 c. water
1 tsp. salt	

Brown hamburger and onion. Add chili powder and salt. Stir in remaining ingredients. Simmer 10 minutes. If desired, use fresh, peeled and seeded tomatoes and simmer longer.

SALMON SOUP

2 T. butter	4 c. milk
1 onion, chopped	salt
2 c. canned salmon	pepper

Cook onions in butter until tender. Add fish, milk, salt and pepper. Heat thoroughly.

OYSTER SOUP

2 c. oysters	1/2 tsp. salt or to taste
4 c. milk	1/8 tsp. pepper
2 T. butter	

Drain liquid from oysters into a saucepan. Bring to a boil and skim. Rinse oysters, removing all shells and grit. If desired use more oysters and cut away the brown pouch. Add oysters and simmer until edges begin to curl. Heat milk almost to boiling. Add butter and seasoning to taste to oysters then add hot milk. Serve at once with salted crackers.

CLAM CHOWDER

12 clams	1 1/2 tsp. salt
1 onion, finely-chopped	1/8 tsp. pepper
2 T. butter	4 c. milk
2 T. flour	3 c. cooked, cubed potatoes

Save juice from clams and set aside. Clean and pick over clams, removing all shell particles. Chop clams finely. Put clams and juice in a sauce pan and cook 10 minutes. Fry onion in butter until a delicate brown. Add flour, salt and pepper and blend till smooth. Add milk, stirring constantly until thickened. Mix in cooked potatoes and clams. Heat thoroughly. Serve at once.

FRESH FISH CHOWDER

2 T. butter	2 c. chopped, fresh fish
1 onion, chopped	4 c. milk
2 c. water	2 tsp. salt
6 cubed potatoes	1/8 tsp. pepper

Melt butter and sauté onion to a light brown. Add water and potatoes. Bring to a boil then simmer 10 minutes. Add fish and simmer 20 minutes. Add milk and season to taste. Heat thoroughly but don't boil.

"To be thoroughly good form at dinner is the very inflorescence of civilized life. Like many other regulations of social life, dinner-table etiquette is arbitrary, but not to know certain things is to argue yourself unknown so far as society life goes. To take soup pushing the spoon from rather than toward yourself; to touch the napkins as little as possible; to accept or decline what is offered instantly and quietly; these and other trifles characterize the well-bred diner-out."

GRANDMA'S

NAVY BEAN
SANDWICHES

Rub cooked beans through a colander;
season; add minced onion or chives, and
butter. Mix to a paste and spread on thin
slices of buttered bread.

ORANGE SANDWICHES

To one cup powdered sugar, add the pulp
and juice of one large orange, one teaspoon
lemon juice. Mix well, then cream it with
two tablespoons sweet butter. Spread
on thin slices of bread.

SANDWICHES

RADISH SANDWICHES

Grandma Martin taught her children to eat radishes with buttered bread. This made them less bitter.

buttered bread   **thinly-sliced radishes**

Lay radish slices on buttered bread. Sprinkle with salt if desired.

SPINACH SANDWICHES

3 c. fresh spinach   **mayonnaise**
1/2 c. diced celery   **salt and pepper to taste**
1/4 c. chopped onion   **white or wheat bread**
2 hard-cooked eggs, chopped

Shred spinach. Add celery, onion and eggs. Moisten with mayonnaise to spreading consistency. Season to taste. Spread between slices of bread.

ONION PEPPER AND OLIVE SANDWICHES

1 onion, chopped   **1 c. grated cheese**
1 green pepper, chopped   **mayonnaise**
1/4 c. chopped olives or dill **salt and pepper to taste**
** pickles**   **white or rye bread**

Combine onion, pepper, olives and cheese. Add enough mayonnaise to moisten. Season to taste. Spread between slices of bread. Add two chopped, hard-cooked eggs if desired.

"Taste may be quite as well displayed on a pine table as in the grouping of silver and china on the table of the rich. The charm of housekeeping lies in the nice attention of little things, not in a superabundance."

EGG SALAD SANDWICHES

4 hard-cooked eggs	3 T. mayonnaise
1/4 c. chopped dill pickle	1/2 tsp. salt or to taste
1/4 c. chopped celery	1/8 tsp. pepper
2 T. minced onion	buttered bread

Combine ingredients. Spread between buttered slices of bread.

CHICKEN SALAD SANDWICHES

2 c. diced, cooked chicken	1/2 c. mayonnaise
2 hard-cooked eggs, chopped	1/2 tsp. salt or to taste
1 c. diced celery or shredded lettuce	1/8 tsp. pepper
2 T. chopped onion or pickles	bread

Combine chicken, eggs, celery and onion. Add mayonnaise. Season to taste and make sandwiches. If desired a chopped, seeded tomato can be added.

Variation for **TURKEY SALAD SANDWICHES:** substitute turkey for chicken.

TUNA SALAD SANDWICHES

1 c. canned (12 oz. can) tuna	2 T. chopped onion
2 hard-cooked eggs	1/3 c. mayonnaise
1 c. chopped tomato	salt and pepper to taste
1/4 c. chopped celery	bread

Combine tuna, eggs, tomato, celery and onion. Mix in mayonnaise. Season to taste and spread on sliced bread for sandwiches. A 3/4 c. of shredded lettuce or diced cucumber can be added if desired.

HAM SALAD SANDWICHES

1 c. chopped, cooked ham
2 hard-cooked eggs
2 T. chopped celery or green
    pepper

2 T. chopped olives or pickles
1/4-1/2 c. mayonnaise
salt and pepper to taste
bread

Combine ham, eggs, celery and olives. Moisten with enough mayonnaise for desired spreading consistency. Season to taste. Spread on bread for sandwiches.

CHOPPED HAM AND CHEESE SANDWICHES

1 c. finely-chopped, cooked
    ham
1 c. grated cheese
1/4 c. cream or mayonnaise

2 T. chili sauce or catsup
1/2 tsp. dry mustard
1 tsp. chopped, fresh parsley
rye or wheat bread

Mix ham and cheese well. Add remaining ingredients. Mix well. Spread between slices of buttered bread. Serve hot or cold.

BROILED BACON CHEESE AND TOMATO SANDWICHES

buttered bread
American cheese, sliced thin
tomato slices

salt and pepper
bacon

Cover each slice of buttered bread with a slice of cheese. Put a slice or two of tomato on cheese and sprinkle with salt and pepper. Lay two strips of bacon on tomatoes. Broil until cheese melts and bacon is crisp.

"Sandwiches hot, or sandwiches cold, sandwiches dainty, or sandwiches bulky—everybody loves a sandwich."

CLUB SANDWICHES

toast
butter or mayonnaise
lettuce

sliced tomatoes
crisp bacon slices
sliced chicken breast

Arrange lettuce, tomato slices and bacon on toast spread with butter c
mayonnaise. Cover with lettuce and a slice of chicken breast. Ad
mayonnaise and cover with another slice of toast. Cut diagonally an
serve.

HOT ROAST BEEF SANDWICHES

buttered toast
thin slices of hot roast beef

well-seasoned gravy
fresh parsley

Cover buttered toast with a slice of hot roast beef. Cover with gravy an
garnish with parsley. Hot roast pork or chicken may be used.

BAKED BISCUIT SANDWICHES

2 c. flour
1 T. baking powder
1/2 tsp. salt
1/4 c. shortening

3/4 c. milk
chopped, cooked ham or other
    cooked meat

Combine dry ingredients. Rub shortening in with fingertips. Add mill
and mix to a stiff dough. Roll out on a floured board to 1/4-inch thick
Cut into rounds. Spread half of the rounds with meat. Moisten edge
with water, milk or gravy and top with another round. Bake at 425° ap
proximately 12 minutes. Cheese, raisins or other fruit may be used in
stead of meat.

Variation for **SAUSAGE BISCUIT SANDWICHES:** Rol
biscuit dough 1/2-inch thick and cut into rounds. Lay a small, cooked
sausage on each round. Moisten edges of dough. Fold over and pres
together with sausage in center. Bake at 425° approximately 12 minutes

LEFTOVER MEAT SANDWICHES

chopped leftover meat
chopped onion
mayonnaise

shredded lettuce or chopped
celery
bread

Mix chopped meat and onion with enough mayonnaise to moisten. Spread on bread and top with crisp lettuce leaves and another slice of bread.

SAUTÉED JAM SANDWICHES

Spread jam between two slices of buttered bread. Sauté sandwich in a little butter until brown on both sides. Sprinkle with powdered sugar. Serve hot.

RAISIN SANDWICH FILLING

"This makes a delightful filling for children's school sandwiches"

1 c. brown sugar
1 c. raisins
1/2 c. water

1 T. butter
1 c. chopped nuts

Boil sugar, raisins, water and butter. When thick, stir in chopped nut meats.

"There is no end to the variety of sandwiches available to the clever home-maker."

NOTES

GRANDMA'S

LETTUCE SALAD

Take the yolks of three hard-boiled eggs, add salt and mustard to taste; mash it fine; make a paste by adding a dessert-spoon of olive oil or melted butter (use butter always when it is difficult to get fresh oil); mix thoroughly, and then dilute by adding gradually a teacup of vinegar, and pour over the lettuce. Garnish by slicing another egg and laying over the lettuce. This is sufficient for a moderate-sized dish of lettuce.

SALAD DRESSING (EXCELLENT)

Four eggs, one teaspoonful of mixed mustard, one-quarter teaspoonful of white pepper, half that quantity of cayenne, salt to taste, four tablespoonfuls of cream vinegar. Boil the eggs until hard; put them into cold water, take off the shells, and pound the yolks in a mortar to a smooth paste. Then add all the other ingredients, except the vinegar, and stir them well until the whole are thoroughly incorporated one with the other. Pour sufficient vinegar to make it of the consistency of cream, taking care to add but little at a time. The mixture will then be ready for use.

SALADS AND SALAD DRESSINGS

LETTUCE SALAD

In 1933 when Kraft's Mayonnaise sales started slipping they came out with Miracle Whip salad dressing.

1 head lettuce, chopped	2 1/2 T. sugar
1 onion, chopped	2 T. cream or milk
1/2 c. grated cheese	2 T. vinegar
1/2 c. salad dressing	1 tsp. mustard

Toss lettuce, onions and cheese. Combine remaining ingredients to make dressing. Pour dressing over all and toss lightly.

MIXED GREEN SALAD

6 lettuce leaves	1 c. thinly-sliced Chinese
6 romaine leaves	cabbage
6 escarole leaves	2 T. minced onion

Rub bowl with garlic. Add greens and onion. Toss with French or other salad dressing.

SPINACH LETTUCE SALAD

2 c. shredded spinach	1/2 c. mayonnaise or salad
2 c. shredded lettuce	dressing
1/2 c. chopped celery	salt to taste

Mix and chill. Add mayonnaise as needed.

"To prevent a vegetable salad from becoming sodden when it has to stand for a few hours, place a saucer upside down in the bottom of the bowl before filling it with salad. The moisture will run underneath and the salad will remain fresh and crisp."

DANDELION SALAD

4 c. dandelion greens	2 c. water
3 slices bacon	1/4 c. vinegar
2 T. sugar	1 egg
1 1/2 T. flour	1/4 c. finely chopped onions
1 tsp. salt	3 hard-cooked eggs

Wash and chop dandelion. Fry bacon until crisp. Remove bacon from drippings, saving drippings to make dressing. Combine sugar, flour and salt. Beat egg in water and vinegar and add to dry ingredients. Pour into drippings and cook until thickened, stirring constantly. Cool dressing slightly. Toss dandelion with bacon, onions and chopped eggs. Pour dressing over all and mix lightly.

CABBAGE AND CARROT SLAW

6 c. shredded cabbage	1/3 c. cream
1/2 c. chopped carrots	1/3 c. sugar
1/2 c. chopped onion	1/3 c. vinegar
1 chopped green pepper	1/2 tsp. salt

Toss vegetables. Combine remaining ingredients and add just before serving.

Variation for **SLAW DRESSING:** Use 2/3 c. mayonnaise or salad dressing, 3 T. vinegar, 3 T. sugar and 1/4 tsp. salt.

CABBAGE PINEAPPLE SALAD

3 c. shredded cabbage	1/2 c. chopped nuts
1 c. diced pineapple	mayonnaise
1 c. diced marshmallows	

Combine cabbage, pineapple, marshmallows and nuts. Moisten with mayonnaise. Mix lightly.

GRANDMA HORST'S
KIDNEY BEAN SALAD

1/2 c. mayonnaise
1/4 tsp. dry mustard
1/2 tsp. honey
4 c. cooked kidney beans

1 onion, chopped fine
1 cucumber, diced
4 hard-boiled eggs, chopped

Combine mayonnaise, mustard and honey to make dressing. Mix with remaining ingredients.

PEA SALAD

2 c. canned peas
1 c. diced celery
1/2 c. diced cheese

2 T. finely-chopped onions
salad dressing or mayonnaise
salt and pepper

Combine peas, celery, cheese and onion; add enough salad dressing or mayonnaise to moisten. Season to taste.

POTATO SALAD

4 c. diced, cooked potatoes
1 c. diced celery
1 onion, chopped
3 hard-cooked eggs, chopped
1/2 c. diced sweet pickles

1 tsp. salt or to taste
1/8 tsp. pepper
1/8 tsp. paprika
3/4 c. mayonnaise or salad
    dressing

Combine all ingredients but mayonnaise. Mix mayonnaise in lightly. If desired marinate potatoes in 1/2 c. French dressing and use only 1/2 c. mayonnaise.

"Definition of a salad: A little bit of anything or everything, seasoned, mixed with a good dressing and served tastefully."

MACARONI SALAD

3 c. cooked macaroni	1/4 c. chopped onions
3 hard-cooked eggs, chopped	3/4 c. mayonnaise
1 c. diced celery	1 tsp. salt or to taste
1/2 c. diced or shredded	1/8 tsp. pepper
carrots	1/8 tsp. paprika

Mix and chill.

Variation for **CHICKEN MACARONI SALAD:** Add 2 c diced, cooked chicken.

Variation for **OLIVE MACARONI SALAD:** Omit hard-cooked eggs and add 3/4 c. chopped olives.

EGG SALAD STUFFED TOMATOES

8 medium tomatoes	2 tsp. salt
16 hard-cooked eggs	3 T. lemon juice or vinegar
1 c. finely-chopped celery	1 T. mustard
3 T. minced onion	1/2 c. mayonnaise

Wash tomatoes. Remove the stem and then cut each tomato in fourths without cutting all the way through. Press back the petals and sprinkle the inside with salt. Chill. Meanwhile chop the eggs and add remaining ingredients. Mix well. Put some of the egg mixture in the center of each tomato.

FRUIT SALAD

1 c. diced pineapple	2 bananas, sliced
1 c. grapes	fruit salad dressing
3 oranges, cut in chunks	

Combine fruit. Moisten with fruit salad dressing (see dressings). Add 1 c. diced marshmallows and 1/2 c. chopped nuts, if desired.

MELON SALAD

3 oz. lime gelatin
2 c. hot water

1 1/2 c. cantaloupe or honey
    dew melon balls

Dissolve gelatin in water. Chill. When slightly thickened, fold in melon balls. Turn into a bowl or mold. Chill until firm. Serve on crisp lettuce with mayonnaise, if desired.

CELESTIAL SALAD

1 c. marshmallows
1/2 c. blanched almonds
1 c. pineapple

1/2 c. mayonnaise
1 c. whipped cream

Mix marshmallows, almonds, pineapples and mayonnaise. When ready to serve fold in whipped cream.

WALDORF SALAD

2 c. diced apples
1 T. lemon juice
1 c. diced celery

3/4 c. mayonnaise or salad
    dressing
1/2 c. chopped walnuts

Sprinkle apples with lemon juice. Add remaining ingredients, mixing well. Serve on individual salad plates or lettuce leaf if desired.

CARROT CABBAGE AND TURNIP SALAD

1 c. shredded carrots
1 c. shredded cabbage

1 c. shredded turnips
salt and pepper to taste

Combine and season to taste. Serve with French dressing.

"Most persons think of salads as side issues, when in truth they should be an inspired part of one or two meals daily."

GRANDMA HORST'S
APPLE SALAD

Grandma added a note that yellow apples don't get as brown as red apples. She als
noted that pineapple chunks can be use instead of all apples.

8 apples, diced	1/2 c. mayonnaise
1 c. nuts	1/2 c. sugar
1/2 c. raisins	1/4 c. peanut butter
1 c. marshmallows	1/4 c. cream

Combine apples, nuts, raisins and marshmallows. Mix togethe
mayonnaise, sugar, peanut butter and cream and pour over salad. Mill
may be used instead of cream.

CREAM CHEESE APPLES

2 c. sugar	8 oz. cream cheese
2 c. water	mayonnaise
1 c. red cinnamon candy	1/4 c. chopped nuts
6 medium apples	

Combine sugar, water and candy. Boil three minutes then drop in peeled
and cored whole apples. Boil slowly, turning frequently, until apples are
tender and well colored but not falling apart. Drain. Chill. Moisten sof
cream cheese with a little mayonnaise. Add nuts. Stuff apples with
cheese mixture. Serve on crisp lettuce with mayonnaise if desired
Three cinnamon sticks and red food coloring can be substituted fo:
candy.

CREAM CHEESE PEARS

6 large pear halves	1/2 c. chopped nuts
6 T. cream cheese	lettuce

Combine cream cheese and nuts. Fill pear cavities. Serve on lettuce
plain, with mayonnaise or with a fruit salad dressing.

CRANBERRY SALAD

4 c. fresh cranberries
2 c. sugar
2 T. unflavored gelatin
1 c. cold water

1/4 tsp. salt
1 1/2 c. diced celery
1 c. chopped nuts

Wash cranberries. Cover with water and cook until tender. Add sugar. Cook five minutes. Soften gelatin in 1 c. cold water. Add gelatin and salt to cranberries. Stir until dissolved. Chill until partially set. Add celery and nuts. Mix thoroughly. Pour into a mold, bowl or cake pan. Serve with mayonnaise if desired.

CARROT SALAD

3 oz. lemon gelatin
1 1/2 c. boiling water
1 c. grated carrots

1/2 c. chopped celery
1 c. crushed pineapple,
    drained

Add boiling water to gelatin and stir until dissolved. Cool then add remaining ingredients. Pour into cake pan and cut in squares and serve on lettuce. If desired, add 1/2 c. chopped nuts.

CIDER GELATIN SALAD

2 1/2 c. cider
2 T. unflavored gelatin
1 c. chopped apples

1/2 c. chopped celery
1/4 tsp. salt
1/4 c. chopped nuts

Soak gelatin in 1/2 c. cold cider about five minutes. Bring remaining cider to a boil and add gelatin mixture. Stir until gelatin is dissolved. Cool until gelatin starts to congeal. Stir in remaining ingredients. Pour into a mold, bowl or cake pan. Chill until firm.

"Many fruit salads are improved by serving on lettuce leaves or other vegetable leaves. Celery is a most happy addition to many fruit salads, especially to apple salad."

GINGER ALE FRUIT SALAD

2 T. unflavored gelatin	1 c. grapes
1/4 c. cold water	1 c. cubed pineapples
1/2 c. boiling water	1 apple
1/4 c. lemon juice	1 orange
2 T. sugar	1/4 c. nuts
1 c. ginger ale	

Soak gelatin in cold water five minutes and dissolve in boiling water. Add lemon juice, sugar and ginger ale. Halve grapes; peel and chop apples. Separate oranges into sections and remove membranes. When first mixture begins to thicken, fold in fruit and nuts. Pour into a bowl, mold or cake pan.

FROZEN FRUIT SALAD

8 oz. cream cheese	1 1/2-2 c. pineapple
2 T. cream	1/2 c. maraschino cherries
1/3 c. mayonnaise	1/2 c. chopped pecans
2 T. lemon juice	1 c. whipping cream
2 T. sugar	

Mix cream cheese and cream. Add mayonnaise, lemon juice and sugar. Stir in pineapple, cherries and nuts. Whip cream and fold into salad. Freeze in a cake pan. May be garnished with maraschino cherries or nuts.

STRAWBERRY CHEESE SALAD

2 c. strawberries	12 oz. cream cheese, softened
2 T. sugar	1/2 c. whipping cream
2 tsp. lemon juice	

Crush berries. Add sugar and lemon juice. Gradually mix in cream cheese. Whip cream and fold into strawberry mixture. Freeze in an 8x8 cake pan. Cut into squares to serve.

CREAM CHEESE SALAD

2 c. crushed pineapple
1 T. unflavored gelatin
2 T. cold water
3 oz. lemon gelatin
2 T. lemon juice

1/8 tsp. salt
1/2 c. chopped nuts
1 c. chopped celery
6 oz. cream cheese
1 c. whipping cream

Drain juice from pineapple. Add enough water to make two cups. Heat to boiling. Soften gelatin in 2 T. cold water. Add lemon gelatin. Pour boiling juice and water mixture over gelatin. Stir until dissolved. Add lemon juice and salt. Mix thoroughly. Cool until partially set. Add nuts and celery to pineapple. Stir in softened cream cheese. Add to gelatin mixture and mix well. Whip cream and fold into salad.

CHICKEN APPLE SALAD

2 c. cold, cooked, diced
    chicken
1 c. diced apples
1/2 c. diced celery

1/2 c. chopped nuts
3/4 c. mayonnaise or salad
    dressing
salt to taste

Combine chicken, apples, celery and nuts. Add mayonnaise, adding extra if needed. Mix well. Season to taste.

CHICKEN AND HAM SALAD IN TOMATOES

1 1/2 c. diced, cooked chicken
1 1/2 c. diced, cooked ham
2 T. minced onion
3/4 c. chopped celery
1/4 c. French dressing

6 medium tomatoes
salt
1/2 c. mayonnaise
1 T. mustard

Combine chicken, ham, onion, celery and French dressing. Let stand one hour, then drain. Scoop centers out of tomatoes. Sprinkle tomatoes with salt. Turn upside down on a plate and refrigerate. Combine mayonnaise and mustard. Stir into chicken mixture. Place tomato shells on lettuce. Fill with chicken and ham mixture.

HAWAIIAN CHICKEN SALAD

2 1/2 c. cooked chicken, cut
    into 1/2-inch squares
2 c. pineapple chunks
1 c. celery, cut into 1/2-inch
    pieces

3 T. cooking oil
2 T. lemon juice
1/4 tsp. salt
1/3 c. mayonnaise
1/4 c. slivered almonds

Combine chicken, pineapple and celery. Mix cooking oil, lemon juice and salt and marinate salad one hour. Add mayonnaise and mix well. Serve on lettuce or other greens and sprinkle almonds on top.

ROAST MEAT SALAD

2 c. cold, cooked meat, diced
1 c. cooked potatoes
1 onion, chopped
2 hard-cooked eggs
1/2 c. celery, diced

1 green pepper, chopped
2 tsp. mustard
2/3 c. mayonnaise
salt to taste
1/8 tsp. pepper

Mix and chill. Shredded lettuce and chopped tomato, may be added.

SALMON SALAD

2 1/2 c. canned salmon
1 c. finely-chopped celery
1/2 c. mayonnaise

lettuce
sliced olives

Flake salmon and mix with celery and mayonnaise. Arrange on lettuce leaves and garnish with olive slices. If desired, serve with a slice of lemon and a spoonful of mayonnaise on each serving.

DUCK SALAD

2 c. chopped, roasted duck
4 oranges, seeded and sliced

lettuce
1/2 c. French dressing

Arrange duck and orange slices on lettuce. Pour dressing on top.

HAM CHEESE AND GREEN PEPPER SLICES

1 c. finely-chopped, cooked ham	1/4 c. chopped fresh parsley
1 c. finely-chopped celery	salt and pepper
6 oz. cream cheese	3 medium green peppers

Mix ham, celery, softened cream cheese and parsley thoroughly. Add salt and pepper if desired. Cut tops off peppers. Take out insides but leave whole. Pack ham mixture into peppers. Chill. Slice. Serve on lettuce with French dressing.

UNCOOKED TOMATO RELISH

4 c. peeled, chopped tomatoes	1 tsp. salt
1/2 c. chopped onion	1 tsp. mustard seed
1/2 c. chopped celery	1/4 tsp. cinnamon
1/4 c. chopped green pepper	1/4 tsp. nutmeg
1/2 c. vinegar	1/8 tsp. cloves
1 T. sugar	

Combine all ingredients, mixing well. Cover and refrigerate. Will keep several weeks in refrigerator.

"A very useful makeshift lemon squeezer is fashioned by placing the prongs of one fork over another, and while you hold them in place by the handles, turn the lemon around the prongs, just as you do with the squeezer."

COOKED SALAD DRESSING

2 T. flour	a few grains cayenne
1 T. sugar	1 egg, well-beaten
1 tsp. salt	1 1/4 c. milk or water
1 tsp. mustard	1/4 c. vinegar
1/4 tsp. paprika	2 T. butter

Combine dry ingredients in a heavy saucepan. Add egg. Mix thoroughly. Add milk, vinegar and butter. Cook, stirring constantly, until thick and smooth. Cool and use or refrigerate. Thin with cream or milk before serving, if necessary.

Variation for **HAM SALAD DRESSING:** Add 1/2 c. finely-chopped cooked ham.

Variation for **PEANUT BUTTER SALAD DRESSING:** Add 1/3 c. peanut butter after cooling slightly. Mix well.

FRENCH DRESSING

1 c. cooking oil	1 tsp. salt
1/2 c. vinegar	1 tsp. paprika
2 T. sugar	1/8 tsp. pepper
1 tsp. dry mustard	

Combine all ingredients in a glass jar. Cover and shake until well-blended. Use or refrigerate.

Variation for **BLEU CHEESE DRESSING:** Crumble 1/2 lb. bleu cheese into French dressing and mix well.

"The oil or fat used in dressing salad is very nourishing and the amount should be regulated by the fuel needs of the body. A manual worker needs more oil than a brain worker."

RED FRENCH DRESSING

1 c. cooking oil	1 1/2 tsp. dry mustard
1/2 c. vinegar	1 tsp. salt
2/3 c. chili sauce or catsup	1 tsp. paprika
2 T. minced onions	1/8 tsp. pepper
2 T. sugar	

Put in a glass jar. Cover and shake until well-blended. Shake each time before using.

ITALIAN DRESSING

2/3 c. salad oil	1/2 tsp. onion salt
1/4 c. vinegar	1/4 tsp. pepper
1/2 tsp. salt	1/2 clove garlic, minced

Beat oil and vinegar. Add remaining ingredients and mix well.

THOUSAND ISLAND DRESSING

1 c. mayonnaise	2 T. minced onion
1/3 c. chili sauce or catsup	1/2 tsp. paprika
1/2 c. finely chopped sweet pickles, olives or peppers	1/2 tsp. salt
	1/8 tsp. pepper

Mix well. Serve or refrigerate. If desired add two chopped hard-cooked eggs before serving. Well-drained pickle relish can be used instead of chopped sweet pickles.

SOUR CREAM DRESSING

1/2 c. sour cream	1/2 tsp. salt
1 T. vinegar	1/4 tsp. paprika
1 T. chopped onion or olives	1/8 tsp. pepper

Mix ingredients until light. Use or refrigerate.

BACON SALAD DRESSING

Combine one part vinegar to two parts bacon fat. Mix well. Crumble in bacon which was fried crisp in the fat. Mix and refrigerate.

FRUIT SALAD DRESSING

1 1/2 c. salad dressing	1/3 c. crushed pineapple
3 oz. cream cheese, softened	

Combine and mix until smooth.

COOKED FRUIT SALAD DRESSING

1/2 c. pineapple juice or peach juice from canned peaches	1 egg, well-beaten
	3 T. sugar
	1 1/2 tsp. lemon juice

Heat pineapple juice. Combine egg and sugar. Add hot pineapple juice slowly, stirring constantly. Cook in a heavy saucepan over low heat and stir until thick and smooth. Remove from heat and add lemon juice. Mix thoroughly. Chill. Any fruit juice can be used.

HONEY DRESSING

2/3 c. cooking oil	1 tsp. salt
1/3 c. lemon juice	2/3 c. honey

Beat oil, lemon juice and salt. Add honey slowly while beating. Serve with fruit salad.

"Avoid over-dressing salads."

GRANDMA'S

BEEFSTEAK PIE

Take some fine tender steaks, beat them
a little, season with a saltspoonful of pepper
and a teaspoonful of salt to a two-pound steak;
put bits of butter, the size of a hickory nut,
over the whole surface, dredge a teaspoonful of
flour over, then roll it up and cut it in pieces two
inches long; put rich pie paste around the sides and
bottom of a tin basin; put in the pieces of steak,
nearly fill the basin with water, add a piece of butter
the size of a large egg, cut small, dredge in a
teaspoonful of flour, add a little pepper and salt,
lay skewers across the basin, roll a top crust to half
an inch thickness, cut a slit in the centre; dip
your fingers in flour and neatly pinch the top and
side crust together all around the edge.
Bake one hour in a quick oven.

BEEF LAMB AND PORK

ROAST BEEF AND GRAVY

beef for roasting   pepper
3/4 tsp. salt per pound of
    meat

Sprinkle beef with salt and pepper. Put in a roasting pan and add 1 c. water. Bake at 325°, allowing 30 minutes per pound. A meat thermometer will show 170° for well done roast. To make gravy remove meat. Skim fat off pan drippings. Mix 2 T. flour to 2 T. water for each cup of liquid. Water can be added if necessary. Mix with drippings, stirring constantly. Blend well and bring to a boil. Season to taste.

PAN-BROILED STEAK

1-inch thick steak   salt and pepper
butter

Trim off excess fat. Heat frying pan until sizzling hot. Grease with removed fat. Sear steak quickly on both sides, turning repeatedly. When evenly seared on both sides reduce heat. Remove fat as it accumulates. A well-done 1-inch steak will require approximately 12 minutes after heat is reduced. Remove steak to platter and smear with butter; sprinkle with salt and pepper.

STEAK ONIONS AND TOMATOES

2 lbs. steak   2 tsp. salt
3 large onions   1/4 tsp. pepper
3 c. canned or fresh, peeled
    tomatoes

Cut meat in serving sized pieces. Melt a little beef fat in a skillet. Put steak in. Place onions on top. Add tomatoes, salt and pepper. Simmer on low heat until meat is tender—approximately one hour.

SWISS STEAK

1/3 c. flour	2 T. shortening
2 tsp. salt	2 1/2 c. canned or fresh,
1/8 tsp. pepper	peeled tomatoes
2 lbs. round steak	1/4 c. chopped green pepper
1 1/2 c. chopped onions	

Combine flour, salt and pepper. Pound flour mixture into steak with potato masher or side of a plate. Cut meat into serving sized pieces. Brown steak and onions in shortening in a heavy pan. Cover and simmer approximately one hour, adding a little water as needed. Add tomatoes and green peppers and cook approximately 30 minutes longer. Juice can be thickened like gravy or 1 c. sour cream may be added.

BAKED STEAK

2 1/2 lb. sirloin steak	2 large onions
2 tsp. salt	1 green pepper
1/8 tsp. pepper	1 1/2 c. ketchup

Place steak in a single layer in a baking pan. Add salt and pepper. Cut onions and pepper into round slices and put on meat. Pour ketchup over everything. Bake uncovered in a preheated 400° oven approximately one hour.

BAKED FLANK STEAK

3 T. vinegar	1 flank steak
1 tsp. salt	1 onion, sliced
1 tsp. sugar	1/2 c. water
1/2 tsp. dry mustard	

Combine vinegar, salt, sugar and mustard. Spread mixture on steak. Top with onion slices. Add water, pouring beside steak. Bake at 350° for 1 1/2 hours.

GRANDMA HOOVER'S
MEAT LOAF

Grandma Hoover's stepmother gave her an old diary with 25 handwritten recipes in it.
The collection consisted of cake and cookie recipes, doughnuts, potato salad and
dressing, and this meat loaf recipe.

2 lbs. ground beef	1/2 c. bread crumbs
2 eggs	2 tsp. salt
1 c. milk	1/4 tsp. pepper

Mix slightly-beaten eggs with ground beef. Add remaining ingredients
and mix well. Bake in a moderate oven (350°) for 1 1/2 hours.

Variation for **ONION MEAT LOAF:** Add 1 chopped onion. If
desired, use 3/4 c. milk and omit eggs. Cracker crumbs or oatmeal may
be used instead of bread crumbs.

Variation for **OLIVE MEAT LOAF:** Add 1/3 c. chopped
stuffed olives. Tomato juice or water can be substituted for milk.

Variation for **SPINACH MEAT LOAF:** Delete milk and add 1
c. canned or chopped spinach and 1/2 c. chopped mushrooms.

GRANDMA HORST'S
MEAT LOAF PIE

1 lb. ground beef	1/4 c. chopped onion
2/3 c. milk	1 tsp. salt
1 egg, beaten	2 c. mashed potatoes
2 slices bread, cubed	1/4 c. shredded cheese

Combine beef, milk, egg, bread, onion and salt. Mix well. Press into a
9-inch pie pan. Bake at 350° for 35-40 minutes. Spread potatoes over
meat and sprinkle with cheese. Return to oven until cheese melts.

PORCUPINE MEATBALLS

2 lbs. ground beef	2 tsp. salt
1 c. uncooked rice	1/4 tsp. pepper
1 onion, chopped	1/4 tsp. paprika
1/4 c. chopped green pepper	4 c. tomato juice

Mix all ingredients except tomato juice. Form into meat balls about the size of walnuts. Place in a large skillet and pour tomato juice on top. Cover. Bring to a boil then reduce heat. Cook over low heat approximately 50 minutes. Break a meatball open to check if rice is done. Add a little more water if necessary. A half cup of catsup may be added.

Variation for **BREAD CRUMB MEATBALLS:** Omit rice and add 1 1/2 c. soft bread cubes and two well-beaten eggs.

AMERICAN TOMALES

6 c. boiling water	2 c. canned or fresh, peeled
2 c. corn meal	tomatoes
1 lb. ground beef	1 tsp. chili powder
1 onion, chopped	1 1/2 tsp. salt
1/2 red or green pepper, chopped	1/8 tsp. pepper

Slowly pour corn meal into boiling water, stirring constantly. Cook 15 minutes. Brown ground beef, onion and green pepper. Add tomatoes and seasoning. Simmer 10 minutes. Fill a well-greased baking pan with alternate layers of corn meal mush and meat mixture. Bake at 400° approximately 25 minutes.

"When meat is eaten a salad of green vegetables, or a liberal serving of one green raw vegetable, like lettuce or celery, should always be taken."

GRANDMA MARTIN'S
BEEF POT PIE

Grandma Martin often made this for their midday meal on Saturday. She served it with green beans and fruit.

1 or 2 qts. canned beef	salt to taste
2 big potatoes	2 qts. water
chopped onion	

Pot Pie Dough:

1 egg	1/2 tsp. salt
milk	flour

Boil beef, potatoes, onion and salt in water. To make pot pie dough put egg in a one cup measure and fill with milk. Beat egg and milk; add salt and enough flour to make a stiff dough. Roll pot pie dough on floured surface to 1/8-inch thickness. Cut into 2-inch squares. Drop into boiling stew and cook 20 minutes or until done.

BEEF STEW AND DUMPLINGS

3 lbs. 1-inch beef cubes	2 c. diced carrots, scraped
flour for dredging	2 onions, sliced
3 T. shortening	1 c. sliced celery
1 T. salt	flour and water paste (about
1/8 tsp. pepper	1/3 c. flour)
4 c. boiling water	1 recipe plain dumplings
8 medium potatoes, peeled	(see next recipe)

Dredge beef cubes in flour and brown in shortening. Add seasonings and water. Simmer covered until meat is tender, approximately 2 hours. Cut potatoes and carrots in chunks and add along with onions about 45 minutes before the end of cooking time. Add more water if necessary. Cover and continue cooking. Fifteen minutes before serving add celery and enough flour and water to make a medium thick gravy. Drop dumplings from teaspoon on top of stew. Cover tightly and cook rapidly without uncovering for 12-15 minutes. Pour stew in center of platter and arrange dumplings around the edge.

PLAIN DUMPLINGS

1 1/2 c. flour	1 egg, beaten
1/2 tsp. salt	7/8 c. milk
2 1/2 tsp. baking powder	

Combine dry ingredients. Add egg to milk, then to dry ingredients. Stir until blended. Drop by teaspoonfuls on top of stew. Be sure there is enough gravy to cook dumplings without scorching the meat. Cover tightly at once and cook rapidly. Do not remove cover until dumplings have steamed 12-15 minutes. Makes 18 dumplings.

SCALLOPED BEEF

3 T. butter	3 c. chopped, cooked beef
3 T. flour	2 T. minced onion
1/2 tsp. salt	1 T. chopped fresh parsley
1/8 tsp. pepper	1 1/2 c. bread crumbs
1 1/2 c. milk	

Melt butter. Blend in flour, salt and pepper. Slowly add milk, stirring constantly, until sauce thickens. Add beef onion and parsley. Place a layer of bread crumbs in a greased baking dish. Put a layer of meat mixture on crumbs. Keep alternating layers ending with crumbs on top. Bake at 425° until crumbs are brown—approximately 15 minutes.

BEEF HASH

2 c. chopped, cooked beef	1 tsp. Worcestershire sauce
3 c. cooked potatoes, diced	1/4 tsp. salt
1/2 c. milk	1/8 tsp. pepper
1/2 c. chopped onion	1 T. butter

Mix all ingredients but butter. Melt butter in a skillet and spread mixture evenly. Fry slowly until well-browned—approximately 30 minutes. Fold like an omelet and place on a platter. Chopped green peppers may be added.

CREAMED DRIED BEEF

The original recipe reads, "Soak beef in cold water 15 minutes. Drain. Pick into thin pieces."

1/4 c. butter
1/4 c. flour
2 c. milk

1/2-3/4 lb. thinly-sliced dried beef

Melt butter. Stir in flour. Slowly add milk, stirring constantly; add dried beef and heat through. Serve on toast, biscuits, rice or baked or mashed potatoes. If desired, add parsley.

FRIED LIVER

Dip sliced beef liver in milk. Roll in flour. Put liver in hot skillet with melted shortening. Sprinkle with salt and pepper. Fry until well-browned on both sides—approximately 6-8 minutes.

SCRAPPLE

2 c. ground beef
2 c. ground pork
3 c. meat broth
2 tsp. salt

1/4 tsp. pepper
1 tsp. sage
few grains of cayenne
1 c. corn meal

Combine beef, pork and broth. Heat to boiling. Add seasoning. Slowly add corn meal, stirring constantly. Cook 30 minutes. Pour into a bread pan or other mold. Chill until firm. Slice and fry on a greased griddle until golden brown, turning once. Eat plain, with syrup or with catsup.

"For ordinary dinners the following bill of fare is sufficient: One kind of soup, one kind of fish, two entrees, a roast, a boil, game, cheese, desserts, ices, and coffee."

BREADED VEAL CUTLETS

2 lbs. veal cutlets	1 egg
1 1/2 tsp. salt	2 T. cold water
1/8 tsp. pepper	2 T. butter
3/4 c. dry bread crumbs	2 T. flour

Sprinkle cutlets with salt and pepper. Roll in bread crumbs. Beat egg with cold water. Dip crumbed cutlets into egg mixture, then roll into crumbs again. Heat butter in skillet and cook cutlets until thoroughly browned on both sides. Remove to platter. Mix flour with a little water and thicken pan drippings. If desired, grated parmesan cheese may be added to bread crumbs.

Variation for **DEEP FRIED VEAL CUTLETS:** Fry seasoned and crumbed cutlets in 380° degree deep fat, approximately seven minutes. Drain.

LAMB STEW

2 1/2 lbs. cubed lamb	1 onion, chopped
1 c. cubed carrots	2-3 tsp. salt
1 c. cubed turnips	1/8 tsp. pepper
3 c. cubed potatoes	

Cover meat with boiling water and cook slowly for 1 1/2 hours or until tender. Add remaining ingredients and cook 30 minutes longer. Thicken with a little flour mixed to a paste with cold water.

"Broiling or baking is better. The least harmful way of using a greasy frying pan is to brown food that has been cooked some other way. There is no need of doing this, but many love the flavor—habits are peculiar entities and hard taskmasters, and often great troublemakers."

LAMB CURRY AND RICE

2 1/2 lbs. 1-inch lamb cubes	1/4 c. flour
3 sliced onions	1 tsp. curry powder
1 tsp. chopped thyme	2 tsp. salt
1 tsp. chopped parsley	1/4 tsp. pepper
3 T. butter, melted	3 c. cooked rice

Brown lamb cubes. Cover with boiling water. Add onion, thyme and parsley. Simmer two hours or until meat is tender. Remove meat. Combine melted butter, flour, curry powder, salt and pepper. Pour into broth, stirring constantly. Bring to a boil. Make a mound of hot, cooked rice on a platter. Place meat and gravy around rice.

PORK ROAST

pork roast	salt and pepper

Rub meat with salt and pepper. Place fattiest side up. Bake at 325° until tender, allowing 30-35 minutes per pound. If a meat thermometer inserted into thickest portion of roast shows 170°, the roast is well-done.

FRIED PORK CHOPS

6 pork chops, 3/4 to 1-inch thick	1/4 tsp. pepper
1 tsp. salt	1 T. butter

Put chops in a hot skillet and sear rapidly on both sides. Reduce heat and cook slowly, 20-25 minutes, turning often. Smear with butter and sprinkle with salt and pepper. A slice of orange may be placed on top of each chop when almost done.

Variation for **PORK CHOPS AND SOUR CREAM:** After chops are tender, skim fat from skillet and add 1/2 c. sour cream. Cook over low heat 10 minutes more, basting chops several times.

BAKED PORK CHOPS AND POTATOES

8 small potatoes	2 T. butter
1 tsp. salt	3 c. milk
1/8 tsp. pepper	8 pork chops, 3/4-inch thick
1/4 c. flour	

Wash and peel potatoes. Slice thin. Place a layer of potatoes in greased baking dish. Sprinkle with half of the flour, salt and pepper. Repeat. Pour in milk. Lay chops on top. Sprinkle with salt and pepper. Bake at 350° approximately 1 1/4 hours.

FRIED HAM

center cut ham slices 1/4, 1/2 or 1-inch thick

Cut the fat on the edge in several places. Place in a hot skillet and brown quickly on both sides. Reduce heat and cook until tender—about 10 minutes if 1/4-inch thick, 15 minutes if 1/2-inch thick and 30 minute if 1-inch thick. If desired, sliced apples may be fried in ham fat and served with ham.

BAKED HAM WITH SWEET POTATOES AND PINEAPPLE

1/2 ham, 5-6 lbs.	6 medium sweet potatoes
1 c. brown sugar	1 c. crushed pineapple

Rub fat side of ham with brown sugar. Peel sweet potatoes and arrange around ham. Pour crushed pineapple over ham. Bake at 325° allowing approximately 25 minutes per pound or until internal temperature reaches 160°.

"Select a butcher carefully. The choice of meats is such a big subject that the housewife with her thousand and one important daily duties can scarcely expect to become expert in the field of choosing meats."

SPARERIBS WITH BARBECUE SAUCE

spareribs	1/2 c. Worcestershire sauce
salt and pepper	1 T. vinegar
1 onion, chopped	1 T. sugar
1/2 c. chopped parsley	1/2 tsp. chili powder
1/2 c. catsup	

Cut ribs into convenient sizes. Sprinkle with salt and pepper. Combine remaining ingredients and pour over meat. Water can be added if needed. Bake at 350° approximately 1 1/4 hours.

SPARERIBS AND SAUERKRAUT

2 lbs. spare ribs	4 c. sauerkraut
1 tsp. salt	

Cut spareribs. Sprinkle with salt. Put in a kettle and cover with cold water. Bring to a boil then reduce heat and simmer 30 minutes. Add sauerkraut and bring to a boil again. Reduce heat and simmer, uncovered, 30 more minutes.

SAUSAGE AND CABBAGE

1 1/2 lbs. sausage	1 tsp. salt
4 c. shredded cabbage	1/8 tsp. pepper

Brown sausage in skillet. Remove most of the fat. Add cabbage, salt and pepper. Cook six minutes, stirring frequently. Serve plain or on mashed potatoes.

Variation for **GROUND BEEF AND CABBAGE:** Substitute ground beef for sausage. Add another teaspoon of salt to meat.

"The distinction between the gentleman and the boor is more clearly noted at the table than anywhere else. Nothing reflects more upon home training than bad manners here. If, then, we would merit the title of lady or gentleman, it is necessary that we be able, naturally and easily, to show our good breeding by gentility at the table. Here especially, it may be said, good manners cannot be assumed for an occasion. Children must be taught by parents, both by precept and example, to be attentive and polite to each other at every meal—to observe proper rules of etiquette regularly. If they are so taught, there is no danger that they will appear rude, awkward or unmannerly when they are entertaining, or are entertained as guests. This every day encouragement of the observances of simple and sensible table manners promotes the comfort and cultivation of the family, and takes the embarrassment out of important occasions."

GRANDMA'S

CHICKEN POTPIE

Skin and cut up the fowls into joints, and put the neck, legs and back-bones in a stew-pan, with a little water, and onion, a bunch of savory herbs, and a blade of mace; let these stew for an hour, and, when done, strain off the liquor; this is for gravy. Put a layer of fowl at the bottom of a pie-dish, then a layer of ham, then one of forcemeat and hard-boiled eggs, cut in rings; between the layers put a seasoning of pounded mace, nutmeg, pepper and salt. Pour in about half a pint of water, border the edge of dish with puff-crust, put on the cover, ornament the top and glaze it by brushing over it the yolk of an egg. Bake for about an hour and a half, and, when done, pour in at the top the gravy made from the bones.

FISH CHICKEN AND STUFFING

BAKED FISH

fish fillets
milk
dry bread crumbs

butter or cooking oil
salt and pepper

Dip serving sized portion of fish into milk. Roll into bread crumbs and place in a greased baking dish. Dot each piece with butter or a teaspoon of cooking oil. Sprinkle fish with salt and pepper. Bake uncovered at 350° for 40 minutes or until fish flakes easily. Fish can be baked plain, rubbed with cooking oil or topped with a strip of bacon. May be sprinkled with lemon juice or paprika. Add sliced onions or tomatoes, if desired.

BROILED FISH

fish fillets
cooking oil

salt and pepper
lemon juice

Rub fish with cooking oil. Sprinkle with salt and pepper. Place fillets on a hot broiler with skin side down. Brown and turn. Fish is done when it flakes easily. Turn several times if necessary. Sprinkle broiled fish with lemon juice.

DEEP FRIED FISH

1-1/2 lbs. boneless fish fillets
1 c. flour
1 tsp. salt
1/4 tsp. pepper

2/3 c. milk
1 egg
1 T. lemon juice
shortening

Combine flour, salt and pepper. Beat egg in milk and add to flour. Add lemon juice. Mix. Heat shortening to 375°. Dip serving-sized fish in batter and fry in deep fat for 3-5 minutes.

Variation for **SAUTÉED BATTER FISH:** Place batter dipped fish in a hot skillet with a little melted shortening until well-browned on both sides.

PAN FRIED FISH

fish fillets   cornmeal or bread crumbs
salt and pepper   shortening or cooking oil

Wash fish. Sprinkle with salt and pepper then roll in cornmeal. Fry in hot shortening. Fry slowly until brown, turning once.

SMOTHERED SALMON

3 T. butter   2 c. salmon
3/4 c. chopped onion   2 thin slices lemon
3/4 c. diced celery   1/2 c. boiling water
1 tsp. salt

Sauté onion and celery in butter. Add salt. Place salmon in the center of a baking pan. Place lemon slices on top. Arrange onion and celery around salmon. Add water. Cover. Bake at 350° approximately 30 minutes. Uncover and bake 10 more minutes.

HALIBUT WITH CHEESE SAUCE

halibut steak   2 T. flour
salt   1/4 tsp. salt
paprika   1 1/4 c. milk
2 T. butter   1 c. grated cheese

Place thick slices of halibut steak in a greased skillet. Sprinkle with salt and paprika. Dot with a little butter. Cover and cook over low heat for 30 minutes. Melt 2 T. butter and blend in flour and salt. Add milk slowly, stirring constantly until it thickens. Add cheese and stir until melted. Remove fish to a serving dish. Pour cheese sauce over fish. Sprinkle with buttered browned bread crumbs, if desired. Garnish with paprika and parsley.

CREAMED TUNA

2 T. butter
2 T. flour
1/4 tsp. paprika

3/4 c. cream or milk
2 c. tuna
salt, if desired

Melt butter. Add flour and paprika. Stir until mixed, then add cream. Continue stirring until sauce thickens. Add fish and salt to taste. Serve on buttered toast or mashed potatoes.

CREAMED SHRIMP AND PEAS

2 T. butter
2 T. flour
1 tsp. salt
1/8 tsp. pepper

1/8 tsp. paprika
1 c. milk
1 c. cooked or canned shrimp
1 c. cooked or canned peas

Melt butter. Blend in flour, salt, pepper and paprika. Slowly add milk and bring to a boil, stirring constantly. Add shrimp and peas. Heat through. Serve on buttered toast or biscuits.

ROAST CHICKEN AND GRAVY

1 roasting chicken,
    approximately 4 lbs.
2 tsp. salt

1/8 tsp. pepper
butter or cooking oil
1 T. flour

Wash chicken, inside and out. Wipe dry. Rub with butter or oil. Rub with salt and pepper and sprinkle breast with flour. Place chicken on its back in a roaster with 1/2-inch of water in it. Stuff, if desired, packing lightly. Fasten legs close to the body with skewers or by tying. Bake at 325°, allowing 25 minutes per pound. To make gravy remove chicken and skim fat off drippings. Mix 2 T. flour and 2 T. cold water for each cup of liquid. Water can be added if necessary. Mix flour mixture with pan drippings, stirring constantly. Blend well and bring to a boil. Season to taste.

FRIED CHICKEN

3/4 c. flour	3 lbs. chicken, cut up
2 tsp. salt	1/2 c. shortening
1/4 tsp. pepper	

Combine flour, salt and pepper. Dip chicken into cold water, then into flour mixture. Melt shortening in skillet and add chicken. Brown both sides then reduce heat. Cover and cook until tender—about 45 minutes after browning. Turn occasionally. For a crisper crust uncover the last 15 minutes.

CHICKEN GOULASH

1 chicken	1 green pepper
2 c. canned or fresh peeled	2 tsp. salt
tomatoes	1/4 tsp. pepper
1 onion	

Cook chicken until tender. Remove chicken from bones and cut into small pieces. Save a little broth. Return chicken to broth and add remaining ingredients. Cook until vegetables are desired tenderness or cook vegetables separately and add to chicken.

CHICKEN AND DUMPLINGS

3 1/2-4 lbs. chicken	1 T. baking powder
1 tsp. salt	1 tsp. salt
1/4 tsp. pepper	3 T. shortening
2 c. flour	3/4 c. milk

Cut chicken in pieces. Put pieces in a kettle and cover with water. Add 1 tsp. salt and pepper. Cover. Simmer until tender, allowing 20-25 minutes per pound. When chicken is almost tender combine flour, baking powder and salt. Work shortening in with fingertips. Add milk. Drop dough, a tablespoon at a time, into boiling broth. Cover and cook 12 minutes. Do not remove cover while cooking. Serve immediately.

CHICKEN PIE

1 chicken, cut up
1 onion, chopped
1 sprig parsley, chopped
1/4 c. butter
1/4 c. flour
2 tsp. salt
1/4 tsp. pepper

3 c. broth, add cream or milk
    if more is needed
2 c. flour
1/2 tsp. salt
2 tsp. baking powder
2 T. butter
1 egg
1 c. milk

Cook chicken, onion and parsley until chicken is tender. Debone chicken. Drain broth and save. Melt 3 T. butter and blend in flour, salt and pepper. Stir in broth and bring to a boil. Add chicken and heat through. Pour into a baking pan. Combine 2 c. flour, salt and baking powder. Work butter into flour. Add well-beaten egg and milk. Mix quickly and pour over chicken. Bake at 400° approximately 30 minutes. One c. sliced carrots can be added to chicken during the last 20 minutes of cooking.

CHICKEN À LA KING

1/4 c. butter
1 c. fresh or canned
    mushrooms
1/4 c. flour
1 tsp. salt

1/4 tsp. pepper
2 c. milk
2 c. cooked chicken, diced
1/2 green pepper, thinly-sliced
1/2 red pepper, thinly-sliced

Sauté mushrooms in butter. Blend in flour. Add salt and pepper. Slowly stir in milk. Add chicken and peppers. Stir frequently until sauce thickens. Serve over toast or biscuits. Chicken broth can be used in place of some of the milk. Cooked turkey, beef or pork can be used instead of chicken.

Variation for **CREAMED CHICKEN:** Omit mushrooms and peppers. Serve over toast, hot biscuits or mashed potatoes. One half cup grated cheese may be added.

CHICKEN CHOP SUEY

1 c. diced celery	2 c. cubed, cooked chicken
2 large onions, diced	1/4 c. water
1 c. canned or fresh	2 T. soy sauce
mushrooms	1 T. corn starch
1/4 c. butter	

Sauté celery, onions and mushrooms in butter. Add chicken and heat through. Combine water, soy sauce and corn starch and add to chicken mixture, stirring constantly until thickened. Serve on hot rice. For chicken chow mein, serve on chow mein noodles.

Variation for **BEEF CHOP SUEY:** Use cubed beef, beef cut in strips or ground beef instead of chicken.

Variation for **PORK CHOP SUEY:** Substitute pork for chicken.

COUNTRY STYLE CHICKEN

3 lb. chicken, cut up	1 large onion
1/2 c. flour	2 c. cubed carrots
2 tsp. salt	2 c. canned or fresh peeled
1/4 tsp. pepper	tomatoes
6 T. butter	2 c. boiling water
6 medium potatoes	

Mix 1 tsp. salt and 1/4 tsp. pepper with flour. Roll chicken in flour. Melt butter in a skillet and brown chicken on both sides over high heat. Peel and quarter potatoes and coarsely-chop onion. Place potatoes, onions and carrots in a large kettle. Add remaining tsp. of salt. Place chicken on vegetables. Top with tomatoes and boiling water. Cover tightly and bring to a boil. Reduce heat and simmer until tender— approximately 1 1/2 hours.

"When putting chicken and gravy into a serving dish top it with fresh ground pepper."

CHICKEN AND RICE CREOLE

1/4 c. shortening	2 tsp. salt
1 large onion	1/2 tsp. paprika
1 chicken, cut up	1/4 tsp. pepper
flour	3 c. boiling water
2 carrots, sliced	1 c. uncooked rice
1 c. canned or fresh, peeled	
tomatoes	

Brown onion in shortening, then remove. Flour chicken pieces and brown in shortening. Place chicken in the center of a large covered baking dish. Combine carrots, tomatoes, salt, paprika, pepper and boiling water and pour around chicken. Sprinkle rice evenly around chicken. Top with fried onions. Cover. Bake at 350° until rice is soft and chicken tender—approximately one hour. Remove cover last 10 minutes.

ROAST TURKEY

The baking time and temperature is current information. Roasting times used to be much longer. If using a "modern" turkey with a salt solution in it, not much salt is needed.

10-15 lb. turkey	salt and pepper
cooking oil	

Wash turkey inside and out. Rub breast with cooking oil. Rub salt and pepper on the inside and outside of the turkey. Place on back in a roaster with 1/2-inch of water in it. Stuff if desired. Bake at 325°. Bake an unstuffed turkey 3-3 1/2 hours, a stuffed turkey 3 3/4-4 1/2 hours. Or bake until temperature probe inserted into the breast reaches 170° or thigh temperature reaches 180°. A twenty pound turkey will take 3 1/2 - 4 hours unstuffed and 4 1/2-5 hours stuffed. When checking the temperature make sure the thermometer is not against bone or poked into the cavity.

STUFFING INFORMATION

Stuffing can be used to stuff turkey or chicken or it can be baked separately. To bake place in a greased baking pan or mold and bake at 350° approximately 45 minutes or until set.

STUFFING

2/3 c. butter
1 c. chopped onions
3/4 c. diced celery
1 tsp. salt

1/4 tsp. pepper
2 tsp. poultry seasoning
8 c. roasted bread cubes

Sauté onion and celery in butter for five minutes. Add salt, pepper and poultry seasoning. Mix well, then add bread cubes. Moisten with 1 c hot water, milk or broth, if desired.

Variation for **BRAZIL NUT STUFFING:** Add 1 1/2 c chopped brazil nuts with seasonings.

GRANDMA HORST'S
CHICKEN STUFFING

1 lb. loaf of bread, toasted
   and cubed
2 c. diced chicken
2 c. diced boiled potatoes
1 c. diced boiled carrots
1 c. diced celery and leaves

1 onion chopped
4 eggs
4 c. chicken broth
3 c. milk
1 1/2 tsp. salt

Combine bread, chicken, potatoes, carrots, celery and onion. Beat eggs. Add broth, milk and salt to eggs. Bake at 350° 1 1/2 hours or until set.

MUSHROOM STUFFING

1/4 lb. mushrooms
1 onion, chopped finely
1/4 c. butter

2 c. bread cubes
1/4 tsp. salt
1/8 tsp. pepper

Chop mushrooms. Cook mushrooms and onion in butter, about five minutes. Add bread cubes, salt and pepper. Moisten with a little water.

110

SAUSAGE STUFFING

1/2 lb. sausage
4 c. bread cubes
1 sprig parsley, chopped
1 tsp. sage or poultry
    seasoning

1/2 tsp. onion salt
1/4 tsp. pepper
1 egg
1/2 c. milk or broth
1/4 c. melted butter

Fry sausage. Mix sausage, bread cubes, parsley, sage, onion salt and pepper. Beat egg in milk. Add melted butter to egg mixture, then add to stuffing. Mix lightly.

CELERY STUFFING

4 c. bread cubes
2 c. celery
1 onion
1/2 c. butter

1 tsp. salt
1/4 tsp. pepper
1/2 tsp. sage

Toast bread and cut into pieces. Sauté celery and onion in butter several minutes. Add seasonings and mix with bread

TOASTED ALMOND STUFFING

1/2 c. butter
1 c. chopped celery
1 c. chopped onion
2 eggs
1 c. milk
8 c. toasted bread cubes

1 tsp. poultry seasoning
1 tsp. salt
1/4 tsp. pepper
1 1/2 c. chopped, toasted
    almonds

Cook celery and onion in butter. Beat eggs in milk and pour over bread cubes. Mix in celery and onions and remaining ingredients.

RAISIN STUFFING

1/4 c. butter
1 c. chopped celery
2 T. chopped onion
1 T. chopped, fresh parsley
3/4 c. milk
2 eggs

1 c. raisins
1 T. grated lemon rind
1/2 tsp. salt
2 1/2 c. fine, dry bread
    crumbs

Sauté celery, onion and parsley in butter. Beat eggs in milk. Add raisins, rind and salt and combine with celery. Pour over bread crumbs. Mix.

GRANDMA'S

WORCESTERSHIRE SAUCE

Ten peppers, one large onion, twenty-four ripe tomatoes, two tablespoonfuls salt, one teaspoonful each of allspice, nutmeg, ginger and cloves, one quart vinegar; chop peppers, onions and tomatoes fine, and let all simmer two hours.

A CHEAP AND GOOD GRAVY

Fry three onions in butter a nice brown; toast a large slice of bread till quite hard, and very brown, but not burnt. Set these, and any bit of meat, or bone of a leg of mutton, etc., and some herbs, on the fire, with water in proportion, and stew till the gravy is thick and rich; add salt and pepper; strain off, and keep cool.

MEAT SAUCES

WHITE SAUCE

1/4 c. butter	1/2 tsp. salt
1/4 c. flour	2 c. milk

Melt butter over low heat. Blend in flour and salt. Slowly add milk, stirring constantly until sauce thickens. This is a medium white sauce. For thin sauce use 2 T. of butter and flour. For thick sauce use 6 T. of butter and flour.

Variation for **CHEESE SAUCE:** Add 1 c. grated cheese after sauce has thickened. Stir until cheese melts. One fourth tsp. dry mustard may be added.

Variation for **PARSLEY SAUCE:** Add 3 T. chopped, fresh parsley.

TARTAR SAUCE

1 c. mayonnaise	1 T. minced onion
2 T. pickle relish, chopped pickles or chopped olives	1 sprig parsley, chopped

Combine ingredients. Serve with fish.

BARBECUE SAUCE

1 onion, chopped	2 T. brown sugar
2 T. butter	2 T. vinegar
1 c. catsup	2 tsp. mustard
1/2 c. water	3/4 tsp. salt
1/4 c. lemon juice	1/4 tsp. red or black pepper
3 T. Worcestershire sauce	

Brown onion in butter. Add remaining ingredients. Simmer 10-15 minutes.

CREOLE SAUCE

1 c. chopped green pepper	2 c. canned or fresh, peeled
3/4 c. chopped onion	tomatoes
1 garlic clove, minced	3/4 tsp. salt
1/4 c. butter	1/4 tsp. pepper
	1/4 tsp. paprika

Sauté green pepper, onion and garlic in butter, about five minutes. Add tomatoes and seasonings. Boil 5-10 minutes. Serve with hot meat.

TOMATO SAUCE

2 c. tomatoes	1/4 c. butter
2 T. chopped onion	1/4 c. flour
1 sprig parsley, finely	1/2 tsp. salt
chopped	1/8 tsp. pepper

Simmer tomatoes, onion and parsley 20 minutes. Strain, if desired. Melt butter over low heat. Add flour, salt and pepper. Add tomatoes, stirring constantly until sauce thickens.

GRANDMA KULP'S
TOMATO GRAVY

Grandma Kulp's family liked to eat tomato gravy on fried potatoes.

1 qt. tomato juice or chunks	2 T. sugar
1/2 tsp. soda	1/2 c. water
2 T. flour	1/3 c. cream

Heat tomato juice and soda. Combine flour and sugar and mix with water. Pour into tomato juice while stirring. Stir until it thickens. Pour in cream and heat through. Season to taste.

"Sauces provide the clever homemaker with an opportunity to get into the diet food values found wanting in the principal items on the menu."

MUSHROOM SAUCE

1/4 c. butter
1 c. fresh or canned
   mushrooms
2 T. chopped onions

1/4 c. flour
2 c. beef or chicken broth
salt and pepper to taste

Melt butter over low heat. Sauté sliced mushrooms and onion about five minutes. Add flour, mixing well. Slowly add broth, stirring constantly until sauce thickens. Season to taste. Serve with roasted or broiled beef or pork or vegetables. Broth may be made by dissolving two bouillon cubes in 2 c. boiling water.

CURRY SAUCE

2 T. butter
2 T. flour
1 T. curry powder

1/2 tsp. onion salt
1/8 tsp. pepper
2 c. milk or broth

Melt butter. Add flour, curry powder, onion salt and pepper. Stir until smooth. Add milk or broth. Bring to a boil, stirring constantly. Broth may be made by dissolving two bouillon cubes in 2 c. boiling water.

SOUR CREAM AND HORSERADISH SAUCE

1 c. sour cream

1/2 c. horseradish

Combine ingredients.

CURRANT JELLY SAUCE

1/2 c. currant jelly
2 T. hot water

2 tsp. lemon juice

Combine and mix well. Grape jelly can also be used.

ONION SAUCE

1 T. butter	1 T. flour
2 T. sugar	1 c. beef broth or bouillon
2 onions, finely-sliced	1 T. vinegar

Brown sugar in butter. Add onions and cook several minutes. Add flour and brown a little before adding broth and vinegar. Cook and stir until smooth. Salt to taste. Strain if desired.

RAISIN SAUCE

2 T. butter	1/3 c. raisins
2 T. flour	2 c. water
1/8 tsp. salt	2 T. lemon juice

Melt butter. Blend in flour, salt and raisins. Slowly add water, stirring constantly. Bring to a boil. Boil five minutes. Remove from heat and add lemon juice. Serve hot with ham.

LEMON BUTTER

1/4 c. butter melted	1/8 tsp. pepper
1 tsp. lemon juice	

Blend together. Serve hot.

DRAWN BUTTER

6 T. butter	1/2 tsp. salt
3 T. flour	1/8 tsp. pepper
2 c. hot water	1 tsp. lemon juice

Melt 3 T. butter. Add flour and cook, stirring constantly until smooth Add hot water, salt and pepper. Bring to a boil and boil five minutes Add remaining butter. Add lemon juice. Serve with fish.

GRANDMA'S

HOW TO BOIL
AND DRESS MACARONI

Put in an iron pot or stew-pan two quarts
of water; let it boil; add two teaspoonfuls of
salt, one ounce of butter; then add one pound
of macaroni; boil till tender; let it be rather
firm to the touch; it is then ready for use, either
for soup, pudding, or to be dressed with cheese.
Drain it in a colander; put it back in the pan, add
four ounces of cheese or more, a little butter,
salt and pepper; toss it well together and serve.
It will be found light and nutritious.

MACARONI SPAGHETTI
NOODLES AND RICE

COOKED MACARONI SPAGHETTI OR NOODLES

Grandma Horst added a pinch of saffron to the water when she made noodles. When ready to serve, she topped them with browned butter. Noodles were often cooked in chicken broth. Chicken was added for chicken and noodles.

1/2 lb. macaroni, spaghetti or noodles	8 c. water
	2 tsp. salt

Drop macaroni, spaghetti or noodles, broken or unbroken, into rapidly boiling, salted water. Boil until tender, stirring occasionally. Pour into a sieve to drain. This recipe can be made bigger or smaller as needed.

MACARONI AND CHEESE

2 c. macaroni	1/2 tsp. salt
1 tsp. salt	1/8 tsp. pepper
3 T. butter	2 c. milk
3 T. flour	1 1/2 c. grated cheese

Cook macaroni in boiling water with 1 tsp. salt for 10 minutes. Melt butter. Blend in flour, salt and pepper. Add milk slowly, stirring constantly until sauce thickens. Stir in cheese. Drain macaroni and mix with cheese sauce. Pour in a baking dish. Top with bread crumbs or six strips of lean bacon if desired. Bake at 375° approximately 40 minutes. Chopped onion or green pepper can be sautéed in butter before adding flour. One half cup dried beef or three chopped, hard-cooked eggs may be added to white sauce.

MACARONI BEEF AND BEANS

1 1/2 lb. ground beef	2 c. cooked macaroni
1 1/2 tsp. salt	2 c. canned tomatoes
1/4 tsp. pepper	1 c. canned kidney beans

Brown ground beef. Add seasoning. Mix remaining ingredients. Bake at 350° approximately one hour.

SPAGHETTI WITH MEAT SAUCE

2 lbs. ground beef or sausage
2 large onions, chopped
1 clove garlic, minced
1 green pepper, chopped
2 sprigs parsley, chopped
1/2 lb. mushrooms
2 1/2 c. tomato juice

1 c. catsup
1 tsp. Worcestershire sauce
2 tsp. lemon juice
2 tsp. salt
1/4 tsp. pepper
8 oz. cooked spaghetti
grated parmesan cheese

Brown meat, onions, garlic, peppers and parsley. Add remaining ingredients except spaghetti and cheese. Simmer covered 1-1/2 hours. Pour sauce over spaghetti; sprinkle with parmesan cheese.

BAKED SPAGHETTI

1/4 c. olive oil
1 c. chopped onion
1 T. chili powder
1/2 tsp. salt
1/8 tsp. pepper

2 1/2 c. canned or fresh,
        peeled tomatoes
3 c. cooked, drained spaghetti
1/4 c. chopped olives
1 1/2 c. grated cheese

Sauté onion in oil. Add chili powder, salt and pepper. Mix well. Add tomatoes and cook over low heat 20 minutes, stirring frequently. Add spaghetti and olives and most of the cheese. Put remaining cheese on top. Bake at 375° approximately 25 minutes.

Variation for **BAKED SPAGHETTI WITH MEAT:** Omit olive oil and add 1 lb. ground beef or sausage. Brown meat with onion.

NOODLES

Most of our Grandmas made their noodles— in much bigger batches of course.

2 c. flour
1 tsp. salt

2 eggs, slightly beaten

Mix flour and salt. Gradually add flour to eggs until a stiff dough is formed. Knead a few minutes on a floured board. Roll out 1/16-inch thick. Let stand 30 minutes. Cut in long 1/4-inch wide strips or other width or shape. Dry thoroughly. Boil in salt water until tender.

NOODLES WITH SALMON

3 T. butter	1 1/2 c. milk
3 T. flour	2 c. salmon
1/2 tsp. salt	1 c. noodles
1/8 tsp. pepper	1/4 c. buttered bread crumbs

Melt butter. Blend in flour and seasonings. Slowly add milk while stirring. Bring to a boil and boil two minutes. Flake well-drained salmon and put in a greased baking dish. Top with noodles then white sauce. Sprinkle crumbs on top. Bake at 375° approximately 30 minutes.

NOODLES WITH HAM AND CHEESE

3 T. butter	2 c. milk
3 T. flour	3/4 c. grated cheese
1/2 tsp. salt	2 1/2 c. cooked noodles
1/8 tsp. pepper	1 c. chopped hams

Melt butter and blend in flour, salt and pepper. Slowly add milk, stirring constantly until sauce thickens. Stir in cheese. Put half of the noodles in a greased casserole. Add half of the ham and pour half of cheese sauce on top. Repeat. Bake at 400° for 25-30 minutes.

COOKED WHITE RICE

1 c. white rice	1/2 tsp. salt
2 c. water or broth	

Combine ingredients. Bring to a boil, then simmer 25 minutes, stirring occasionally. Remove from heat. Let stand, covered, for five minutes. Fluff with a fork before serving. Makes 2 1/2 cups.

COOKED BROWN RICE

1 c. brown rice   1/2 tsp. salt
2 1/2 c. water

Combine ingredients. Bring to a boil, then reduce heat and simmer ap proximately 50 minutes. Makes 2 1/2 cups.

BAKED RICE AND CHEESE

4 c. cooked rice   1/2 c. chopped pimento
1 1/2 c. tomato juice   1/8 tsp. pepper
3/4 c. grated cheese

Combine ingredients. If rice is unsalted, add 1 tsp. salt. Pour into a greased baking dish. Bake at 375° approximately 30 minutes.

SPANISH RICE

6 slices bacon, diced   2 c. canned or fresh, peeled
2 onions, chopped   tomatoes
1 green pepper, chopped   1 tsp. salt
2 c. cooked rice   1/4 tsp. pepper

Cook bacon until crisp. Remove from fat. Add onions and green peppe and cook approximately five minutes. Add remaining ingredients and heat through. Put in a serving dish and sprinkle crisp bacon on top.

RICE AND PINEAPPLE

2 c. cooked rice   3 T. sugar
salt   1 c. diced pineapple
3 T. butter

Put 1/3 of rice in a greased baking dish. Sprinkle lightly with salt. Do with 1 T. butter and sprinkle with 1 T. sugar. Add 1/3 c. of pineap ple. Make three layers, ending with pineapple on top. Bake at 425° ap proximately 20 minutes.

BROILED
POTATOES

Cut whole boiled Irish or sweet
potatoes lengthwise into slices a quarter of an inch thick, and lay upon a gridiron
over a hot fire; brown on both sides, sprinkle
with pepper and salt and lay a bit of butter on each.

TO PRESERVE VEGETABLES FOR WINTER USE

Green string beans must be picked when young; put a layer
three inches deep in a small wooden keg or half barrel;
sprinkle in salt an inch deep, then put another layer of beans,
then salt, and beans and salt in alternate layers, until you have
enough; let the last be salt; cover them with a piece of board
which will fit the inside of the barrel or keg, and place a heavy
weight upon it; they will make a brine. Carrots, beans, beet-
roots, parsnips, and potatoes keep best in dry sand or earth in
a cellar; turnips keep best on a cellar bottom, or they may be
kept the same as carrots, etc. Whatever earth remains
about them when taken from the ground, should not be taken
off. When sprouts come on potatoes or other stored
vegetables, they should be carefully cut off. The young
sprouts from turnips are sometimes served as a salad,
or boiled tender in salt and water, and served with
butter and pepper over. Celery may be kept
all winter by setting it in boxes filled with
earth; keep it in the cellar; it will
grow and whiten in the dark;
leeks can be kept the
same way.

BAKED BEANS

2 c. navy beans
1/3 lb. diced bacon
2 c. hot water
1 1/2 c. brown sugar

2 tsp. salt
3/4 tsp. dry mustard
1/2 tsp. cinnamon
1 onion, chopped

Wash beans and soak overnight. Drain. Cover with water and bring to a boil. Reduce heat and simmer 1 1/2 hours. Drain. Mix in diced bacon. Place in a bean pot or greased baking dish. Mix remaining ingredients and pour over beans. Cover. Bake at 350° until beans are soft—approximately three hours.

MEXICAN BAKED BEANS

2 c. dry beans
1/2 lb. bacon, diced
2 onions, chopped
2 green peppers, chopped

2 c. canned or fresh peeled
    tomatoes
1 tsp. chili powder
1/8 tsp. pepper

Cook beans in salted water until soft—approximately three hours. Place in a baking dish. Fry bacon until brown. Remove from pan. Fry onions in bacon drippings. Add bacon, onions, peppers, tomatoes and seasoning to beans. Mix well. Bake at 350° approximately 1 1/2 hours.

GREEN BEANS AND MUSHROOMS

2 T. butter
1/2 lb. fresh mushrooms

1 T. flour
1 lb. fresh beans

Sauté sliced mushrooms in butter, about five minutes. Add flour and cook a little longer. Add beans and bring to a boil. Reduce heat and cook 10-15 minutes.

GREEN BEANS TOMATO AND ONION

1 qt. fresh green beans	1 tsp. salt
6 slices bacon	1 c. canned or fresh peeled
1 onion, chopped	tomatoes
1 clove garlic	1/2 c. catsup

Wash beans and break into pieces. Fry bacon until crisp. Remove bacon and brown onion and garlic in bacon fat. When brown, combine all ingredients and bring to a boil. Reduce heat and cook approximately 10 minutes.

HARVARD BEETS

1/3 c. sugar	1/2 c. vinegar
3 T. cornstarch	3 T. butter
1/2 c. water	3 c. cooked, diced beets

Combine all but beets and cook until thick. Add 3/4 tsp. salt if beets weren't cooked in salt water. Add beets and heat through. When using fresh beets, cook whole, leaving 1/2-inch of stem and the main tap root on the beets. Cook small beets approximately 30 minutes. Peel and trim root and stem after beets are done cooking.

GRANDMA KULP'S
STEAM FRIED RED BEETS

cooking oil or water	1/2 tsp. salt
2 c. shredded red beets	pepper

Heat cooking oil in a frying pan. Add red beets, salt and pepper. Cook on low heat until moisture is absorbed and beets are slightly browned.

"Put vegetables to cook in enough water so there will be none to throw away when the vegetable is cooked tender."

BROCCOLI WITH ONIONS

1 bunch broccoli	1/4 tsp. salt
3 T. butter	1/8 tsp. pepper
3 T. minced onion	2 tsp. lemon juice

Cut broccoli apart. Peel and slice stem and use too. Cook broccoli in salted water approximately 10 minutes. Drain. Sauté onion in butter until lightly browned. Add salt, pepper and lemon juice. Add broccoli and heat one minute.

"Save small amounts of leftover vegetables. They may be cooked to make delicious cream soups."

SWEET SOUR CARROTS

4 c. sliced carrots	2 T. sugar
1 tsp. salt	2 T. butter
2 T. vinegar	1/8 tsp. cloves

Cook carrots in boiling salted water until tender—approximately 10 minutes. Drain. Combine remaining ingredients and pour over carrots.

GRANDMA HORST'S
BAKED CARROTS

An aunt writes, "I don't remember any rich casseroles. The only casserole I remember was macaroni and cheese on occasion and this baked carrot dish. Food was mostly cooked separate and simply."

2 1/2 c. mashed carrots	1 c. dry bread crumbs
1 T. chopped onion	2 c. milk
3 T. butter, melted	1 tsp. salt
3 eggs, beaten	1/4 tsp. pepper

Mix ingredients together. Bake at 350° for one hour.

FRIED CAULIFLOWER

cauliflower   flour and butter

Cook cauliflower in salted water until fairly tender. Drain. Cut floret
in half. Roll in flour and fry butter, turning once. Sprinkle with salt.

CAULIFLOWER AU GRATIN

1 head cauliflower	1/8 tsp. pepper
1/4 c. butter	2 c. milk
1/4 c. flour	1 c. grated cheese
1 tsp. salt	bread crumbs

Break cauliflower into florets. Cook in salt water approximately 1(
minutes. Drain and put in a greased baking dish. Melt butter. Blend in
flour, salt and pepper. Add milk slowly, stirring constantly until sauce
thickens. Add cheese and stir until melted. Pour sauce over cauliflower
Top with bread crumbs if desired. Bake at 375° approx. 25 minutes.

Variation for **BRUSSELS SPROUTS AU GRATIN:** Use 4
c. cooked Brussels sprouts instead of cauliflower.

Variation for **CABBAGE AU GRATIN:** Use cooked cabbage
instead of cauliflower.

Variation for **PARSNIPS AU GRATIN:** Use 4 c. cooked pars
nips instead of cauliflower.

BAKED CORN

2 T. butter	3/4 c. milk or cream
2 T. flour	2 c. fresh or canned corn
3/4 tsp. salt	2 eggs, well-beaten
1/8 tsp. pepper	

Melt butter. Blend in flour, salt and pepper. Add milk slowly, stirring
constantly until sauce thickens. Add corn and eggs. Mix thoroughly
Put in a greased baking dish. Bake at 375° approximately 40 minutes.

CORN FITTERS

2 c. flour
1 T. baking powder
1 tsp. salt
1 1/2 c. milk

1 egg, well-beaten
1 T. melted butter
2 c. corn

Combine dry ingredients. Add milk and egg. Beat until smooth. Add butter and well-drained corn. Drop by tablespoon onto a hot greased griddle. Bake until bubbles form on the top, then turn and bake on the other side. Turn carefully. Serve at once. Eat plain, with butter or with syrup.

SAUTÉED ONIONS

2 T. butter
2 large onions, sliced

1/2 tsp. salt
1/4 tsp. pepper

Melt butter in skillet. Add onion and sprinkle with seasonings. Mix well. Cover and cook slowly until browned.

CREAMED PEAS

4 c. peas
1 tsp. salt
2 T. butter
2 T. flour

1/4 tsp. salt
1/8 tsp. pepper
1 1/2 c. milk

Bring peas and 1 tsp. salt to a boil in a little water. Cook approximately seven minutes. Melt butter. Add flour, 1/4 tsp. salt and pepper. Add milk slowly, stirring constantly until sauce bubbles. Add drained peas. Heat through. If desired, 1/4 c. chopped onion can be sautéed in butter before flour is added.

Variation for **CREAMED MIXED VEGETABLES:** Use 4 c. mixed vegetables instead of peas.

STUFFED PEPPERS

6 green peppers	1 onion, chopped
1 c. cubed, cooked ham or beef	2 T. butter
	1 tsp. salt
1 c. peeled, chopped tomatoes	1/4 tsp. pepper
1 c. cooked rice	cheese

Wash peppers. Cut a slice from the stem end and remove all insides. Mix all ingredients but cheese. Stuff peppers. Sprinkle peppers with cheese. Put 1/4-inch hot water in a baking dish. Set peppers upright in baking dish. Bake at 375° approximately 30 minutes.

CREAMED POTATOES

2 c. cooked, sliced potatoes	1 T. butter
1 c. milk	small sprig of parsley, chopped
1 1/2 T. flour	

Drain potatoes. Combine milk and flour and pour into potatoes. Cook and stir lightly until thickened. Add butter and parsley.

MASHED POTATOES

6 medium potatoes	1/4 c. hot milk, approximately
1 tsp. salt	1/8 tsp. pepper
3 T. butter	

Peel potatoes and cut in chunks. Cook in salted water until tender. Drain cooked potatoes. Mash until lump free before adding butter. Gradually add milk, beating constantly, until potatoes are light and fluffy. Add more milk if necessary. Sprinkle with pepper. When making mashed potatoes allow one medium potato per person.

Variation for **GREEN ONION MASHED POTATOES:** Add 1/4 c. finely-chopped green onion just before serving. Use about three inches of green stem.

FRIED POTATOES AND ONIONS

3 T. shortening
3 c. thinly sliced or shredded   1 tsp. salt
    potatoes   1/8 tsp. pepper
1 onion, chopped

Heat shortening in frying pan. Combine remaining ingredients and add. Cover and cook slowly until brown on one side. Turn and brown on the other side, keeping lid off. Cooked potatoes may be used too. If cooked potatoes are used sauté onions in shortening several minutes before stirring in potatoes.

BAKED POTATOES

Select medium, even-sized potatoes. Scrub clean. Bake at 400° approximately 50 minutes. Bake longer if larger potatoes are used. Rub skins with butter or cooking oil to soften them. Serve at once.

STUFFED BAKED POTATOES

4 large potatoes   1 onion, chopped
3/4 tsp. salt   grated cheese
1/4 tsp. pepper   paprika
2 T. butter

Bake potatoes. Cut in half lengthwise. Scoop out insides and mash, adding salt and pepper. Save skins. Brown onion in butter. Add mashed potatoes and mix well. Fill potato skins with mashed potato mixture. Sprinkle with cheese and paprika. Reheat at 375° until lightly browned.

Variation for **SAUSAGE STUFFED BAKED POTATOES:**
Omit butter. Brown 1/4-1/2 lb. sausage and onion together. Remove excess grease before adding mashed potatoes. Chopped ham may also be used. If ham is used sauté in butter along with onion.

CHEESE POTATO CAKES

2 c. mashed potatoes   1/4 tsp. salt
1/2 c. grated cheese   1/8 tsp. pepper

Combine ingredients and form into small cakes. Fry in butter.

RAW POTATO PANCAKES

Grandma Horst's family enjoyed potato pancakes. They ate them with honey.

2 1/2 c. grated, raw potatoes   1/2 c. flour
2 eggs, well-beaten   1 T. baking powder
1 T. milk   1 tsp. salt

Mix potatoes with eggs and milk. Combine dry ingredients and add to potatoes. Cook on well-greased griddle until brown on both sides.

SCALLOPED POTATOES

4 c. diced potatoes   1 1/2 tsp. salt
1/4 c. butter   1/4 tsp. pepper
1 onion, chopped   2 c. milk
1/4 c. flour

Cook potatoes five minutes in unsalted water. Drain. Brown onion in butter. Blend in flour, salt and pepper. Slowly add milk and stir constantly until sauce thickens. Combine potatoes and white sauce. Pour into a well-greased baking dish. Bake at 350° approximately 50 minutes.

"The lightest duties oft are found
Lying on the lowest ground;
In the hidden and unnoticed ways,
In household work on common days."

-a verse Grandma Kulp copied into her notebook

POTATOES AU GRATIN

3 T. butter	1 1/2 c. milk
3 T. flour	1 c. grated cheese
1 tsp. salt	3 c. thinly-sliced raw potatoes
1/8 tsp. pepper	1/2 c. buttered bread crumbs
1/8 tsp. paprika	

Melt butter and blend in flour, salt, pepper and paprika. Add milk stirring constantly, until sauce thickens. Add cheese and stir until melted. Layer potatoes and cheese sauce in a well-greased baking dish. Top with bread crumbs. Bake covered at 375° approximately one hour. Uncover and bake 15 minutes longer.

GRANDMA KULP'S
FRIED PARSNIPS

One of the aunts said they also made fried parsnip patties; a combination of mashed parsnips, cracker crumbs, egg, milk and seasoning. Though she didn't remember ingredient amounts, she remembered how good they tasted.

5 medium parsnips	2 T. butter
1 tsp. salt	

Wash and scrape parsnips. Cook whole in salt water until tender but not too soft. Slice. Fry in butter.

GRANDMA KULP'S
SALSIFY

One of Grandma's daughters writes, "We hated to clean salsify."

salsify ("oyster plant")	butter
milk	salt and pepper

Wash salsify and scrape carefully. Slice and cook in a little water. Add milk and a little butter. Season to taste.

GLAZED BAKED SWEET POTATOES

6 medium raw sweet potatoes
3/4 c. brown sugar
3/4 tsp. salt

1 tsp. cinnamon
1 c. water
2 T. butter

Peel sweet potatoes. Cut in half lengthwise and place in a greased baking dish. Combine remaining ingredients and boil several minutes. Pour over sweet potatoes. Bake at 400° until potatoes are tender and syrup thick—approximately one hour. Baste or turn sweet potatoes several times. Sweet potatoes may be cooked first, using only 1/2 c. water in syrup. Bake at 400° for 30 minutes, basting occasionally.

SWEET POTATOES DELUXE

6 medium sweet potatoes
1/4 c. sugar
1 tsp. salt
1/2 tsp. cinnamon

1/4 c. evaporated milk or
  cream
3 T. butter, melted
1/2 c. chopped pecans
marshmallows

Cook potatoes until soft. Peel and mash. Add all but marshmallows. Mix well. Place in a greased baking dish. Top with marshmallows. Bake at 350° until heated through and marshmallows are slightly brown.

GRANDMA HORST'S
SIX LAYER DINNER

2 c. raw, shredded or sliced,
  potatoes
2 c. chopped celery
2 c. ground beef, browned
1/2 onion, chopped

1/2 green pepper, chopped
2 c. tomatoes, peeled and
  chopped
2 tsp. salt
pepper

Layer ingredients in a casserole in the order given. Top with tomatoes. Sprinkle each layer with salt and pepper. Bake at 350° approximately two hours.

STRAWBERRY BAVARIAN CREAM

Take the hulls from two quarts of fine strawberries, and bruise them in a basin with six ounces of pounded sugar; rub this through a sieve, and mix it with a pint of whipped cream, and one ounce and a half of clarified isinglass, or its equal of gelatine. Pour the cream into a mould, previously oiled with oil of sweet almonds, set it on ice, and when it has become quite firm, turn it out on its dish.

RICE CREAM

To a pint of new milk add a quarter of a pound of ground rice, a lump of butter the size of a walnut, a little lemon peel and a tablespoonful of powdered sugar. Boil them together for five minutes, then add half an ounce of isinglass which has been dissolved, and let the mixture cool. When cool add half a pint of good cream whisked to a froth, mix all together, and set it for a time in a very cool place or on ice. When used, turn it out of the basin into a dish and pour fruit juice around it; or some stewed apple or pear may be served with it.

DESSERTS

VANILLA PUDDING

1/4 c. sugar	2 c. milk
3 T. cornstarch	1 T. butter
1/8 tsp. salt	1 tsp. vanilla
1/4 c. cold water	

Mix sugar, cornstarch, salt and water. Add hot milk. Cook and stir until thick and smooth. Add butter and vanilla.

GRANDMA HORST'S
CARAMEL PUDDING

1/4 c. butter	6 c. milk
2 c. brown sugar	6 T. flour
1/2 tsp. salt	4 eggs, well-beaten
2 T. water	2 tsp. vanilla

Melt butter in skillet. Add sugar and salt and stir until sugar melts and browns slightly. Remove from heat and add water. When mixture stops boiling add four cups milk and heat. Mix flour with remaining milk. Add to skillet, stirring constantly until thick. Stir 1/2 cup hot pudding into beaten eggs. Stir eggs into pudding. Mix well. Boil two minutes. Add vanilla. Layer with whipped cream and graham cracker crumbs. Sliced bananas may be added.

GRANDMA MARTIN'S
CHOCOLATE PUDDING
The Martin family enjoyed chocolate pudding on fried potatoes (yes!) at supper-time.

1 c. sugar	1 tsp. salt
1/2 c. cocoa	4 c. milk
1/2 c. flour	

Combine dry ingredients in a saucepan. Stir in milk. Cook, stirring more frequently as mixture heats. Stir constantly as it begins to thicken. Boil one minute.

TAPIOCA PUDDING

1/4 c. minute tapioca	2 c. milk
1/2 c. sugar	1 c. cream
1 T. flour	1 tsp. vanilla
1/4 tsp. salt	

Combine tapioca, sugar, flour and salt. Add milk and mix well. Let stand five minutes. Bring to a boil, stirring constantly. Remove from heat. Cool stirring occasionally. Whip cream and vanilla. Fold into tapioca. A cup of fresh or canned fruit can be added.

GRAHAM CRACKER PUDDING

2 c. milk	1/2 c. whipping cream
1 egg, beaten	1/4 c. sugar
1/3 c. sugar	1/8 tsp. salt
3 T. flour	1 tsp. vanilla
1/2 tsp. salt	2 c. graham cracker crumbs
1 tsp. vanilla	

Add egg to milk in a heavy saucepan. Combine sugar, flour and salt and add to milk. Mix well. Cook and stir until slightly thickened. Remove from heat and add vanilla. Chill. Whip cream. Mix in remaining sugar, salt and vanilla. Fold cream into pudding, reserving some for topping. Mix in graham cracker crumbs. Top with remaining cream. Sliced bananas may be added.

GRAHAM CRACKER FLUFF

1 T. unflavored gelatin	1 c. whipping cream
1/2 c. cold water	1 tsp. vanilla
2/3 c. milk	12 whole graham crackers
1/2 c. sugar	3 T. butter, melted
1 egg, beaten	3 T. sugar

Dissolve gelatin in cold water. Combine milk, sugar and egg in a heavy saucepan. Mix well. Cook and stir until slightly thickened. Add gelatin and stir until smooth. Chill until partially congealed. Whip cream and vanilla until stiff. Fold into chilled mixture. Crush crackers and add butter and sugar. Press into the bottom and sides of a small serving dish, saving some of the crumbs for the top. Pour cream mixture into bowl and top with remaining crumbs.

GRANDMA HORST'S
CREAM SPONGE
One of the aunts wrote, "With lots of milk on hand, Mom often made this dessert."

1 T. unflavored gelatin	1/8 tsp. salt
1/4 c. water	1 c. cream
1 1/2 c. milk	1 tsp. vanilla
1/2 c. sugar	

Combine gelatin and water in mixing bowl. Heat milk, sugar and salt. Pour on gelatin. Stir to dissolve. Chill until partially thickened. Whip cream and vanilla and add.

Variation for **CHOCOLATE SPONGE:** Mix 1 T. cocoa with sugar and salt.

GRANDMA HORST'S
ORANGE SPONGE

1 T. gelatin	1 T. orange rind
1/2 c. cold water	1/2 c. sugar
1/2 c. boiling water	1/4 tsp. salt
1/2 c. orange juice	1/2 c. cream

Soften gelatin in 1/2 c. cold water. Bring 1/2 c. water to a boil and add orange juice, rind, sugar and salt. Pour over gelatin to dissolve. Chill until partially thickened. Whip cream and add.

Variation for **GRAPE SPONGE:** Bring 1 c. grape juice to a boil. Omit orange juice, boiling water and orange rind.

RICE PEACH PUDDING

1 c. cooked rice
1/2 c. powdered sugar

1 c. fresh, sliced peaches
1/2 c. whipping cream

Combine rice, sugar and peaches. Whip cream and fold into rice mixture. Chill before serving. Pineapple can be substituted for peaches. Marshmallows may be added.

MARSHMALLOW PINEAPPLE DESSERT

Commercially made marshmallows as we know them weren't around until the late 40's. People made their own or bought those molded and sold by confectioners. When recipes call for quartered or diced marshmallows, miniature marshmallows—another convenience our grandmothers didn't have in the 20's, 30's and 40's—may be used.

1/2 lb. marshmallows
1 1/2 c. crushed pineapple
2 c. whipping cream

2 T. sugar
2 tsp. vanilla

Cut marshmallows in fourths. Add pineapple. Whip cream. Add sugar and vanilla to cream. Fold into marshmallow mixture. Chill thoroughly before serving. Garnish with maraschino cherries and nuts.

FRUIT AND DUMPLINGS

4 c. fresh blueberries,
    peaches or cherries
3 c. water
2 c. sugar

1 1/2 c. flour
2 tsp. baking powder
1/4 tsp. salt
1/3 c. milk

Boil blueberries, water and sugar until there is plenty of juice. Mix flour, baking powder and salt. Add milk. Drop from a tablespoon into boiling berries. Cover and boil 12 minutes. Can be made with canned fruit. If using sweetened canned fruit, use liquid as part of the water and use 1/2 c. less sugar.

APPLE RINGS

Wash, core and slice apples cross-wise in rounds. Dip slices in sugar and cinnamon and fry slowly in butter until brown, turning once. Eat plain or serve with sausage or pork chops.

CINNAMON APPLES

6 tart apples	1/4 c. red cinnamon candies
2 c. sugar	2 c. water

Wash and peel apples. Cut in half. Combine remaining ingredients. Boil five minutes. Add apples. Cook slowly until tender.

RHUBARB FLUFF

2 c. cooked rhubarb	2/3 c. sugar
2 T. lemon juice	1/2 c. whipping cream

Combine rhubarb, lemon juice and sugar. Cool if rhubarb is still warm. Whip cream and fold into rhubarb mixture.

Though non-dairy whipped topping was not an option for our grandmas until the mid forties, it can be substituted, in many cases for whipped cream.

PEACH FLUFF

6 fresh peaches	1 c. cream, whipped
1/4 c. sugar	1/2 tsp. almond extract
1/2 lb. marshmallows	1/2 tsp. vanilla

Peel and slice peaches. Sprinkle sugar over peaches. Cut marshmallows into small pieces. Add to peaches. Add flavoring to cream and whip. Chill. Two cups of fresh sliced or crushed strawberries may be used instead of peaches.

PEACH GELATIN

3 oz. pkg. orange gelatin
1 c. boiling water
1/2 c. peach juice or water

2 T. lemon juice
2 c. drained, canned peach
   slices

Dissolve gelatin in boiling water. Add peach and lemon juice. When partially thickened, add peaches. Other canned fruits or flavors of gelatin may be used.

Peach gelatin, first made in 1907, was discontinued in 1918 and not reintroduced until the 70's, so our Grandmas used orange gelatin for peach desserts.

PEACH BAVARIAN

3 oz. pkg. orange gelatin
3/4 c. boiling water
1 c. peach juice from canned
   peaches

1 c. crushed, canned peaches
1 c. whipping cream
2 T. powdered sugar
1/2 tsp. almond extract

Dissolve gelatin in boiling water. Add peach juice. Chill until cold and syrupy. Beat until fluffy and thick. Add peaches. Whip cream; add sugar and flavoring. Fold into mixture.

Bavarians and other cream based recipes go well with a graham cracker crust. Crush 12 whole graham crackers and add 3 T. sugar and 3 T. butter. Press around the bottom and sides of a serving bowl or into a cake pan. Fill with a bavarian recipe or other dessert.

PINEAPPLE BAVARIAN

3 oz. pkg. lemon gelatin
3/4 c. boiling water
1/4 c. sugar

1/8 tsp. salt
1 c. crushed pineapple
2 c. cream

Dissolve gelatin in boiling water. Add sugar and salt and stir to dissolve. Cool until partially set. Beat gelatin until light and fluffy. Fold in pineapple. Whip cream and add. Pour into a mold or bowl.

CHOCOLATE BAVARIAN

1 T. gelatin	1/2 c. hot milk
1/4 c. cold water	2 c. cream
2 oz. unsweetened chocolate	1/4 c. sugar
3/4 c. sugar	1 tsp. vanilla
1/8 tsp. salt	

Soften gelatin in water. Melt chocolate in a heavy saucepan over very low heat, stirring constantly. Add sugar, salt and milk. Cook several minutes. Add gelatin to hot mixture. Mix well. Cool until partially thickened. Beat until mixture becomes very light. Whip cream, add sugar and vanilla. Add to chocolate mixture. Pour into a mold or bowl and chill thoroughly before serving.

CITRUS TAPIOCA

1/2 c. baby pearl tapioca	2 T. lemon juice
3 1/2 c. boiling water	1 c. sugar
1/8 tsp. salt	1 c. whipping cream
1 c. crushed pineapple	2 T. sugar
shredded pulp of 2 oranges	1/2 tsp. vanilla

Cook tapioca in water and salt until clear. Cool. Add pineapple, oranges, lemon juice and 1 c. sugar. Whip cream and add 2 T. sugar and vanilla. Top with whipped cream or fold whipped cream into tapioca.

STRAWBERRY MOLD

2 T. gelatin	1 1/4 c. sugar
1/4 c. cold water	1/2 c. whipping cream
1/2 c. boiling water	1 tsp. vanilla
3 c. crushed strawberries	angel food cake

Soften gelatin in water. Dissolve in boiling water. Cool. Add strawberries and sugar. Whip cream and vanilla. Fold into strawberry mixture. Line a mold or bowl with angel food cake slices. Pour strawberry mix over cake. Chill until firm; unmold and garnish with whole strawberries.

RASPBERRY ANGEL FOOD MOLD

1 T. unflavored gelatin
1/4 c. cold water
1/4 c. hot water
1 c. crushed, sweetened red
    raspberries

1 T. lemon juice
1/2 c. sugar
1/4 tsp. salt
1 1/2 c. whipping cream
angel food cake

Soften gelatin in cold water. Add hot water and stir until gelatin dissolves. Add raspberries, lemon juice, sugar and salt. Mix well. Chill until mixture begins to thicken. Whip cream and fold into raspberry mixture. Cut 1/2-inch thick strips of angel food cake. Line bottom and sides of a 9x5-inch loaf pan with strips of cake. Fill with raspberry mixture. Chill until firm. Unmold on a serving dish or plate.

GRANDMA HORST'S
DATE WHIP

1 c. chopped dates
1 c. marshmallows
1 c. crushed graham crackers

1/2 c. chopped nuts
1/2 c. whipping cream

Combine dates, marshmallows, graham crackers and nuts. Whip cream and add. Chill.

BAKED CUSTARD

4 eggs
1/2 c. sugar
1/8 tsp. salt

1 tsp. vanilla
1/4 tsp. nutmeg
4 c. hot milk

Beat eggs. Add sugar, salt, vanilla and nutmeg. Add milk slowly, stirring constantly. Pour into a baking dish or custard cups. Set baking dish into a pan of hot water. Bake at 350° for 35 minutes or until inserted knife comes out clean.

Variation for **CHOCOLATE CUSTARD:** Add 1/2 c. cocoa.

BAKED RICE PUDDING

5 c. milk	1/4 tsp. salt
1/2 c. sugar	1/8 tsp. nutmeg
1/2 c. rice	1 T. butter

Combine and pour into a greased shallow baking dish. Bake at 325° for two hours or until rice is tender. Stir occasionally. One cup of raisins may be added toward the end of baking time.

DATE PUDDING

1 c. brown sugar	1/2 tsp. salt
1 c. water	1/2 c. brown sugar
1 T. butter	1/2 c. milk
1 c. flour	1 c. chopped dates
2 tsp. baking powder	1/2 c. chopped nuts

Combine 1 c. brown sugar, water and butter. Cook three minutes. Combine flour, baking powder, salt and 1/2 c. sugar. Add milk. Mix well. Add dates and nuts. Pour syrup into a 9x9 greased baking dish. Pour batter on syrup and bake at 350° approx. 40 minutes. Serve plain or with whipped cream. Or cut into small squares and mix with cream.

BREAD PUDDING

3 c. bread cubes	1/4 tsp. salt
3 c. milk	1 T. butter
2 eggs, beaten	1 tsp. vanilla
2/3 c. sugar	1 c. raisins
1/2 tsp. cinnamon	

Combine ingredients. Pour into a greased baking dish. Bake at 350° one hour or until an inserted knife comes out clean. Cool. Serve with whipped cream. For chocolate pudding add 3 T. cocoa.

Variation for **SPICED BREAD PUDDING:** Use 1 tsp. cinnamon and 1/2 tsp. nutmeg. Eggs may be omitted.

CREAM PUFFS

1/2 c. butter
1/2 tsp. salt
1 c. boiling water

1 c. flour
4 eggs

Combine butter, salt and water. Heat to boiling. Add flour to boiling mixture. Beat vigorously until mixture leaves sides of saucepan and does not cling to spoon. Remove from heat and cool slightly. Add unbeaten eggs, one at a time. Beat thoroughly after the addition of each egg until mixture is smooth. Drop by tablespoons onto well-greased baking sheet, 2 inches apart. Shape mixture into rounds and pile slightly in the center. Bake at 425° for 30 minutes or until firm and dry. Cool. Cut a slit in the side of each with a sharp knife. Remove any moist strands from centers before filling with sweetened whipped cream, ice cream or fruit. Sprinkle with powdered sugar. Makes approximately 12 cream puffs.

Variation for **ECLAIRS:** Shape cream puff mixture into 4-inch strips on a well-greased baking sheet, 2 inches apart. Bake at 425° for 30 minutes or until firm and dry. When cool, fill with cream filling. Ice by dipping into desired icing or spread icing on top.

BAKED APPLES

Grandma Horst's family ate a lot of apple desserts. They bought bushels of apples each fall then sorted through them every week, using any apples that showed signs of deteriorating.

6 tart apples
6 T. brown sugar
1/2 tsp. cinnamon

1 T. butter
1/2 c. boiling water

Wash apples. Remove cores. Mix sugar and cinnamon. Fill each apple with 1 T. sugar and cinnamon mixture. Dot apples with butter. Put in baking dish. Add water. Bake at 350° until tender—approximately 45 minutes. Baste occasionally. You can also cut apples in half and fill the cavities with sugar and cinnamon.

GRANDMA HORST'S
APPLE TAPIOCA
Grandma sped this up by boiling the apples, sugar and spice before baking.

4 c. water	1 c. brown sugar
1/2 c. minute tapioca	2 tsp. lemon juice
1 tsp. salt	1/3 tsp. nutmeg
3 c. peeled, sliced apples	3/4 tsp. cinnamon

Bring water, tapioca and salt to a boil. Cook until tapioca is clear. Stir frequently. Put apples in a greased a baking dish. Combine remaining ingredients and sprinkle over apples. Pour tapioca on top. Bake at 350° about 45 minutes. Eat warm or chill and serve with whipped cream.

APPLE CRISP

8 c. sliced apples	1/2 c. butter
1/4 c. sugar	3/4 c. flour
1 tsp. cinnamon	1 c. brown sugar
1/4 c. hot water	

Mix apples, sugar and cinnamon and place in a 13x9 baking dish. Pour water into the side of dish. Cream butter; add flour and sugar. Spread crumbs over apples. Bake at 375° approximately 45 minutes.

APPLE DELIGHTS

2 c. flour	1 c. milk
2 tsp. baking powder	1 egg, beaten
1/2 tsp. salt	6 baking apples
1/4 c. shortening	sugar

Mix flour, baking powder and salt. Work in shortening with finger tips. Add milk and beaten egg. Mix well. Put a tablespoon of batter into well greased muffin pans. Peel, halve and core apples. Put on top of batter, cut side up. Fill holes with sugar. Bake at 375° for 30 minutes or until apples are tender. Serve hot with sweetened whipped cream sprinkled with cinnamon.

GRANDMA HORST'S
APPLE CORNBREAD

A hearty wintertime dish they often had for Saturday dinner. The girls remember how
good it tasted after helping outside all morning.

10 -12 apples, peeled	**2 T. sugar**
sugar and cinnamon	**1/2 tsp. salt**
1 c. cornmeal	**1 egg, well beaten**
1 c. flour	**1 c. milk**
1 T. baking powder	**1/4 c. melted shortening**

Slice apples into a 13 x 9 cake pan or a roaster. Sprinkle liberally with
sugar and cinnamon; add one half cup water. In another bowl combine dry
ingredients. Beat egg, milk and shortening and add. Mix. Pour batter
evenly on apples and sugar. Bake at 375° for 50 minutes or until apples
are soft. Eat warm with milk.

APPLE ROLL-UPS

2 c. flour	**soft butter**
2 tsp. baking powder	**brown sugar**
1 tsp. salt	**cinnamon**
1/4 c. shortening	**5 apples, peeled and chopped**
3/4 c. milk	

SAUCE:

1 c. sugar	**1/4 tsp. salt**
1 T. flour	**1 c. hot water**
1 tsp. cinnamon	**2 T. butter**

Combine flour, baking powder and salt. Work shortening in with fingertips. Add milk and mix well. Roll out dough 1/4-inch thick. Spread
with soft butter. Sprinkle with brown sugar, cinnamon and apples. Roll
up like a jelly roll. Cut into 1 1/2-inch slices. Place slices in a greased
pan one inch apart. To make sauce, combine ingredients and boil 3
minutes. Pour over roll-ups. Bake at 375° approximately 40 minutes.

APPLE COBBLER WITH BUTTER SAUCE

8 tart apples
1/2 c. sugar
1 tsp. cinnamon
1/2 tsp. nutmeg
1/4 tsp. salt

2 c. flour
2 tsp. baking powder
3/4 tsp. salt
1/2 c. butter
2/3 c. milk

BUTTER SAUCE:

1 c. sugar
2 T. flour
1/2 tsp. cinnamon

1/8 tsp. salt
2 c. boiling water
2 T. butter

Peel and chop apples. Butter a greased 13x9-pan and fill with apples. Combine sugar, spices and 1/4 tsp. salt and sprinkle over apples. Combine flour, baking powder and 3/4 tsp. salt. Mix in butter until mixture is as fine as corn meal. Add milk, mixing until a soft dough is formed. Knead lightly on a floured board. Roll out to fit the size of the pan and place over apples. Brush crust with milk. Bake at 375° approximately 45 minutes. Serve hot with butter sauce, milk or cream. To make sauce mix dry ingredients in a sauce pan. Add boiling water, stirring constantly until blended. Add butter and boil 5 minutes.

PEACH COBBLER

4 c. sliced peaches
2 T. minute tapioca
1/2 c. sugar
1/4 tsp. salt
1/2 tsp. cinnamon
1/8 tsp. nutmeg

1 T. butter
1 1/2 c. flour
2 tsp. baking powder
1/4 tsp. salt
1/4 c. shortening
3/4 c. milk

Mix peaches, tapioca, sugar, salt and spices in a 13x9 baking pan. Dot with butter. Let set 10 minutes. Combine flour, baking powder and salt. Work in shortening. Add milk. Drop batter by tablespoon onto peaches. Sprinkle sugar on top of batter. Bake at 375° for 30 minutes.

Variation for **CHERRY COBBLER:** Substitute cherries for peaches.

PEACH CRUMBLE

6-8 peaches	3/4 c. flour
1/3 c. brown sugar	1/8 tsp. nutmeg
1/3 c. butter	

Peel and halve peaches. Place in a greased baking dish. Mix together remaining ingredients and sprinkle over peaches. Bake at 350° approximately 30 minutes. Serve warm with milk or cream.

GRANDMA KULP'S
STRAWBERRY SHORTCAKE

2 c. flour	3 T. lard or shortening
1/2 tsp. salt	1/2 c. milk
2 T. sugar	1 egg
4 tsp. baking powder	sweetened strawberries

Combine flour, salt, sugar and baking powder. Mix in lard or shortening. Combine milk and egg beating well. Add to flour mixture. Spread in lightly greased pan. Bake in hot (375°) oven for approximately 20 minutes. Serve with fresh, sweetened strawberries and milk.

FRESH FRUIT SHORTCAKE

1 qt. fresh strawberries, raspberries or sliced peaches	4 tsp. baking powder
	1 tsp. salt
	1 T. sugar
1/2 c. sugar, or to taste	1/4 c. butter
2 c. flour	1 c. milk

Sprinkle 1/2 c. sugar over fruit. Combine dry ingredients then cut in shortening. Add milk, stirring just until dough stiffens. Pat to uniform thickness in a greased 8-inch layer cake pan. Bake at 400° approximately 20 minutes. Split and butter while hot. Spread layers with fruit and serve plain, or with whipped cream or milk. Part or all whole wheat flour may be substituted.

Variation for **CANNED FRUIT SHORTCAKE:** Use 1 qt. canned peaches or cherries. Drain juice and add 2 T. cornstarch. Stir until smooth then bring to a boil. Remove from heat. Add fruit and a few drops of almond flavoring. Serve—between halves and on top of warm, split and buttered shortcakes—with cream.

BLUEBERRY PUDDING

1/4 c. butter	1/2 tsp. salt
1/2 c. sugar	1/4 c. milk
1 egg	1 tsp. vanilla
1 c. flour	3 c. blueberries
1 tsp. baking powder	1/3 c. sugar

Cream butter and sugar. Add egg. Add flour, baking powder, salt, milk and vanilla. Put blueberries in a greased, covered baking dish. Sprinkle with 1/3 c. sugar. Spoon batter over berries. Cover. Bake at 350° for approximately 70 minutes. Blackberries or huckleberries can be used.

Variation for **BLACKBERRY PUDDING:** Use 3 c. blackberries instead of blueberries.

CHILDREN LOVE GAMES

"Take advantage of this to give them physical training. Furnish them the apparatus for games which requires a good deal of muscular exercise. Those curious little affairs which require them to sit on the floor or gather about the table and remain in a cramped position, are not advisable.

It is particularly desirable that the games should call them into the open air and sunshine. In this way children lay in a stock of health and strength. Remember that, particularly in our early years, this is infinitely more important than all adornments of the person or study of books."

JELLY ROLL

1 c. cake flour
1 tsp. baking powder
1/4 tsp. salt
3 eggs, separated

3/4 c. sugar
2 T. cold water
1/2 tsp. vanilla

Combine flour, baking powder and salt. Beat egg whites until stiff, then gradually beat in 1/4 c. sugar. Add water to egg yolks, beat until light and thick, gradually beating in remaining sugar. Add vanilla. Fold egg whites into yolks, then fold into flour mixture. Spread into a 11x15 pan buttered on the sides with waxed paper on the bottom. Bake at 375° for 10-12 minutes or until it springs back when lightly touched with finger tips. Turn out on a tea towel sprinkled with powdered sugar. Quickly pull off waxed paper and cut off crisp edges. Place a piece of waxed paper on the cake and roll up cake starting with the narrow side. Wrap in towel. When cool, unroll, remove paper and spread with jelly, lemon or chocolate filling (See fillings) or ice cream. Reroll. Cover and chill for several hours. Makes 8-10 servings.

Variation for **CHOCOLATE JELLY ROLL:** Add 1/4 c. cocoa to flour.

VANILLA ICE CREAM

Homemade ice cream in Grandma Horst's home was not unusual. An ice man passed by their lane once a week. Whenever they wanted to make ice cream they hung a red flag on the mailbox. They did not have a freezer so they stashed the ice block in the barn under a feed bag and covered it with straw, until they were ready to make ice cream. This isn't Grandma Horst's recipe, but probably much like the one she used. One of her daughters writes, "Mom often made homemade ice cream. Her recipe included gelatin which made the ice cream very creamy. It didn't melt to milk again like others did when served."

2 T. unflavored gelatin
1/3 c. cold water
6 c. milk
2 c. sugar

1/2 tsp. salt
4 c. cream
2 T. vanilla

Soften gelatin in water. Heat 2 c. milk. Remove from heat. Add gelatin and stir to dissolve. Add remaining milk. Add sugar and salt and stir until dissolved. Add cream and vanilla. Freeze in a 4-quart or 6-quart ice cream freezer.

Variation for **BUTTER PECAN ICE CREAM:** Heat 1 c. chopped pecans in 1 T. butter until lightly browned. Sprinkle very lightly with salt. Cool. Add to ice cream when its almost done.

CUSTARD ICE CREAM

4 eggs	4 c. milk
1 1/2 c. sugar	3 c. cream or evaporated milk
1/4 tsp. salt	2 tsp. vanilla

Beat eggs well. Add sugar and salt. Add milk, stir well. Cook over low heat, stirring constantly until mixture begins to thicken and coats a spoon. Remove from heat. Chill. Add cream and vanilla. Freeze in a one gallon ice cream freezer.

CHOCOLATE ICE CREAM

2 c. sugar	6 c. milk
1/2 c. cocoa	4 c. cream
1/2 tsp. salt	2 T. vanilla
1 c. water	

Combine sugar, cocoa and salt. Mix with water. Heat and stir until sugar is thoroughly dissolved. Remove from heat and add milk, cream and vanilla. Freeze in a 1-gallon ice cream freezer.

Variation for **CHOCOLATE BANANA ICE CREAM:** Add four ripe bananas, mashed, along with milk and cream. Use 1/2 c. less sugar.

"So many eat cakes with ice cream. Doubling the dessert when the meal has already been great enough is a mistake."

FRESH FRUIT ICE CREAM

2 T. unflavored gelatin	2 c. sugar
1/3 c. cold water	2 T. lemon juice
3 c. milk	3 c. whipping cream
4 c. fresh crushed peaches, strawberries or raspberries	1/2 tsp. almond extract

Soften gelatin in cold water five minutes. Heat milk. Add gelatin and stir until it dissolves. Combine fruit, sugar and lemon juice. Chill Whip cream until thick. Add extract. Fold into fruit mixture. Pour into freezer trays and freeze, removing once to stir. If desired, freeze in a 1 gallon ice cream freezer.

PINEAPPLE ICE CREAM

4 c. milk	1 c. sugar
2 c. cream	1/4 c. lemon juice
2 c. crushed pineapple and juice	1/4 tsp. salt

Combine ingredients. Pour into ice cream freezer and freeze.

ICE CREAM DESSERT

vanilla ice cream	chopped nuts
chocolate ice cream or chocolate syrup	maraschino cherries
	whipping cream

Layer vanilla ice cream in a cake pan. Add a layer of chocolate ice cream or syrup. Sprinkle with nuts and coarsely chopped cherries. Top with sweetened whipped cream. Freeze.

CHOCOLATE MARSHMALLOW DESSERT

1/4 c. cocoa	1 T. vanilla
1 c. milk	1/8 tsp. salt
18 marshmallows	1 c. cream, whipped

Combine cocoa and milk in a saucepan and stir until smooth. Add marshmallows and cook over low heat until melted, stirring constantly. Add vanilla and salt. When cool and slightly stiffened, add whipped cream. Pour into a mold or bowl and freeze.

CHOCOLATE MOUSSE

2 c. whipping cream
1/2 c. powdered sugar
1/8 tsp. salt

2 oz. unsweetened chocolate
1 tsp. vanilla

Whip cream, sugar and salt until stiff. Melt chocolate. Add chocolate and vanilla to cream. Mix well. Freeze without stirring.

CHERRY MOUSSE

2 c. whipping cream
1/4 c. powdered sugar

1/2 tsp. almond flavoring
1 c. drained, canned cherries

Whip cream. Add sugar and flavoring. Fold in cherries. Pour into a mold, bowl, or cake pan. Freeze without stirring.

STRAWBERRY MOUSSE

4 c. strawberries
1 1/2 c. sugar
1 T. lemon juice
2 T. unflavored gelatin

1/4 c. cold water
1/2 c. boiling water
1/8 tsp. salt
2 c. whipping cream

Wash and hull strawberries. Mash very well or rub through a sieve. Add sugar and lemon juice and let stand. Soften gelatin in cold water for five minutes. Combine gelatin and hot water, stirring to dissolve gelatin. Add gelatin and salt to strawberries. Mix well. Set mixture in a pan of cold water and stir until it begins to thicken. Beat cream. Fold in stiffly beaten cream. Pour into a mold or bowl and freeze without stirring.

PINEAPPLE ORANGE MOUSSE

1 c. crushed pineapple	1/2 c. sugar
1/2 c. pineapple juice	1/8 tsp. salt
1 c. orange juice	2 c. whipping cream

Combine pineapple, juices, sugar and salt. Whip cream; fold into pineapple mixture. Pour into mold, bowl or cake pan; freeze without stirring.

ORANGE SHERBET

1 T. unflavored gelatin	1/2 c. light corn syrup
1/2 c. milk	1/4 tsp. salt
1 1/4 c. orange juice	1 1/2 c. thin cream or milk
1/4 c. lemon juice	2 tsp. grated orange rind
2/3 c. sugar	

Soften gelatin in a small kettle with milk. After five minutes turn on heat and stir constantly until gelatin dissolves. Remove from heat and let stand. Combine juices, sugar, corn syrup and salt. Stir until sugar is dissolved. Add cream or milk, rind and gelatin mixture. Stir in several drops of yellow food coloring if desired. Mix well. Pour into two ice trays. Freeze to mush—about one hour. Place in a bowl and beat until smooth. Return to trays and freeze until firm—about one hour.

GRAPE SHERBET

3 c. milk	1/4 c. lemon juice
1 c. grape juice	1/8 tsp. salt
3/4 c. sugar	

Combine all ingredients. Mix well. Freeze in a bowl or cake pan until mushy. Beat until mixture becomes light and creamy. Return quickly to freezer and freeze until firm.

FRESH CHERRY SHERBET

1 1/2 c. pitted red cherries	1 T. gelatin
2 1/2 c. water	1/4 c. cold water
2/3 c. sugar	1 T. lemon juice

Cook cherries, water and sugar five minutes. Soften gelatin in cold water. Add gelatin to cherries and stir until dissolved. Add lemon juice. Freeze until mushy—about one hour. Place in a chilled bowl and beat until light. Freeze until firm.

CHRISTMAS SHERBET

1 c. sugar	2 1/2 c. red raspberries
2 c. water	1/4 c. orange juice
3 oz. pkg. raspberry gelatin	1/4 c. lemon juice

Combine sugar and water and boil five minutes. Add gelatin; stir until dissolved. Cool until slightly thickened. Press raspberries through a sieve and add to gelatin mixture. Add juices and mix well. Pour into ice tray and freeze one hour. Place in a chilled bowl and beat until smooth. Return to tray. Freeze until firm.

Ices are frozen desserts distinguished from sherbets in that they contain no milk, cream or gelatin. Freeze ices then remove from freezer and beat until light and creamy. Return quickly to freezer and freeze until firm. Serve as a dessert or earlier in the meal.

GRAPE ICE

2 c. water	2 c. grape juice
2/3 c. sugar	1/4 c. lemon juice

Boil water and sugar five minutes. Cool. Add juices. Freeze.

"Eat all cold desserts slowly. All frozen desserts should be well melted in the mouth—that is the way to get the flavor."

GINGER ALE ICE

2 c. water
3/4 c. sugar
2 c. ginger ale

1 c. orange juice
1/2 c. lemon juice

Boil water and sugar 5 minutes; cool. Add ginger ale and juices; freeze.

Variation for **COCA COLA ICE:** Substitute coca cola for ginger ale. Omit orange juice.

LEMON ICE

4 c. water
1 1/2 c. sugar

1 c. lemon juice
1/8 tsp. salt

Boil water and sugar five minutes. Cool. Add lemon juice and salt. Freeze.

Variation for **ORANGE LEMON ICE:** Substitute 2 c. orange juice for 2 c. water. Add orange juice with lemon juice.

PINEAPPLE ICE

2 c. water
2/3 c. sugar

2 c. crushed pineapple
1/4 c. lemon juice

Boil water and sugar five minutes. Cool. Add pineapple and lemon juice. Freeze.

PINK FRUIT ICE

3 c. pineapple juice
3 c. orange juice
3 c. red carbonated beverage

1/2 c. lemon juice
2 c. sugar

Mix well making sure sugar is dissolved; freeze.

GRANDMA'S

MAPLE SUGAR SAUCE

Melt over a slow fire, in a small
teacup of water, half a pint of maple
sugar; let it simmer, removing all scum; add
four tablespoonfuls of butter mixed with a
level teaspoonful of flour and one of grated nutmeg; boil for a few moments, and serve with
boiled pudding.

DESSERT SAUCES

BUTTERSCOTCH SAUCE

1/4 c. butter
1 1/4 c. brown sugar
2/3 c. corn syrup

1/8 tsp. salt
3/4 c. evaporated milk

Combine all but evaporated milk. Cook slowly to the very soft ball stage (230°). Remove from heat. Add evaporated milk.

MAPLE PECAN SAUCE

2 T. butter
3/4 c. sugar
1/4 c. water
3 T. white corn syrup

1/4 c. cream or milk
3/4 tsp. maple flavoring
1/2 c. pecans

Melt butter in saucepan. Add sugar, water and corn syrup. Boil to 230° or until a small amount forms a very soft ball when dropped into cold water. Remove from heat. Slowly add cream, flavoring and nuts. Serve hot or cold on ice cream or pudding.

HARD SAUCE

1/4 c. butter
1 c. powdered sugar

1/4 tsp. vanilla
1/8 tsp. salt

Cream butter and sugar; add vanilla and salt. Pack into a small bowl and chill. When ready to serve, turn out in a small serving dish. Serve with apple dumplings or warm rolls.

Variation for **CREAM HARD SAUCE:** Whip 1/2 c. cream and add to hard sauce.

"Sauces are dressings served with foods when it is necessary to develop flavor, provide moisture, add richness, give color, or impart attractiveness."

SPICED SAUCE

1/3 c. brown sugar
1-inch stick cinnamon
1 T. grated lemon peel
small piece root ginger
2 whole cloves

1 1/2 c. water
1 T. cornstarch
2 T. water
1 T. lemon juice

Combine sugar, cinnamon, lemon peel, ginger, cloves and 1 1/2 c. water. Simmer, covered, for 20 minutes, stirring occasionally. Strain. Blend together cornstarch and 2 T. water and stir into mixture. Boil one minute. Remove from heat and stir in lemon juice.

COCOA SAUCE

1/4 c. cocoa
1 c. water
1 c. sugar

1/4 tsp. salt
1 T. butter
1 tsp. vanilla

Cook cocoa and water together until smooth and thick. Add sugar and salt and cook a few minutes longer. Add butter and vanilla.

CHOCOLATE SAUCE

1 c. sugar
1 T. cornstarch
1/4 tsp. salt
1 c. water

1/2 c. milk
2 oz. unsweetened chocolate, chopped
1 tsp. vanilla

Mix dry ingredients. Add water, milk and chocolate. Cook until thickened, stirring constantly. Remove from heat. Add vanilla.

CHOCOLATE MINT SAUCE

2 c. sugar
1/8 tsp. salt
2 oz. unsweetened chocolate
3/4 c. milk

1 T. butter
1/4 c. crushed peppermint candy

Combine all ingredients but candy and heat slowly, stirring until sugar is dissolved and chocolate melted. Bring to a boil and boil, uncovered until a small amount forms a very soft ball (230°) when dropped into cold water. Remove from heat. Add candy and beat slightly. Serve warm. Dilute with a small amount of milk or cream if necessary.

FRESH APPLE SAUCE

8 medium apples	1/4 tsp. cinnamon
1 c. water	1/8 tsp. nutmeg
1/2 c. sugar	1/8 tsp. salt

Peel, core and quarter apples. Put in a saucepan with water. Boil until apples are soft. Add remaining ingredients and cook five minutes longer.

CHERRY SAUCE

2 T. sugar	2 c. canned cherries and juice
2 T. cornstarch	2 T. lemon juice
1/4 tsp. salt	1/4 tsp. almond extract

Mix dry ingredients in a saucepan. Add cherries and juice and cook and stir until mixture comes to a boil. Remove from heat and add lemon juice and almond extract. Two drops of red food coloring may be added.

CRANBERRY SAUCE

4 c. cranberries	1 3/4 c. sugar
2 c. water	

Bring water to a boil; add berries. Cover and cook until outer skins burst. Add sugar and simmer 10 minutes. Pour into a mold or bowl; chill. If desired, strain cranberries through a sieve after they're cooked before adding sugar. Heat strained cranberries, add sugar and simmer ten minutes.

Variation for **CRANBERRY SAUCE WITH APPLES:** Peel and slice 4 apples. Cook with cranberries.

LEMON SAUCE

1 c. sugar	1/4 c. lemon juice
2 T. cornstarch	1 tsp. grated lemon peel
1 3/4 c. hot water	2 T. butter

Mix sugar and cornstarch in a saucepan. Add boiling water gradually, stirring all the time. Cook about 10 minutes. Add lemon juice, lemon peel and butter. Serve hot.

Variation for **LEMON RAISIN SAUCE:** Add 1/2 c. raisins.

ORANGE SAUCE

1 T. cornstarch	1 c. orange juice
1/2 c. sugar	1 T. lemon juice
1 tsp. grated orange peel	2 T. butter

Mix cornstarch, sugar, peel and orange juice. Boil 5 minutes. Remove from heat. Add lemon juice and butter. Serve hot.

PINEAPPLE MARSHMALLOW SAUCE

1/2 c. sugar	1 tsp. grated lemon rind
1 T. cornstarch	1 c. crushed pineapple
1 c. pineapple juice	12 large marshmallows
1/4 c. lemon juice	

Combine sugar and cornstarch in a saucepan. Stir in pineapple juice, lemon juice and rind. Cook, stirring constantly until thickened. Add pineapples and diced marshmallows. Mix thoroughly. Serve with pudding, frozen desserts or plain cake.

RASPBERRY SAUCE

1/2 c. sugar	2 T. cornstarch
1/2 c. water	2 T. water
1 c. raspberry jelly or jam	

Combine sugar and 1/2 c. water. Bring to a boil, stirring until sugar is dissolved. Add jelly. Blend cornstarch and 2 T. water and stir into mixture. Bring to a boil again. Serve hot or cold.

RHUBARB SAUCE

2 c. 1-inch diced rhubarb   1/2 c. sugar
water

Put rhubarb in a saucepan. Cover the bottom with water. Sprinkle sugar on rhubarb. Cook slowly, stirring constantly, until soft.

RHUBARB SAUCE AND PINEAPPLE

4 c. diced rhubarb   14 oz. can pineapple cubes
1 1/2 c. sugar

Place rhubarb and sugar in a saucepan. Add juice from pineapple. Bring to a boil. Reduce heat and simmer until rhubarb is soft. Place pineapple cubes in a bowl. Pour rhubarb sauce on top. Chill well before serving.

FRESH STRAWBERRY SAUCE

1/4 c. butter   12 large strawberries, mashed
1/2 c. powdered sugar

Cream butter and sugar. Add strawberries and beat. Serve on cake.

TABLE ETIQUETTE

"The hour of dining should be made an hour of solid pleasure and comfort; the dining room, the table, and all the appurtenances belonging thereto, should be as cheerful as possible. The room should be comfortable, bright and cozy, and at the table the mistress should wear her brightest smile. If you have trials do not bring them to the table; brooding over them impairs digestion and sends husband and children to business and to school gloomy and morose instead of strengthened and refreshed."

GRANDMA'S

PUFF PASTE

One quart of flour, one pint of butter, one tablespoonful of salt, one and one-fourth cupfuls of ice water. Do not use any more water than specified. Before using the butter, mix well in cold water, to get all the salt out, and let it harden. Roll it out, and put half of the butter over it in small pieces; turn in the ends and roll it thin; do this twice, and touch it no more than can be avoided; use the last half of the butter for the last time you roll it. Then put on ice for at least an hour before using it. If it sticks, put it on a tin sheet before putting on the ice. The least flour you use in rolling, the nicer will be your paste. Bake in a quicker oven than for a short crust, and lay a paper over the top to keep it from scorching.

EGGLESS SQUASH PIE

Stew the squash till very dry; press through a colander; to each pint of squash allow one tablespoonful each of butter and cinnamon, one cup of sugar, one teaspoonful of ginger, a little salt, and a few crackers rolled very fine. Add milk according to judgment.

PIES AND TARTS

PLAIN PASTRY

1 1/2 c. flour	1/2 c. shortening
1/2 tsp. salt	1/4 c. cold water

Combine flour and salt. Work in shortening. Work water in lightly. Turn half of pastry onto a lightly floured board. Roll 1/8-inch thick. Shape pastry to fit pie pan. Roll remainder of dough for a top crust or roll and cut into strips for a lattice top. If making a pie without a top crust the leftover dough can be pressed in a muffin tin for tart shells. If a baked crust is needed, fit pie crust into a pie pan as usual, crimping edges if desired. Prick the bottom and sides of pie shell with a fork. Bake at 375° for 15 minutes, or until lightly browned.

Variation for **CHEESE PASTRY:** Add 2 c. grated cheese with shortening. Use only 1/3 c. shortening.

GRAHAM CRACKER PASTRY

1 1/4 c. graham cracker crumbs	1/4 c. sugar
	1/4 c. melted butter

Mix well. Press into pie pan. Bake at 375° approximately 10 minutes or chill and use unbaked.

MERINGUE

2 egg whites	1/2 tsp. cornstarch
3 T. powdered sugar	1 tsp. vanilla

Beat egg whites until almost stiff. Combine sugar and cornstarch and gradually add while beating. Add vanilla. Beat until stiff. Put on top of pie and bake at 325° until golden brown—approximately 20 minutes. Baking meringue at higher temperatures makes it tough and shriveled. Watery meringue is underbaked.

"Pastry should be crisp, flaky, evenly browned and tender. Thorough chilling of pastry before its uses aids in insuring these characteristics."

SWEETENED WHIPPED CREAM

1 c. whipping cream	1/2 tsp. vanilla
2-3 T. powdered sugar	1/8 tsp. salt

Whip cream until stiff. Mix in powdered sugar, vanilla and salt. Cream when whipped, approximately doubles in volume.

APPLE PIE

pastry for a double pie crust	1/4 tsp. nutmeg
4 c. thinly sliced apples	1/8 tsp. salt
1 c. sugar	1 tsp. lemon juice
1 T. flour	1 T. butter
1/2 tsp. cinnamon	

Line a 9-inch pie pan with pastry. Fill with apple slices. Mix sugar, flour, cinnamon, nutmeg, salt and lemon juice. Sprinkle over apples. Dot with butter. Roll out top crust about one inch larger than pie pan. Make three slits in crust to vent steam. Moisten the edge of the crust already in the pan. Cover with top crust. Finish by pressing edges together with a fork. Brush top crust with milk and sprinkle with sugar. Bake at 375° approximately 45 minutes.

OPEN FACED APPLE PIE

Open faced apple pies were the norm in Grandma Hoover and Grandma Martin's homes. One of Grandma Martin's daughters recalls attractive pies with apples arranged in circles.

pastry for one pie	1/4 tsp. cinnamon
4 large, tart apples	1/4 tsp. nutmeg
1 c. sugar	1 T. butter

Wash and peel apples. Cut into quarters, removing cores. Arrange apple quarters in a pastry-lined pie pan. Combine sugar and spices and pour over apples. Dot with butter. Bake at 425° for 10 minutes. Reduce heat to 350° and bake 20 minutes longer.

BANANA CREAM PIE

3/4 c. sugar
1/3 c. flour
1/8 tsp. salt
2 c. milk
2 eggs, beaten

2 T. butter
1 tsp. vanilla
2 or 3 bananas
1 baked pie crust
sweetened whipped cream

Combine sugar, flour and salt in a heavy saucepan. Stir in milk. Add beaten eggs and mix well. Cook, stirring constantly until thick and smooth. Remove from heat and add butter and vanilla. Slice bananas into the bottom of baked pie crust. Pour cooled pudding over bananas. Chill. Top with sweetened whipped cream.

BLUEBERRY PIE

3 c. fresh blueberries
1 c. sugar
2 T. cornstarch <u>or</u>
    1/4 c. flour

1/8 tsp. salt
1 T. lemon juice
pastry for a double-crust pie
1 T. butter

Mix berries with sugar, cornstarch, salt and lemon juice. Line pie pan with pastry. Fill with blueberry mixture. Dot with butter. Moisten the edge of the pie crust. Cover with top crust. Cut several slits in top crust so steam can escape. Seal edge. Bake at 350° approximately 45 minutes.

Variation for **BLACKBERRY PIE:** Substitute blackberries for blueberries.

Variation for **GOOSEBERRY PIE:** Substitute gooseberries for blueberries.

Variation for **HUCKLEBERRY PIE:** Substitute huckleberries for blueberries.

BUTTERMILK PIE

A pie our Grandmas made to use up buttermilk—a byproduct of making butter.

2 eggs
1 c. sugar
2 T. flour
2 c. thick buttermilk

1 tsp. soda
1 tsp. lemon flavoring
pastry for 1 pie

Beat eggs. Add sugar and flour. Dissolve soda in buttermilk and add to egg mixture. Add flavoring. Mix well. Pour into pie shell. Bake at 400° for 10 minutes, then at 350° for 30 minutes or until inserted knife comes out clean.

BUTTERSCOTCH PIE

2 c. milk
3 T. cornstarch
1/8 tsp. salt
1 egg

2 T. butter
1 c. brown sugar
1 tsp. vanilla
1 baked pie crust

Stir cornstarch and salt into milk in a heavy saucepan. Add well-beaten egg. Mix well. Melt butter in a skillet. Add brown sugar and brown well. Add to other ingredients. Cook, stirring frequently until warm, then stir constantly, until mixture is thick and smooth. Cool slightly and add vanilla. Pour into a baked pie shell. Cool. Top with whipped cream.

CHERRY PIE

2 1/2 c. canned sour cherries
2/3 c. sugar
1/3 c. cherry juice

3 T. flour or minute tapioca
1/8 tsp. salt
pastry for a double crust pie

Combine all but pastry. If using tapioca let set 15 minutes. Pour into an unbaked pie shell. Moisten edge and put top crust on. Press edges together and trim. Cut several slits or designs in top crust to vent steam. Brush top with milk and sprinkle with sugar.

CHOCOLATE CREAM PIE

1 c. sugar
3 T. cornstarch
3 T. cocoa
1/2 tsp. salt, scant
2 c. milk

1 egg, beaten
1 T. butter
1 tsp. vanilla
1 baked pie crust

Combine dry ingredients in a heavy saucepan. Add milk and eggs. Mix well. Cook and stir until thick and smooth. Remove from heat and add butter and vanilla. Pour into baked pie shell. Top with sweetened whipped cream or meringue. A half cup of chopped pecans may be added before pouring into pie shell.

CUSTARD PIE

3 eggs, beaten
3/4 c. sugar
1/8 tsp. salt

2 1/2 c. milk
1 tsp. vanilla
pastry for 1 pie

Combine all but pastry; mix well. Pour into pastry lined pie plate. Bake at 450° in a preheated oven approximately 35 minutes or until inserted knife comes out clean.

GRANDMA KULP'S
ELDERBERRY PIE

Grandma Kulp didn't make pies very often. When she did, she usually made what was in season. When elderberries ripened in the fall, the family enjoyed elderberry pie.

2 1/2 c. elderberries
pastry for 1 pie
3/4 c. sugar
2 T. flour

1/8 tsp. salt
1/4 c. flour
3 T. sugar
2 T. soft butter

Wash and stem elderberries. Put in unbaked pie shell. Mix 3/4 c. sugar, 2 T. flour and salt. Sprinkle over berries. Combine remaining ingredients and sprinkle on pie. If desired, omit crumbs and cover with crust.

GRANDMA MARTIN'S
GROUND CHERRY PIE

Grandma Martin often made pies on Saturday. When she finished it wasn't unusual for the children to have a dozen pies to carry down to the cellar.

pastry for double crust pie	**2/3 c. brown sugar**
1/3 c. sugar	**1 tsp. cinnamon**
1/3 c. flour	**1 T. lemon juice**
3 1/2 c. ground cherries	**2 T. butter**

Line pie pan with pastry. Combine sugar and flour and sprinkle over bottom of pastry. Add ground cherries. Combine brown sugar and cinnmaon. Sprinkle on top with lemon juice. Dot with butter. Put on top crust and seal edges. Bake at 400° for 15 minutes, then at 350° for 40 minutes or until done. If desired, omit top crust and make crumbs of 3 T. flour, 3 T. sugar, 2 T. butter. Sprinkle on top.

LEMON MERINGUE PIE

1 c. sugar	**2 tsp. grated lemon rind**
1/4 c. cornstarch	**2 T. butter**
1/8 tsp. salt	**2 egg yolks**
2 c. water	**1 baked pie crust**
1/3 c. lemon juice	

MERINGUE

2 egg whites	**1 tsp. lemon or vanilla fla-**
3 T. powdered sugar	**voring**
1/2 tsp. cornstarch	

Mix sugar, cornstarch and salt in a heavy saucepan; mix well. Cook, over medium heat, stirring constantly, until smooth and thick. Remove from heat. Add lemon juice, rind and butter. Slowly add beaten yolks while stirring. Cook 2 minutes. Pour into a baked pie crust. To make meringue, beat egg whites until stiff. Combine sugar and cornstarch and add gradually while beating. Add vanilla; beat until stiff. Top lemon filling with meringue. Bake at 325° until meringue is golden brown.

MINCE MEAT PIE

3 c. mince meat pie filling   pastry for a double crust pie

Fill pastry with mince meat. Cover with top crust that has vent holes cut in it. Seal edges. Bake at 425° approximately 30 minutes.

MOLASSES PIE

3 eggs
1 1/2 c. baking molasses
2 T. melted butter
3/4 c. brown sugar
3 T. flour

1/2 tsp. salt
1/2 tsp. cinnamon
1/4 tsp. nutmeg
pastry for 1 pie

Beat eggs. Add molasses and butter. Combine sugar, flour, salt and spices. Add to first mixture. Mix thoroughly. Pour into pastry-lined pie pan. Bake at 425° for 15 minutes. If desired, the pie may be covered with a layer of pecans at this time. Reduce heat to 350° and bake approximately 20 minutes longer. This pie can also be made with a top crust.

GRANDMA HOOVER'S
MOLASSES CRUMB PIE

pastry for 1 pie
3/4 c. boiling water
1/2 tsp. soda
1/2 c. molasses
1 egg yolk
3/4 c. flour
1/2 c. brown sugar

1/4 tsp. salt
1/2 tsp. cinnamon
1/8 tsp. nutmeg
1/8 tsp. ginger
1/8 tsp. cloves
2 T. butter

Line pie pan with pastry. Dissolve soda in boiling water. Add molasses. Beat yolk and add while stirring. Pour into unbaked pie shell. Mix flour, sugar, salt, spices and butter. Sprinkle on top. Bake at 425° for 15 minutes. Reduce heat and bake at 350° approximately 20 minutes longer. The whole egg may be used.

GRANDMA HORST'S
OATMEAL PIE

1 c. sugar	1 tsp. vanilla
3/4 c. molasses	1 c. oatmeal
1/4 c. butter	1/4 c. chopped nuts
2 eggs	pastry for 1 pie
3/4 c. milk	

Beat together sugar, molasses and butter. Beat in eggs. Add milk and vanilla. Mix well. Stir in oatmeal and nuts. Pour into pastry-lined pie pan. Bake at 350° approximately 50 minutes.

OLD FASHIONED CREAM PIE

1 c. white or brown sugar	2 c. cream
1/4 c. cornstarch	pastry for 1 pie
1/4 tsp. nutmeg	butter
1/8 tsp. salt	

Combine dry ingredients. Add cream and mix well. Pour into a pastry-lined pie pan. Dot with bits of butter. Bake at 350° for 40 minutes or until done.

PEACH PIE

pastry for a double crust pie	1/4 tsp. cinnamon
3 1/2 c. sliced fresh peaches	1/4 tsp. nutmeg
1 c. sugar	1/8 tsp. salt
2 T. flour or 2 1/2 T. minute tapioca	1 tsp. lemon juice
	1 T. butter

Line a 9-inch pie pan with pastry. Fill with peach slices. Combine sugar, flour, spices, salt and lemon juice. Sprinkle over peaches. Dot with butter. Moisten edge of crust. Cover with top crust and seal the edge. Cut several slits in the top crust. Brush with milk and sprinkle with sugar. Bake at 400° or 15 minutes, then at 350° for 45 minutes.

GELATIN PEACH PIE

2 1/2 c. canned, sliced peaches
1 1/2 c. peach juice and water

3 oz. pkg. orange gelatin
1 baked pie crust

Drain peaches. Add enough water to juice to make 1 1/2 cups. Bring liquid to a boil. Remove from heat and dissolve gelatin in liquid. Add peaches. When slightly thickened pour into cooled, baked pie crust. Chill until firm. Top with sweetened whipped cream.

PECAN PIE

1 c. corn syrup
1/2 c. sugar
1/8 tsp. salt
1/4 c. butter, melted

3 eggs, beaten
1 tsp. vanilla
1 c. pecans
pastry for 1 pie

Combine corn syrup, sugar, salt, melted butter, beaten eggs and vanilla. Mix well. Stir in nuts. Pour into pastry-lined pie pan. Bake at 350° approximately 55 minutes.

Variation for **WALNUT PIE:** Use walnuts instead of pecans.

PINEAPPLE CREAM PIE

3/4 c. sugar
1/3 c. flour
1/8 tsp. salt
2 c. milk
1 egg, well-beaten

1 c. crushed pineapple
2 T. butter
1 tsp. vanilla
1 baked pie crust

Combine sugar, flour and salt in a heavy saucepan. Add milk, stirring constantly. Add beaten egg. Mix well. Cook, stirring frequently, until warm, then stirring constantly until thick and smooth. Add well-drained pineapple. Heat through. Remove from heat and stir in butter and vanilla. Pour into a baked pie crust. Cool. Top with whipped cream.

Variation for **COCONUT CREAM PIE:** Omit pineapple. Add 1 c. coconut with butter and vanilla; use coconut flavor instead of vanilla.

PUMPKIN PIE

1 1/2 c. mashed pumpkin	1/2 tsp. salt
1 c. cream or rich milk	1 tsp. cinnamon
1 c. sugar	1/2 tsp. ginger
1 T. flour	1/4 tsp. nutmeg
1 egg, beaten	pastry for 1 pie

Combine ingredients and mix well. Pour into pastry-lined pie pan. Bake at 425° for 10 minutes. Reduce heat and bake at 350° for 30 minutes or until filling is firm.

RHUBARB PIE

3 c. diced rhubarb	1 egg, well-beaten
1 c. sugar	1 T. lemon juice
3 T. flour	2 T. melted butter
1/4 tsp. salt	pastry for a double-crust pie

Combine all ingredients. Pour into pastry-lined pie pan. Moisten edges. Cover with top crust. Press edges of top and bottom crust together and trim. Make some slits in the top to let steam escape. Bake at 350° for 40-45 minutes or until rhubarb is soft.

SOUR CREAM RAISIN PIE

1 c. raisins	1/2 tsp. cinnamon
1 c. sour cream	2 tsp. nutmeg
1 egg, well-beaten	1/4 tsp. salt
1 c. sugar	pastry for a double-crust pie

Mix together raisins, sour cream and egg. Combine dry ingredients and add to raisin mixture. Mix well. Pour into pastry-lined pie pan. Wet edges of pastry. Put top crust on. Press edges of crusts together. Trim edges. Cut several slits in top crust to let steam escape. Bake at 425° for 10 minutes. Reduce heat to 350° and bake 20 more minutes.

RAISIN PIE

1 3/4 c. water
1 1/2 c. raisins
3/4 c. sugar
1/4 tsp. nutmeg
1/8 tsp. salt

2 T. cornstarch
1/4 c. water
2 T. lemon juice
1 T. butter
pastry for a double crust pie

Bring water, raisins, sugar, nutmeg and salt to a boil; boil several minutes. Mix cornstarch and 1/4 c. water. Add to raisin mixture while stirring. Cook until thick and clear. Remove from heat and add lemon juice and butter. Pour into a pastry-lined pie pan. Wet edges of pastry then cover with top crust. Press edges together and trim. Make several slits in the top to let steam escape. Bake at 400° for 25 minutes. Pie filling can be poured into a baked pie shell and topped with whipped cream.

GRANDMA HORST'S
SHOE FLY PIE

1 c. baking molasses
3/4 c. hot water
1/2 tsp. soda
1 egg, beaten
1 c. flour

2/3 c. brown sugar
1/4 tsp. soda
2 T. butter or other
       shortening
pastry for 1 pie

Dissolve 1/2 tsp. soda in water and add molasses. Add egg and stir well. Combine flour, brown sugar and 1/4 tsp. soda. Work in butter. Mix half of the crumbs with the molasses mixture. Pour into a pastry-lined pie pan; top with remaining crumbs. Bake at 375° about 35 minutes.

"To run short of food when we entertain is as serious as to have it poorly cooked"

GRANDMA MARTIN'S
SUGAR MILK PIE

When Grandma Martin made pies on Saturday she often made some of these for supper.

2/3 c. sugar	2 c. creamy milk
1/3 c. flour	pastry for one pie

Combine sugar and flour; put in pie shell. Add milk, mixing milk, sugar and flour with fingers. Bake at 350° for 40 minutes or until set.

GRANDMA MARTIN'S
VANILLA PIE

This makes four pies. With 17 children one pie would never have been enough.

pastry for 4 pies	2 c. sugar
1 c. sugar	1/2 c. shortening
1 c. molasses	1 c. sour milk
2 c. cold water	1 T. soda
1 egg	1 egg
1 T. vanilla	3 1/4 c. flour

Line four pie pans with pastry. Mix 1 c. sugar, molasses, water, egg and vanilla; divide equally among four pies. Mix remaining ingredients using enough flour to make soft cake dough. Drop dough into liquid in pie pans. Bake at 350° approximately 40 minutes.

GRANDMA HOOVER'S
COCONUT PIE WITHOUT CRUST

Grandma Hoover cut this recipe out of an Indiana newspaper. There is no date on it, but an advertisement on the back reads: "Cozy living room, pleasant dining room, two nice bedrooms with bath between, all floors nicely carpeted, small but compact kitchen, full basement, double garage, nice lot." The selling price? $3,000!

2 eggs	1 c. coconut
2 T. sugar	1/4 tsp. salt
1/4 c. flour	1 tsp. vanilla
2 c. milk	

Beat eggs until light. Mix in sugar and flour. Add milk, coconut, salt and vanilla. Pour into a pie pan. Bake at 350° for 45 minutes or until pie is set and the top is golden.

APPLE TURNOVERS

Roll out plain pastry dough into 6-inch circles. On half of the circle arrange thin slices of apple. Sprinkle with sugar and cinnamon. Dot with butter. Moisten the rim of dough. Fold over and press edges together with fork. Prick top. Bake at 400° until apples are tender—approximately 25 minutes.

PEACH TURNOVERS

Roll out pastry and cut 6-inch circles. Arrange peach slices on one half of the circle. Sprinkle with sugar and flour. Dot with butter. Moisten dough edges; fold over and press edges firmly together. Bake at 425° approximately 20 minutes.

FRUIT TURNOVERS

Roll out plain pastry. Cut into 5 or 6-inch circles. Place 1-2 T. of thickened fruit pie filling on half of the round. Moisten edges. Fold over. Press edges firmly together. Bake at 400° until golden brown—approximately 25 minutes.

FRUIT TARTS

Roll plain pastry 1/8-inch thick. Turn muffin tins upside down and cover each cup with pastry. Bake at 400° until lightly brown. Cool. Fill tart shells with any thickened fruit or pudding. Top with whipped cream.

SOUR CREAM TARTS

1 c. sugar
1 1/2 T. cornstarch
1/8 tsp. salt
1/4 tsp. nutmeg

1 1/2 c. sour cream
1 c. chopped nuts
baked individual pastry shells

Combine dry ingredients in a heavy saucepan. Add sour cream. Cook, stirring constantly, until thick and smooth. Cool. Add nuts. Pour into baked individual pastry shells.

TEACH YOUR OWN CHILDREN

"Some parents allow their children to acquire the very rude and unmannerly habit of breaking in upon their conversation and those of older persons with questions and remarks of their own. It is very uncivil to allow them to do so. So, even among their own age, let them speak without interrupting. If one begins to tell a story or bit of news, teach them to let him finish it; and if he makes mistakes that ought to be corrected, do it afterwards. Don't allow them to acquire the habit of being interrupters. Most of those who allow their own children to form this disagreeable habit will be exceedingly annoyed at the same conduct in other folks' children. The fault is that of the parents in not teaching their children. If they interrupt at home, tell them to wait till they can converse without annoying, and see that they do it."

GRANDMA'S

TO MAKE
SMALL SPONGE CAKES

The weight of five eggs in flour, the
weight of eight in pounded loaf sugar;
flavor to taste. Let the flour be perfectly
dry, and the sugar well pounded and sifted.
Separate the whites from the yolks of the eggs,
and beat the latter up with the sugar; then whisk
the whites till they become rather stiff, and mix
them with the yolks, but do not stir them more than
is just necessary to mingle the ingredients well together.
Dredge in the flour by degrees, add the flavoring;
butter the tins well, pour in the batter, sift a little
sugar over the cakes, and bake them in rather a quick
oven, but do not allow them to take too much color,
as they should be rather pale. Remove them from
the tins before they get cold and turn them on
their faces, where let them remain until quite
cold, when store them away in a closed tin
canister or wide-mouthed glass bottle.

CAKES-COFFEE CAKES
AND CUPCAKES

ANGEL FOOD CAKE

1 1/2 c. egg whites   1 1/2 c. sugar
   (approximately 12)   1 tsp. vanilla
1/4 tsp. salt   1 c. flour
1 tsp. cream of tarter

Add salt to egg whites and beat until frothy. Add cream of tarter. Beat until stiff but not dry. Fold in sugar a little at a time with a wire whisk. Add vanilla. Fold in flour gradually. Put in an ungreased angel food cake pan. Bake at 350° approximately one hour.

Variation for **COCOA ANGEL FOOD CAKE:** Substitute 1/4 c. cocoa for 1/4 c. flour. Add cocoa with flour.

Variation for **LEMON ANGEL FOOD CAKE:** Substitute grated rind of 1/2 of a lemon for vanilla. Ice with lemon flavored icing. One fourth of an orange rind can be used instead of lemon.

GRANDMA HORST'S
APPLE CAKE

Grandma Horst kept a black and white composition book to write in recipes friends and relatives shared with her. Katie L. was the apparent donor of this recipe.

2 c. brown sugar   1 tsp. soda
3/4 c. butter   1/2 tsp. salt
2 eggs   3 1/2 c. chopped apples
2 c. flour   1 c. chopped nuts
2 tsp. cinnamon

Cream sugar and butter. Beat in eggs. Combine flour, cinnamon, soda and salt and add. Mix well. Add apples and nuts. If desired, use 1/2 c. of the sugar, 1 tsp. cinnamon and the nuts and make crumbs. Sprinkle on top before baking. Pour into a greased 13x9-inch pan. Bake at 350° for 45 minutes or until done.

DUTCH APPLE CAKE

1 1/2 c. flour	1 egg, beaten
1 T. baking powder	4 or 5 tart cooking apples
1/2 tsp. salt	1/2 c. sugar
2 T. sugar	1 T. cinnamon
3/4 c. milk, scant	3 T. butter
1/3 c. butter, melted	

Combine dry ingredients. Mix together milk, butter and egg and add to dry ingredients. Mix quickly. Spread into a buttered 11x7-inch pan. Peel and core apples and cut into sixteenths. Press sharp edges of apple wedges into dough. Mix sugar and cinnamon together and sprinkle over apples. Dot with small pieces of butter. Bake at 375° approximately 40 minutes—until apples are soft and cake well browned. Serve warm with lemon sauce if desired.

GRANDMA KULP'S
APPLESAUCE CAKE

One of Grandma's daughters said this was the only cake she remembered her mother making.

1 c. sugar	1 tsp. soda
1/2 c. shortening	2 c. flour
1 egg	1 tsp. cinnamon
1 c. applesauce	1 tsp. cloves

Cream sugar and shortening. Beat in egg. Dissolve soda in applesauce and add. Add remaining ingredients and mix well. Put in a greased 13x9-inch cake pan. Bake at 350° approximately 35 minutes. Less cloves can be used.

"Don't pack flour in the measuring cup. Most young cooks make the mistake of using too much flour."

BANANA CAKE

1 1/2 c. brown sugar
1/2 c. butter
2 eggs
3 bananas, mashed
2 c. flour

2 tsp. baking powder
1/2 tsp. soda
1/2 tsp. salt
3/4 c. buttermilk or sour milk
1 tsp. vanilla

Cream sugar and butter. Beat in eggs one at a time. Add mashed bananas. Combine dry ingredients and add alternately with buttermilk. Add vanilla. Mix well. Pour into a greased 13x9-inch cake pan. Bake at 350° approximately 40 minutes.

Grandma's milk wasn't pasteurized so it soured more readily. To make sour milk put a tablespoon of vinegar or lemon juice in a cup measure and fill it up with milk. Let stand several minutes.

BLACK WALNUT LAYER CAKE
Though not sure if this is Grandma Horst's recipe, she, according to a daughter made the best black walnut cake.

1/2 c. butter
2 c. brown sugar
3 eggs, separated
3 c. flour
1/2 tsp. salt

1 T. baking powder
1/2 tsp. cinnamon
3/4 c. milk
1 c. chopped black walnuts

Cream butter and sugar. Beat in egg yolks. Combine dry ingredients and add alternately with milk. Add finely chopped black walnuts. Fold in well-beaten egg whites. Turn into three well-greased 8-inch layer-cake pans. Bake at 350° until lightly browned—approximately 25 minutes.

Variation for **BUTTERNUT LAYER CAKE:** Substitute butternuts for black walnuts.

GRANDMA MARTIN'S
BURNT SUGAR CAKE

1/2 c. sugar	2 1/2 c. flour
1/2 c. water	2 tsp. baking powder
1 1/2 c. sugar	1/2 tsp. salt
1/2 c. butter	3/4 c. water
4 eggs, separated	1 tsp. vanilla

ICING

2 c. sugar	2 egg whites, beaten
1 c. water	reserved burnt sugar mix

Melt and brown 1/2 c. sugar in a frying pan. Add 1/2 c. water. Set aside. Cream 1 1/2 c. sugar and butter. Add well-beaten egg yolks. Mix dry ingredients and add alternately with water and 1/3 c. of the reserved burnt sugar mix. Add vanilla. Fold mixture into two stiffly-beaten egg whites. Pour into two round layer cake pans. Bake at 350° for approximately 30 minutes. To make icing, boil sugar and water to hard crack (290°). Pour into two stiffly-beaten egg whites, beating constantly. When mixture begins to thicken, add remaining burnt sugar mixture. Drizzle hot icing on cooled cakes. Add water if icing gets too stiff. Maple flavoring can be added.

BUTTER CAKE

3/4 c. butter	1 T. baking powder
2 c. sugar	1/2 tsp. salt
3 eggs	1 c. milk
3 c. flour	1 tsp. vanilla

Cream butter and sugar. Beat in eggs. Combine dry ingredients and add alternately with milk. Add vanilla. Beat thoroughly. Pour into a greased 13x9-inch cake pan or into round layer cake pans. Bake at 350° for 35-40 minutes. Ice with favorite icing.

GRANDMA HORST'S
CARROT NUT CAKE

1 c. cooking oil	2 tsp. baking powder
2 c. sugar	1 tsp. soda
4 eggs	1 tsp. salt
2 c. flour	3 c. grated carrots
2 tsp. cinnamon	1 c. chopped nuts

Mix together cooking oil, sugar and eggs. Combine and add dry ingredients. Mix well. Add carrots and nuts. Pour into a 13x9-inch cake pan or an angel food cake pan. Bake at 350° approximately one hour.

GRANDMA HORST'S
CHOCOLATE CAKE

Grandma Horst had four different chocolate cake recipes in her composition book. She got this recipe from one of her daughters.

1 3/4 c. sugar	1 tsp. soda
3/4 c. shortening	1 tsp. baking powder
3 eggs	1/2 tsp. salt
2 1/4 c. flour	1 c. water
3/4 c. cocoa	1 tsp. vanilla

Cream sugar and shortening. Beat in eggs. Combine dry ingredients and add alternately with water and vanilla. Mix well. Pour into a greased 13x9-inch cake pan. Bake at 350° approximately 35 minutes.

FINE SUGAR KEY TO FINE TEXTURE

"Coarse texture in a cake is often caused by the use of coarse sugar. In fact it is almost impossible to make a fine textured cake with coarse sugar. If you cannot buy extra fine sugar from your grocer, take the time to roll the sugar you have with your rolling pin, to make it as fine as possible. Do not use pulverized sugar."

RICH CHOCOLATE LAYER CAKE

1 1/4 c. shortening or butter
1 c. brown sugar
1/3 c. sugar
3/4 c. cocoa
1 tsp. vanilla

3 eggs
2 c. cake flour
1 tsp. soda
1/2 tsp. salt
2/3 c. sour milk

Cream shortening and sugars. Add cocoa and vanilla. Beat in eggs. Add dry ingredients alternately with sour milk. Pour into two greased 9-inch round cake pans. Bake at 350° approximately 30 minutes.

One fourth cup cocoa and 1 1/2 tsp. of shortening can be substituted for each ounce of chocolate.

CHOCOLATE AND WHITE LAYER CAKE

1 1/2 c. sugar
2/3 c. shortening
3 eggs
3 c. flour
1 T. baking powder
1/2 tsp. salt
1 c. milk

1 tsp. vanilla
3 oz. unsweetened chocolate, melted
2 T. sugar
1/4 c. hot water
1/2 tsp. soda
2 T. butter

Cream sugar and shortening. Add eggs and beat well. Combine flour, baking powder and salt and add alternately with milk, beating until smooth. Add vanilla. Pour a generous third of batter in a greased 9-inch layer pan. Combine remaining ingredients. Cool slightly then add to remaining batter. Pour into two greased 9-inch layer pans. Bake at 350° approximately 30 minutes. Put white layer in the middle. Ice with chocolate or white icing—or both.

"If you want your cakes to look nice and high use 8-inch cake pans rather than 9-inch."

GRANDMA HOOVER'S
DARK SYRUP CAKE

2 c. dark syrup	1 T. soda
3/4 c. lard or other	1/2 tsp. salt
shortening	3 1/2 c. flour
3 eggs, beaten	1/4 c. cocoa
1 c. sour milk	1 tsp. baking powder

Beat syrup and shortening until smooth. Add eggs. Combine sour milk, soda and salt and add. Combine flour, cocoa and baking powder and add. Mix well. Bake in a greased 13x9 cake pan at 350° approximately 45 minutes.

GRANDMA HOOVER'S
DATE CAKE

This was one of the recipes given to Grandma Hoover by her stepmother when Grandma married her stepmother's brother. About five years later when her stepmother's youngest brother—also her husband's youngest brother—got married, they had this for their wedding cake.

1 c. chopped dates	3 T. shortening
2 tsp. soda	2 eggs
1 c. boiling water	1 1/2 c. flour
1 c. sugar	1 c. chopped nuts

Sprinkle soda over dates then pour boiling water over soda and dates. In another bowl, cream sugar, shortening and eggs. Stir in flour and chopped nuts. Add dates. Mix well. Pour into a greased 9x9-inch cake pan. Bake at 350° approximately 20 minutes.

"Push the mixture [cake batter] well to the side and corners of the pan leaving a slight depression in the center so that the cake may rise evenly."

GRANDMA HOOVER'S
EGGLESS, MILKLESS, BUTTERLESS CAKE

Grandma Hoover clipped this recipe from an old newspaper. Telephone numbers listed in the help wanted ads on the back help date the recipe. Some of the phone numbers were: J-1832, 340, 260, R-2825 and 457.

1 c. brown sugar	1/8 tsp. salt
1 c. water	1/4 c. hot water
1 c. raisins	1 tsp. soda
1/3 c. shortening	2 c. flour
1/4 tsp. cinnamon	1/2 tsp. baking powder

Boil sugar, water, raisins, shortening, cinnamon and salt for 3 minutes. Cool and add remaining ingredients. Mix well. Pour into a well-greased tube pan. Bake at 350° approximately 45 minutes. Ice with plain or maple flavored icing.

FRUIT CAKE

1 c. butter	2 T. milk or fruit juice
1 c. brown sugar	2 c. chopped nuts
3 large eggs	2 c. raisins, dates or currants
2 c. flour	2 c. citron
2 tsp. baking powder	1 c. candied pineapple
1/2 tsp. salt	1 c. candied cherries
1 tsp. cinnamon	1/2 c. flour
1 tsp. mace	

Cream butter and sugar. Add eggs and beat thoroughly. Combine and add dry ingredients. Add milk. Mix well. Add nuts. Mix remaining ingredients with 1/2 c. flour and add, mixing well. Pack into a well-greased or waxed paper-lined angel food cake pan. Bake at 300° until top appears dry—approximately 2 hours.

GRANDMA HOOVER'S
GINGERBREAD CAKE

1/2 c. butter	1/2 tsp. salt
1/2 c. sugar	1 tsp. ginger
1 egg, beaten	1 tsp. cinnamon
1 c. molasses	1/2 tsp. cloves
2 1/2 c. flour	1 c. hot water
1 1/2 tsp. soda	

Cream butter and sugar. Add beaten egg and molasses. Combine dry ingredients and add. Add hot water last and beat until smooth. Pour into a greased 13x9-inch cake pan. Bake at 350° for approximately 35 minutes.

GRANDMA KULP'S
LADY WASHINGTON GINGERBREAD

Grandma Kulp copied this recipe for her youngest son's wife including a note saying this was one of his favorites. She also wrote that she always dilutes the molasses with Karo syrup.

1/2 c. shortening	1 tsp. soda
1/2 c. brown sugar	1 T. ginger
3 eggs, well-beaten	1/2 tsp. cinnamon
1 c. molasses	1/2 tsp. nutmeg
1/2 c. warm milk	1/2 tsp. mace
1/2 c. hot coffee	juice of one orange (1/3 c.)
3 c. flour	grated rind of one orange

Cream shortening and sugar then add eggs. Stir in molasses, milk and coffee. Combine dry ingredients and add. Mix well. Stir in juice and rind of orange. Pour into a greased cake pan. Bake at 350° approximately 45 minutes. One cup raisins may be added.

"If a recipe calls for 2 c. cake flour use only 1 3/4 c. all purpose flour."
-A hint Grandma Horst wrote in her personal cookbook.

HONEY CAKE

1/2 c. shortening
1 c. honey
2 eggs, beaten
2 c. flour

1 tsp. soda
1/2 tsp. salt
1/2 tsp. cinnamon
1/2 c. sour milk

Cream shortening. Add honey and eggs. Combine dry ingredients and add alternately with sour milk. Mix thoroughly. Pour into a well-greased cake pan. Bake at 350° approximately 45 minutes.

GRANDMA HORST'S
MARBLE CAKE

2 2/3 c. sugar
3/4 c. shortening
3 eggs
1 1/3 c. water
4 c. cake flour
4 tsp. baking powder

1 tsp. salt
1 tsp. vanilla
1/2 c. cocoa
1/3 c. sugar
boiling water

Cream sugar and shortening. Beat in eggs. Add water. Combine flour, baking powder and salt and add. Mix well. Add vanilla. Pour into a greased 15x10-inch cake pan. Mix cocoa and sugar with just enough boiling water to make a thick syrup. Mix well. Pour in streaks over cake, then go through the opposite way with a knife or spatula to marble the cake. Bake at 350° approximately 40 minutes. If not using cake flour omit 1/2 c. flour.

"When the baking is finished, the cake will break away from the sides of the pan, and it will spring back quickly when pressed lightly by the finger. The new cook will find it safer to test with a clean toothpick. Insert this in the center of the cake. If it comes out clean, the cake is done."

ORANGE CAKE WITH ORANGE TOPPING

1 orange	2 c. flour
1 c. dates	1 tsp. soda
1/2 c. nuts	1/2 tsp. salt
1/2 c. butter	3/4 c. orange juice
1 c. brown sugar	1 c. sugar
2 eggs	1/3 c. orange juice
1 tsp. maple flavor	

With a sharp knife remove the bright colored layer of peel from the orange. Combine with dates and nuts. Chop finely. Cream butter and brown sugar. Add eggs and maple flavor, beating well. Add fruit and nut mixture. Combine flour, soda and salt and add alternately with orange juice. Turn into a greased 13x9-inch cake pan. Bake at 350° until done—approximately 45 minutes. Mix sugar and 1/3 c. orange juice and spread on hot cake. Serve hot or cold.

ORANGE LAYER CAKE

1 1/2 c. sugar	1/2 tsp. salt
1/2 c. butter	1 c. boiling water
2 eggs	1/4 tsp. soda
3 c. flour	juice from 1 orange (1/3 c.)
2 tsp. baking powder	1 tsp. grated orange rind

Cream sugar and butter. Beat in eggs. Combine flour, baking powder and salt and add. Dissolve soda in boiling water. Add juice and rind to water and add to first mixture. Beat thoroughly. Pour into two well-greased layer cake pans. Bake at 350° approximately 30 minutes. Put orange filling (see fillings) between layers. Ice if desired.

Variation for **LEMON LAYER CAKE:** Substitute lemon juice and rind for orange juice and rind. Fill with lemon filling. Ice if desired.

PINEAPPLE UPSIDE DOWN CAKE

2/3 c. sugar
1/4 c. butter
1 egg
1 tsp. vanilla
1 1/2 c. flour
1/2 tsp. salt

2 tsp. baking powder
1/2 c. milk
3 T. soft butter
3/4 c. brown sugar
pineapple rings

Cream sugar and butter. Add egg and vanilla. Beat well. Combine dry ingredients and add alternately with milk. Spread soft butter thickly on the bottom and sides of a 13x9-inch cake pan. Sprinkle sugar over butter. Arrange well-drained pineapple rings over sugar. Pour batter evenly over pineapples. Bake at 350° approximately 45 minutes. Invert pan on a baking sheet or large platter. Serve with whipped cream.

Variation for **APPLE UPSIDE DOWN CAKE:** Peel three apples and slice thinly. Spread slices in an overlapping layer in buttered pan. Mix 2 tsp. cinnamon with brown sugar and sprinkle over apples. Top with cake batter.

POUND CAKE

This recipe calls for the traditional method of testing the doneness of a cake by inserting a toothpick. Some old recipes suggested using a clean broom straw to check cakes. Though available since the late 1800s, toothpicks caught on slowly. "Dandies", well-dressed young men, finally created a demand by asking for toothpicks at eating establishments.

1 c. butter
1 1/2 c. sugar
5 eggs
2 c. flour

2 tsp. baking powder
1/2 tsp. salt
1 tsp. vanilla

Cream butter and sugar. Beat eggs in one at a time. Combine dry ingredients and add. Add vanilla. Beat thoroughly. Turn into a greased tube pan or a bread pan. Bake at 350° until toothpick comes out clean— about one hour. One cup chopped nuts or 2/3 c. coconut may be added.

PUMPKIN CAKE

1 1/2 c. sugar	1 tsp. baking powder
1/2 c. shortening	1 tsp. soda
2 eggs	1 tsp. salt
1 c. mashed pumpkin	1 tsp. cinnamon
2 c. flour	1/4 c. sour milk

Cream sugar and shortening. Add eggs and pumpkin. Beat thoroughly. Combine dry ingredients and add alternately with sour milk. Mix well. Turn into two round layer cake pans. Bake at 350° approximately 25 minutes. Bake longer if baked in an oblong cake pan. Good with spiced whipped cream. Chopped nuts may be added to batter.

SOUR CREAM RAISIN CAKE

1 c. sour cream	1/2 tsp. salt
1 c. sugar	1 tsp. cinnamon
2 eggs	1 tsp. nutmeg
2 c. flour, divided	1/4 tsp. cloves
1 tsp. baking powder	1 c. raisins
1/2 tsp. soda	1 tsp. vanilla

Beat sour cream, sugar and eggs. Save 2 T. flour then combine dry ingredients and add. Mix raisins with 2 T. flour and add, along with vanilla. Mix well. Pour into well-greased layer cake pans. Bake at 350° approximately 30 minutes. This good filled with almond filling (see fillings).

"The woman in the house has opportunity daily for satisfying her creative urge in sewing, in decorating her home, and particularly in cooking. When she bakes tender flaky biscuits or a delicate feathery cake she has the double pleasure of creating something worthwhile and of giving pleasure to those who mean the most to her—her family."

SPICE CAKE

1/2 c. butter	1/2 tsp. nutmeg
1 1/2 c. brown sugar	1/4 tsp. cloves
1 egg	2 c. flour
1/2 tsp. salt	2 tsp. baking powder
1 tsp. cinnamon	1 c. milk

Cream butter and sugar. Add egg, salt and spices and beat thoroughly. Combine flour and baking powder and add alternately with milk. Bake at 350° approximately 35 minutes. Ice with brown sugar icing or serve with whipped cream.

Variation for **RAISIN SPICE CAKE:** Add 1 c. raisins with spices.

SPONGE CAKE

4 eggs, separated	1 tsp. lemon rind
1 c. sugar	1/2 tsp. salt
2 T. lemon juice	1 c. flour

Beat egg yolks until thick and lemon colored. Gradually add half of the sugar, beating thoroughly. Add lemon juice and rind. Beat egg whites and salt until they start to peak. Fold in the other half of the sugar, then the yolk mixture. Fold the flour in gently. As soon as batter is mixed pour it into an ungreased angel food cake pan. Sprinkling powdered sugar on top will make a nicer crust. Bake in a preheated oven at 350° approximately 45 minutes. Invert cake to cool.

> *"God has for you…*
> *A light for every shadow,*
> *A plan for each tomorrow,*
> *A key for every problem,*
> *A balm for every sorrow."*
>
> *-a verse Grandma Kulp copied into her notebook*

GRANDMA HORST'S
HOT MILK SPONGE CAKE

3 eggs, separated
1 1/2 c. sugar
3/4 tsp. orange flavoring
1/3 tsp. lemon flavoring

1 1/2 c. flour
1 1/2 tsp. baking powder
1/4 tsp. salt
3/4 c. hot rich milk

Beat egg yolks until thick. Gradually add half of the sugar, beating thoroughly, then add flavorings. Combine flour, baking powder and salt and fold into egg mixture. Add stiffly beaten egg whites. Add hot milk. Pour into a tube pan. Bake at 350° approximately 40 minutes.

GRANDMA HOOVER'S
THUMB CAKE

Grandma Hoover made this cake as a little girl. (Did the cake get richer as her thumb got bigger?)

1 c. sugar
butter the size of your thumb
2 eggs
1 1/2 c. flour

1 tsp. soda
2 tsp. cream of tarter
1/2 c. milk
1 tsp. vanilla

Cream sugar and butter. Beat in eggs. Combine flour, soda and cream of tarter and add alternately with milk. Add vanilla. Mix well. Pour into two 8-inch round cake pans. Bake at 350° approximately 25 min-utes.

COURAGE

"One may possess physical courage, so that in times of danger, a railroad accident, a steamboat collision or a runaway horse, the heart will not be daunted or the cheek paled, while on the other hand, one may be morally brave, not afraid to speak a word for the right in season, though unwelcome, to perform a disagreeable duty unflinchingly or to refuse to do a wrong act, and yet be a physical coward, trembling and terrified in a thunderstorm, timid in the dark, and even scream at the sight of a mouse. Courage both moral and physical, is one of the finest attributes of character, and both can be cultivated and gained if desired and sought after."

GRANDMA HORST'S
WALNUT CAKE

A couple of Grandma Horst's daughters mentioned the delicious hickory nut cake she used to make. We couldn't find a recipe—unless she used this one and substituted hickory nuts for walnuts.

2 c. sugar	1/2 tsp. salt
1/2 c. shortening	1 c. water
2 large eggs	1 tsp. vanilla
3 c. flour	1 c. finely-chopped walnuts
1 T. baking powder	

Cream sugar and shortening. Beat in eggs. Combine dry ingredients and add alternately with water and vanilla. Mix well. Add nuts. Pour into a greased 13x9-inch cake pan. Bake at 350° approximately 35 minutes.

WHITE LAYER CAKE

2 c. sugar	1/2 tsp. salt
2/3 c. shortening	1 c. milk
3 c. flour	1 tsp. vanilla
1 tsp. baking powder	4 egg whites

Cream sugar and shortening until light and fluffy. Combine flour, baking powder and salt and add alternately with milk. Add vanilla and mix well. Beat egg whites until stiff. Fold into cake batter. Pour into two greased layer cake pans. Bake at 350° approximately 30 minutes. Ice with white or chocolate icing. May be sprinkled with coconut or chopped nuts.

PETITS FOURS

Bake a sponge or pound cake in a shallow pan so the finished cake is not more than an inch high. Cool. Slice into 1-inch strips. Cut into squares, circles, triangles or other shapes. Cut each shape in half crosswise. Remove a portion of the inside and fill with whipped cream, custard or other filling. Put cakes together again and dip into thin icing or icings. Designs may be made with icings of different colors. Garnish with nuts, maraschino cherries, etc.

DATE FILLED COFFEE CAKE

In many of Grandma's cookbooks coffee cakes were called tea cakes.

1 c. chopped dates
1/4 c. chopped nuts
1 c. brown sugar
1/4 c. water
1 tsp. lemon juice
2/3 c. butter
3/4 c. brown sugar

1 egg
3 c. flour
1/2 tsp. soda
1/2 tsp. salt
1/3 c. buttermilk or sour milk
1 tsp. lemon or almond flavoring

In a heavy saucepan cook dates, nuts, 1 c. brown sugar, water and lemon juice until smooth and thick. Cream butter and remaining sugar. Add well-beaten egg. Combine dry ingredients and add alternately with milk. Add flavoring; mix well. Spread half of the batter into a greased 13x9-inch cake pan. Add date filling then top with rest of batter. Bake at 350° for 30-35 minutes.

SOUR CREAM COFFEE CAKE

1 egg
1 c. sugar
1 c. sour cream
1/2 tsp. soda
2 c. flour

2 tsp. baking powder
1/2 tsp. salt
1/2 tsp. cinnamon
1/4 tsp. nutmeg
2 T. melted butter

TOPPING

1/2 c. sugar
2 T. flour
1/2 tsp. cinnamon

1 T. butter
1/2 c. pecan pieces

Beat egg and add sugar. Stir together sour cream and soda. Combine dry ingredients and add to first mixture alternately with sour cream. Add butter. Spread into a greased 9-inch square cake pan. Blend topping ingredients and sprinkle over batter. Bake at 350° approximately 30 minutes. Serve hot.

STREUSEL COFFEE CAKE

1 1/2 c. flour
1 T. baking powder
1/2 tsp. salt
2 T. sugar

3/4 c. milk, scant
1/3 c. butter, melted
1 egg, beaten

TOPPING

3 T. butter, melted
1/2 c. brown sugar
1/4 c. flour

1 1/2 tsp. cinnamon
1/3 c. chopped nuts

Combine dry ingredients. Mix together milk, butter and egg and pour onto dry ingredients. Mix quickly. Spread in a greased 8x8-inch pan. Blend topping ingredients thoroughly and sprinkle over the batter. Bake at 350° approximately 30 minutes.

RAISED STREUSEL COFFEE CAKE

1 1/2 pkg. or 1 1/2 T. yeast
1 T. sugar
1 c. warm milk
4 1/2 c. flour

1/4 c. butter
1/2 c. sugar
1/2 tsp. salt
2 eggs

Dissolve yeast and 1 T. sugar in warm milk; add 1 1/2 c. flour. Beat until smooth. Cream butter, add sugar and salt; add to yeast mixture. Add well beaten eggs and remaining flour. Knead lightly. Place in a well-greased bowl, cover and let rise in a warm place—about 2 hours. Roll 1/2-inch thick and place in two well-greased shallow pans. Let rise again until light—about 1 1/2 hours. Prick tops with fork; brush with melted butter and sprinkle with cinnamon topping or honey nut topping (see following recipes). Let rise in a warm place about 1/2 hour. Bake at 400° approximately 15 minutes. Makes two cakes.

"Small cakes may be dipped, one side at a time, into icing, and rolled in coconut or nuts."

CINNAMON TOPPING

6 T. butter	1 1/2 tsp. cinnamon
3/4 c. sugar	1/8 tsp. salt
6 T. flour	

Cream butter and sugar. Add remaining ingredients and stir until well mixed and crumbly.

HONEY NUT TOPPING

1/4 c. butter	1/4 c. honey
1/4 c. sugar	1/2 c. chopped nuts
1/4 c. flour	

Cream butter and sugar. Add flour and honey. Beat well and add nuts.

CUPCAKES

None of the recipes mentioned cupcake liners. Either they weren't available or not widely used.

1/2 c. shortening	2 tsp. baking powder
1 c. sugar	1/2 tsp. salt
3 eggs	1/2 c. milk
1 3/4 c. flour	1 tsp. vanilla

Cream shortening, sugar and eggs until light and fluffy. Combine dry ingredients and add alternately with milk. Add vanilla. Beat thoroughly. Spoon into greased muffin tins. Bake at 350° approximately 25 minutes. Cool and ice. Makes 18 cup cakes.

FILLED CUPCAKES

Make any cupcake recipe. Cool. Cut cakes in half, crosswise. Remove a portion of the inside of the cakes. Fill with whipped cream. Put pieces back together. Ice with icing of choice. Serve immediately.

WHITE CUPCAKES

1 1/2 c. sugar	1/2 tsp. salt
1/2 c. butter	1 c. milk
2 1/2 c. flour	1 tsp. vanilla
2 tsp. baking powder	3 egg whites

Cream sugar and butter. Combine dry ingredients and add alternately with milk. Beat thoroughly. Add vanilla. Fold in stiffly beaten egg whites. Place in well greased muffin tins. Bake at 350° approximately 25 minutes.

Variation for **RAINBOW CAKES:** Spread tinted icing on white cup cakes. Top with coconut if desired.

Variation for **SNOWBALLS:** Cover entirely with icing and roll in coconut.

CHOCOLATE CUPCAKES

1/2 c. shortening	2 c. flour
1 1/2 c. sugar	1 1/2 tsp. soda
2 eggs	1/2 tsp. salt
1/2 c. cocoa	1 c. sour milk or buttermilk
hot water	1 tsp. vanilla

Cream shortening and sugar until light and fluffy. Beat in eggs one at a time. In a measuring cup add enough hot water to cocoa to make a smooth paste then add hot water to make one cup. Add to creamed mixture. Combine dry ingredients and add alternately with sour milk. Add vanilla. Mix thoroughly. Spoon into well-greased muffin tins. Bake at 350° approximately 25 minutes.

Variation for **FILLED CHOCOLATE CUPCAKES:** While cupcakes are hot, remove a marshmallow sized portion from the center top of the cupcake and insert a marshmallow. Ice with chocolate or white icing.

GRANDMA HOOVER'S
QUICK CUPCAKES

1/2 c. soft butter	1 2/3 c. flour
1 1/3 c. brown sugar	1 T. baking powder
2 eggs	1/2 tsp. cinnamon
1/2 c. milk	1/2 tsp. nutmeg

Put ingredients in bowl in order given. Do not stir until everything has been added. Beat several minutes. Nuts or raisins may be added. Pour into greased muffins tins. Bake at 350° approximately 30 minutes.

CHOCOLATE CHIP CUPCAKES

This recipe predates chocolate chips. One and one third cups of chocolate chips can be substituted for the squares of chocolate.

1 c. sugar	1/2 tsp. salt
1/2 c. shortening	3/4 c. milk
2 eggs	1 1/2 tsp. vanilla
2 1/4 c. flour	8 oz. semi-sweet chocolate
2 tsp. baking powder	

Cream sugar and shortening. Beat in eggs. Combine dry ingredients and add alternately with milk. Add vanilla and mix well. Chop squares of chocolate into pieces. Stir into batter. Spoon into greased muffin tins. Bake at 350° approximately 25 minutes. Ice if desired.

"Shortening is creamed by pressing it with the back of the spoon against the sides of the bowl, and then stirring until uniformly plastic. Sugar is stirred in with simple, rhythmic, rotary motions in which the spoon goes around and around. Egg yolks are stirred in, then beaten, using rhythmic motions, the spoon describing vertical circles. Milk is also stirred in. Flour is cut or folded, a motion similar to beating, but done more slowly. Egg whites are also folded in."

GRANDMA KULP'S
POPOVER CUPCAKES

This recipe, found, interestingly enough, among Grandma Hoover's cookbooks, was signed by Grandma Kulp and included this note: "This we started when we were all at home yet. When·the girls started to do the baking it was omitted. A while ago I started to make them once again and Mary Ann,(a daughter) said, 'This is the kind we couldn't keep without hiding them.' "

2 c. sugar	1 tsp. vanilla
1 c. sour cream	2 tsp. baking powder
3 T. cocoa	1/2 tsp. soda
2 eggs	flour to make medium dough

Mix everything together, beating well. Put in greased muffin tins. Bake at 350° approximately 25 minutes.

SPICE CUPCAKES

2 c. brown sugar	1 tsp. soda
1 c. butter	1 tsp. cinnamon
4 eggs	1/2 tsp. cloves
2 1/2 c. flour	1 c. buttermilk
1 T. cocoa	1 c. raisins

Cream sugar and butter. Beat eggs and add. Combine dry ingredients and add alternately with buttermilk. Mix well. Stir in raisins. Spoon into well-greased muffin tins. Bake at 350° approximately 25 minutes.

ORANGE CUPCAKES

1/3 c. soft shortening	2 c. flour
1 c. sugar	2 tsp. baking powder
2 eggs	1/2 tsp. salt
1/2 tsp. orange or lemon	1/3 c. orange juice
extract	1/3 c. water

Beat together shortening, sugar, eggs and extract. Combine dry ingredients and add alternately with orange juice and water. Mix well. Spoon into greased muffin tins. Bake at 350° approximately 30 minutes. Ice with orange icing, orange cream cheese icing or butter icing.

GRANDMA'S

GINGER SNAPS

Two cups of molasses, one-quarter
cup of brown sugar, one large cup of
butter, one-half cup of sour milk, two
tablespoonfuls of saleratus, three teaspoonfuls
of ginger. Melt the molasses and butter together,
and pour hot upon one quart of flour; then add
ginger and saleratus. Mix the saleratus with the
sour milk.

GRAHAM GINGER COOKIES

One cup of molasses, one cup of sugar, one full cup of
shortening, one-fourth cup of water, one tablespoonful of ginger, one teaspoonful of soda and a
pinch of salt. Add equal portions of graham and
white flour enough to make a dough to
roll nicely.

COOKIES AND PAN COOKIES

GRANDMA HORST'S
APPLE NUT COOKIES

1 1/2 c. brown sugar	1 c. nuts
1/2 c. shortening	2 c. flour
1 egg	1/2 tsp. salt
1/2 c. apple juice or water	1 tsp. cinnamon
1 apple, grated	1/2 tsp. nutmeg
1 c. raisins	1/2 tsp. cloves

Cream sugar, shortening and egg. Add juice, grated apple, raisins and nuts and mix well. Combine and add dry ingredients. Bake at 375° approximately 12 minutes.

GRANDMA HOOVER'S
BRAN COOKIES

A recipe Grandma Hoover doubled ingredients on. The end of the recipe reads, "These are very fine."

1 1/2 c. bran	1/2 tsp. salt
2 c. flour	2/3 c. raisins
1 c. sugar	1 c. sour milk
1 1/2 tsp. soda	2 eggs, beaten
1/2 tsp. nutmeg	2/3 c. butter, melted

Combine dry ingredients. Add raisins and milk. Add eggs and butter, mixing well. Drop onto buttered baking sheet. Bake at 375° approximately 12 minutes.

"Almost everyone has a favorite time when nothing else tastes so good as a cookie. Midmorning, maybe when the dishes are washed and the beds made, or lunch time, or after school, or on Saturdays when the grass is mowed or the snow shoveled from the sidewalks."

BLACK WALNUT COOKIES

3/4 c. shortening
2 c. brown sugar
2 eggs, beaten
1 c. chopped black walnuts
1 tsp. vanilla

3 c. flour
1 tsp. soda
1/2 tsp. salt
1/3 c. milk

Cream shortening and sugar. Add eggs, then nuts and vanilla. Stir well. Combine dry ingredients and add alternately with milk. Beat vigorously. Drop by teaspoons on greased baking sheet. Bake at 350° approximately 12 minutes. English walnuts may be substituted for black walnuts.

GRANDMA MARTIN'S
BUTTERMILK COOKIES

2 c. brown sugar
1 c. shortening
2 eggs
1 tsp. vanilla
1 c. buttermilk

5 c. flour, more as needed
1 tsp. baking powder
1 tsp. baking soda
1/2 tsp. salt

Cream sugar and shortening. Beat in eggs and vanilla. Add buttermilk. Combine and add dry ingredients. Drop by teaspoon on a greased baking sheet. Bake at 375° approximately 12 minutes.

CHOCOLATE CHIP COOKIES

Perhaps a more accurate name would be chocolate chunk cookies. Commercial chocolate chips weren't made until 1939 and not widely used through the 1940s. Before that, if our grandmothers made chocolate chip cookies, they cut up squares of semi-sweet chocolate.

12 squares (12 oz.) semi-
    sweet chocolate
1 c. shortening
1/2 c. brown sugar
1 c. white sugar
2 eggs, well-beaten

2 c. flour
1 tsp. salt
1 tsp. soda
1 c. broken nutmeats
2 tsp. vanilla

Cut each square of chocolate into pieces. Cream shortening. Add sugars, creaming until light and fluffy. Add eggs and mix well. Combine dry ingredients and add, mixing well. Add chocolate, nuts and vanilla. Drop from a teaspoon onto greased baking sheet. Bake at 375° for 10-12 minutes. Two cups chocolate chips can be used instead of the squares.

COCOA DROP COOKIES

3/4 c. butter	1/2 c. cocoa
1 1/2 c. sugar	3 1/2 c. flour
2 eggs	1 T. baking powder
1 tsp. vanilla	1/2 tsp. salt

Cream butter and sugar. Add egg, vanilla and cocoa. Mix well. Combine dry ingredients and add alternately with milk to first mixture. Bake at 350° approximately 12 minutes. One cup of nuts may be added to batter. Eat plain or ice.

COCONUT ORANGE COOKIES

Though obsolete now, almost all of our Grandmas' recipes with coconut in the ingredients spelled it cocoanut.

3/4 c. shortening	1/2 tsp. salt
1 1/4 c. sugar	1/2 tsp. soda
2 eggs	3/4 c. orange juice
1 c. coconut	2 T. grated orange peel
2 1/2 c. flour	

Cream shortening and sugar. Beat in eggs. Beat in coconut. Combine dry ingredients and add alternately with orange juice to creamed mixture. Beat until smooth. Add orange peel. Drop by teaspoons on ungreased baking sheet. Sprinkle with additional coconut and orange peel, or ice. Bake at 375° approximately 12 minutes.

"Add interest to drop cookies by pressing a teaspoon of thick jam into top of cookies when almost done baking."

GRANDMA HOOVER'S
FRUIT JUMBLES

When Grandma Hoover got married in November of 1929, her stepmother gave her a 1928 diary with handwritten recipes in it. This recipe is from that diary. The only instructions given were "drop in pans". Grandma Hoover later shared this recipe in a small neighborhood cookbook.

1 1/2 c. brown sugar	1 tsp. vanilla
1/2 c. butter	3 c. flour
3 eggs	1 lb. chopped dates
1 tsp. soda	1/4 c. chopped nuts
1 T. warm water	

Cream sugar and butter. Add eggs. Dissolve soda in 1 T. warm water and add, along with vanilla. Add flour, mixing well. Stir in dates and nuts. Bake on a greased baking sheet at 350° approximately 10 minutes.

GRANDMA HOOVER'S
ICED CARROT COOKIES

1/2 c. shortening	juice and grated rind of 1/2 orange
2 c. brown sugar	
1 egg, beaten	2 1/2 c. flour
1 c. cooked, mashed carrots	2 1/2 tsp. baking powder

ICING:

juice and grated rind of 1/2 orange	milk (if needed) to make spreadable
2 1/2 c. powdered sugar	

Cream shortening and sugar. Mix in egg, carrots, juice and rind. Add flour and baking powder. Mix well. Bake at 375° approximately 10 minutes. Cool slightly and ice.

LACE WAFERS

2 T. butter
1 c. sugar
2 eggs
1/2 tsp. salt
1/2 tsp. nutmeg

2 1/2 c. oatmeal
2 1/2 tsp. baking powder
1 tsp. vanilla
1/4 tsp. maple or almond
    flavoring

Cream butter, sugar and eggs together. Combine salt, nutmeg, oatmeal and baking powder. Add to first mixture and mix thoroughly. Add flavorings. Drop by teaspoons on greased baking sheets, two inches apart. Bake at 350° for 12-15 minutes. Makes approximately 5 dozen.

MACAROONS

2 egg whites
1 c. powdered sugar
1/2 tsp. almond flavoring

1 c. coconut
1 c. finely chopped almonds
    or walnuts

Beat egg whites until stiff and dry. Fold sugar in gradually. Add flavoring, coconut and finely-chopped nuts. Drop by teaspoons onto well-greased baking sheet. Bake at 350° approximately 10 minutes.

SOFT MOLASSES COOKIES

2 1/2 c. flour
2 tsp. baking powder
1 tsp. soda
1/2 tsp. salt
1 tsp. cinnamon
1 tsp. ginger

1/4 tsp. nutmeg
2/3 c. shortening
1/2 c. sugar
1 egg
1/2 c. molasses
1/2 c. hot water

Combine flour, baking powder, soda, salt and spices. Cream shortening and sugar; add egg. Beat until fluffy. Add dry ingredients and molasses mixed with hot water, alternately. Mix well. Drop by teaspoons onto a greased baking sheet. Flatten with a glass dipped in sugar. Bake at 350° approx. 10 minutes.

WHOLE WHEAT MOLASSES COOKIES

1 c. shortening	1/2 tsp. salt
1 c. brown sugar	1 tsp. ginger
2 c. molasses	1 tsp. cinnamon
2 tsp. soda	1/2 tsp. cloves
2 eggs	7 c. whole wheat flour
1 c. sour milk or buttermilk	

Cream together shortening and sugar. Dissolve soda in molasses and add to the mixture. Beat in eggs, milk, salt, ginger, cinnamon, cloves and flour. Drop on greased baking sheet. Bake at 350° approximately 10 minutes or until done.

GRANDMA HORST'S
NUT SHORTBREAD COOKIES

2 c. sugar	3 c. flour
1 c. butter	2 tsp. baking powder
1 c. cold water	1/2 tsp. salt
1 tsp. vanilla	1 c. chopped nuts

Cream sugar and butter. Add cold water and vanilla. Combine dry ingredients and add. Mix in nuts. Mix well. Bake at 375° approximately 12 minutes. Almond or other flavoring may be used instead of vanilla.

GRANDMA HORST'S
APPLESAUCE OATMEAL COOKIES

1 1/2 c. sugar	1 tsp. soda
1/2 c. shortening	1/2 tsp. salt
1 egg	1 tsp. cinnamon
3/4 c. applesauce	1/2 tsp. nutmeg
1 3/4 c. flour	1/4 tsp. cloves
1 tsp. baking powder	3 c. quick oatmeal

Cream sugar and shortening. Beat in egg. Add applesauce and mix well. Combine all but oatmeal and add, mixing well. Stir in oatmeal. Bake at 350° approximately 12 minutes.

GRANDMA HORST'S

HICKORY NUT OATMEAL COOKIES

Because she had them Grandma Horst often used hickory nuts in baking. Walnuts or other nuts may be substituted in this recipe.

1 1/2 c. sugar	2 1/2 c. flour
1 c. brown sugar	1 1/2 tsp. baking powder
1 1/4 c. shortening	1/2 tsp. soda
3 eggs	1/2 tsp. salt
1/3 c. milk	2 1/2 c. oatmeal
1 tsp. vanilla	1 c. hickory nuts

Cream sugar and shortening. Beat in eggs, milk and vanilla. Combine and add dry ingredients. Mix well. Stir in oatmeal and nuts. Bake at 350° approximately 12 minutes.

RAISIN OATMEAL COOKIES

3/4 c. butter	1 tsp. soda
1 1/2 c. brown sugar	1 tsp. salt
2 eggs	1 tsp. cinnamon
1 tsp. vanilla	2 c. oatmeal
1/4 c. milk	1 c. raisins
2 c. flour	1 c. coconut
1 tsp. baking powder	

Cream butter and sugar until very light. Add well-beaten eggs, vanilla and milk. Combine and add dry ingredients to first mixture. Add oatmeal, raisins and coconut. Mix well. Drop from a teaspoon onto buttered baking sheets. Bake at 375° approximately 10 minutes.

Variation for **ORANGE OATMEAL COOKIES:** Omit cinnamon. Add 1 T. grated orange rind and substitute 1/3 c. orange juice for milk.

GRANDMA HOOVER'S
WHOLE WHEAT OATMEAL COOKIES

1/2 c. butter
1 c. brown sugar
2 eggs
2 tsp. water
7/8 c. whole wheat flour

1/2 tsp. soda
1/2 tsp. cinnamon
2 c. oatmeal
1 c. raisins

Cream butter and sugar. Add eggs and water. Combine and add dry ingredients. Mix well. Add oatmeal and raisins. Drop by teaspoons onto buttered baking sheet. Bake at 350° approximately 12 minutes.

GRANDMA HOOVER'S
PEANUT BUTTER COOKIES

1 c. sugar
1 c. brown sugar
1 c. butter
2 eggs
1 c. peanut butter

1 tsp. vanilla
3 c. flour
2 tsp. soda
1/4 tsp. salt

Cream sugar and butter. Beat in eggs. Add peanut butter and vanilla. Mix well. Combine dry ingredients and add. Roll dough in balls and press twice with a fork. Bake at 350° approximately 10 minutes.

PUMPKIN COOKIES

2 c. brown sugar
1 c. shortening
2 eggs
2 c. mashed pumpkin
4 c. flour

1 tsp. salt
1 tsp. baking powder
1/2 tsp. soda
1 tsp. cinnamon

Cream sugar and shortening. Add eggs and pumpkin. Beat thoroughly. Combine and add dry ingredients. Mix well. Drop by spoon on cookie sheet. Bake at 350° approximately 12 minutes. Good with cream cheese icing.

ROCKS

"These cookies improve on keeping in a stone crock or cooky jar."

1 1/2 c. brown sugar	1/2 tsp. salt
2/3 c. butter	2 1/2 c. flour
2 eggs	1 tsp. soda
1 tsp. cinnamon	1/2 chopped nuts
1 tsp. nutmeg	1 c. chopped raisins
1/4 tsp. cloves	1 tsp. vanilla

Cream butter and sugar. Add eggs and mix well. Combine dry ingredients and add, mixing well. Add nuts, raisins and vanilla. The mixture should be very stiff and might be necessary to hand mix. Drop by teaspoons onto flat, buttered baking sheet. Bake at 350° approximately 15 minutes.

GRANDMA MARTIN'S
SOUR CREAM COOKIES

After dropping the cookies by teaspoon on to the baking sheet Grandma Martin flattened them with a cup dipped in sugar.

2 c. brown sugar	2 tsp. soda
1 c. shortening	1 tsp. salt
2 eggs	1 c. sour cream
5 c. flour	1 tsp. vanilla

Cream sugar and shortening. Beat in eggs. Combine dry ingredients and add alternately with sour cream. Add vanilla. Bake at 375° approximately 10 minutes.

"Make surprise cookies by wrapping strips of rolled dough around Brazil nuts. Or cut dough into squares, heap centers with mincemeat or other fruit filling, fold, press edges firmly together and bake."

SOUR CREAM RAISIN COOKIES

1 c. shortening	1 tsp. cinnamon
2 c. sugar	1/2 tsp. nutmeg
3 eggs, well beaten	1/2 tsp. salt
4 c. flour	1 c. sour cream
1 tsp. soda	1 c. raisins

Cream shortening and sugar. Add eggs and beat until light. Combine dry ingredients and add alternately with sour cream to dry ingredients. Stir in raisins. Bake at 375° for 10-12 minutes. This recipe can be made with water instead of sour cream and baking powder instead of soda.

SUGAR COOKIES

2 c. sugar	2 tsp. baking powder
3/4 c. shortening	1/2 tsp. salt
2 eggs	1/2 tsp. nutmeg
4 c. flour	3/4 c. milk

Cream sugar and shortening. Add eggs. Combine dry ingredients and add alternately with milk. Mix thoroughly. Drop by teaspoons onto well-greased baking sheet. Sprinkle with sugar before baking. Bake at 350° approximately 12 minutes.

BROWN SUGAR COOKIES

1/2 c. butter	2 c. flour
1 c. brown sugar	2 tsp. baking powder
4 eggs	1/2 tsp. salt
2/3 c. milk	1 c. chopped nuts

Cream butter and sugar. Add eggs, yolks and whites beaten separately, and milk. Combine and add dry ingredients. Add nuts. Mix thoroughly. Drop by teaspoon onto a well-oiled baking sheet. Bake at 350° approximately 12 minutes.

WHOLE WHEAT SUGAR COOKIES

1 c. shortening	4 c. whole wheat flour
2 c. sugar	1 tsp. baking powder
2 eggs	1 tsp. salt
1 c. milk	1/4 tsp. nutmeg or cinnamon
1 tsp. soda	

Cream shortening. Add sugar and eggs. Dissolve soda in milk and add alternately to mixture with flour and baking powder. Add salt and nutmeg. Mix well. Drop on greased cookie sheet or roll in balls. Bake approximately 12 minutes at 375°.

CUTOUT BUTTER COOKIES

1 c. butter	1 tsp. salt
2 c. sugar	4 tsp. baking powder
3 eggs	1 1/2 tsp. vanilla
5 c. flour	

Cream butter, sugar and eggs until light. Combine dry ingredients and add to first mixture. Add vanilla. Mix until smooth. Chill. Roll to 1/4-inch thick on slightly floured board. Cut with cookie cutter. Sprinkle with sugar before baking or ice when cool. Bake at 350° approximately 10 minutes. Makes 5 dozen cookies.

Variation for **CHOCOLATE BUTTER COOKIES:** Add 1/2 c. cocoa mixed with 3 T. hot water to Butter Cookies recipe when eggs are added.

Variation for **COCONUT BUTTER COOKIES:** Add 1 c. coconut along with dry ingredients in Butter Cookies recipe.

Variation for **SPICE BUTTER COOKIES:** Add 1/2 tsp. cinnamon, 1/4 tsp. nutmeg and 1/8 tsp. cloves to dry ingredients in Butter Cookies recipe.

GINGER SNAPS

1 c. sugar	1 tsp. cinnamon
1 c. molasses	2 tsp. soda
1 c. butter	1 T. vinegar
1 egg	1 tsp. vanilla
1 T. ginger	5 c. flour

Combine sugar, molasses, butter, egg, ginger, cinnamon and soda. Mix well. Mix in vinegar and vanilla. Add flour and beat well. Roll thin on a floured surface and cut with a cookie cutter. Bake at 350° for 8-10 minutes. Sprinkle with sugar before baking.

HONEY COOKIES

This was a recipe Grandma Hoover cut out of a newspaper.

1 c. honey	2 1/4 c. flour
1/4 c. butter	1/2 tsp. cinnamon
1/3 c. chopped nuts	1/4 tsp. cloves
grated rind of 1 lemon	2 tsp. baking powder

Warm honey and butter together until butter melts. Add nuts and lemon rind. Combine flour and spices and add. Mix thoroughly. Add baking powder after mixture cools, mixing well. Let stand overnight in a cool place. Roll thin and cut cookies in desired size and shape. Place on a greased baking sheet. If desired, decorate cookies with almond halves. Bake at 350° for 8-10 minutes.

LEMON COOKIES

3/4 c. butter	3 c. flour
1 1/2 c. sugar	1 tsp. baking powder
2 eggs, well-beaten	1/4 tsp. soda
6 T. lemon juice	1/2 tsp. salt
1 lemon rind, grated	

Cream butter and sugar. Add eggs, lemon juice and rind. Combine dry ingredients and add to first mixture. Mix thoroughly. Turn onto a lightly floured board. Roll 1/8 to 1/4-inch thick. Cut with cookie cutter. Place on slightly greased baking sheet. Bake at 375° approximately 8 minutes. Ice if desired.

BUTTERSCOTCH COOKIES

1/2 c. shortening	3 c. flour
2 c. brown sugar	1 tsp. cream of tarter
2 eggs, well-beaten	1 tsp. salt
1 tsp. vanilla	1/2 tsp. soda

Cream shortening and sugar. Add eggs. Mix well. Add vanilla. Combine dry ingredients and add to first mixture. Mix thoroughly. Form into rolls 2-inches in diameter. Chill overnight. Cut into thin slices. Place on a lightly-greased baking sheet. Bake at 375° approximately 10 minutes.

Variation for **BUTTERSCOTCH COCONUT COOKIES**: Add 1 cup coconut along with dry ingredients.

CHOCOLATE WALNUT COOKIES

1/2 c. butter	2 1/2 c. flour
1 c. sugar	1 tsp. baking powder
1 egg	1/2 c. chopped walnuts
2 T. milk	2 oz. melted unsweetened
1 tsp. vanilla	chocolate

Cream butter, sugar and egg. Add milk and vanilla. Combine flour and baking powder and add gradually. Add walnuts and chocolate. Form into a roll. Chill and slice thin. Bake at 350° approximately 10 minutes.

"There is one important point to remember: Do not feed a child too many cakes and cookies, so that plain foods are slighted."

GRANDMA HORST'S
DATE PINWHEELS

Most of Grandma's recipes using dates began, "Pit dates...". Some recipes even called for seeding raisins.

2 c. brown sugar	4 c. flour
1 c. shortening	1 tsp. soda
3 eggs	1 tsp. salt

DATE FILLING

2 1/2 c. chopped dates	1 c. water
1 c. sugar	1 c. chopped nuts

Cream sugar and shortening. Add eggs. Beat until fluffy. Combine dry ingredients and add. Mix well. Chill. Combine filling ingredients and cook and stir approximately five minutes. Cool. Divide dough in half and roll out one half at a time, into 1/4-inch thick rectangles. Spread each rectangle with half of the cooled filling mixture. Roll up tight like a jelly roll. Chill thoroughly. Cut into 1/4-inch thick slices using a sharp knife. Place on a buttered baking sheet. Bake at 375° approximately 10 minutes.

JAM OATMEAL COOKIES

3 c. oatmeal	1 tsp. soda
1 c. brown sugar	1/3 c. hot water
1 1/2 c. flour	1/2 c. melted shortened
1 tsp. salt	jam
1/2 tsp. cinnamon	

Combine oatmeal, sugar, flour, salt and cinnamon. Dissolve soda in hot water and add. Add shortening. Mix well. Chill. Roll out 1/4-inch thick on slightly-floured board. Cut into circles and place on baking sheet. Make a slight depression in the center of cookies and fill with jam. Bake at 350° for 12-15 minutes.

WHOLE WHEAT ICEBOX COOKIES

3 1/2 c. whole wheat flour
1/2 tsp. salt
2 tsp. baking powder
2/3 c. butter

1 1/3 c. sugar
2 tsp. grated orange rind
2 T. strained orange juice
3 eggs beaten

Combine dry ingredients. Cream butter and sugar. Sprinkle in rind and add juice and eggs. Mix well. Add dry ingredients and mix to a smooth dough. Shape into a firm cylindrical roll. Wrap in wax paper and chill in refrigerator overnight or longer. Slice thin with sharp knife and place about 1/2 inch apart on greased baking sheet. Bake at 350° for 12-15 minutes.

BROWNIES

1 c. butter
2 c. sugar
3 eggs
1 tsp. vanilla

1/4 c. cocoa
1 c. flour
1 c. chopped walnuts

Cream butter and sugar. Add eggs and vanilla and cocoa. Add flour and nuts and mix well. Spread into a greased, 13x9-pan. Bake at 350° approximately 30 minutes. Good sprinkled with powdered sugar.

FUDGE BROWNIES

1/2 c. butter
2 c. sugar
4 eggs, well-beaten
4 oz. unsweetened chocolate,
    melted

1 1/2 c. flour
1/2 tsp. salt
1/2 c. milk or cream
2 tsp. vanilla
1 1/2 c. chopped nuts

Cream butter and sugar. Add well-beaten eggs and melted chocolate. Combine flour and salt, add alternately with milk. Mix well. Add vanilla and nuts. Spread in a greased 13x9-inch pan. Bake at 350° approximately 30 minutes. Ice with chocolate fudge icing. (See icings.)

BUTTERSCOTCH SQUARES

1 1/2 c. flour	2 c. brown sugar
2 tsp. baking powder	2 eggs
1 tsp. salt	2 tsp. vanilla
3/4 c. butter	1 c. chopped nuts

Combine dry ingredients. Cream butter and sugar. Add eggs and vanilla. Beat well and add to dry ingredients. Mix in nuts. Spread into a greased, 13x9-pan. Bake at 350° approximately 30 minutes.

CHOCOLATE RAISIN SQUARES

1/2 c. butter	1/2 tsp. salt
1 c. sugar	2/3 c. raisins
2 eggs, well-beaten	1/2 c. nuts
1/2 c. flour	1 tsp. vanilla
3 T. cocoa	

Cream butter and sugar. Add eggs. Beat thoroughly. Combine dry ingredients and add to first mixture. Add raisins, nuts and vanilla. Mix thoroughly. Pour into a well-greased 8x8-inch pan. Bake at 350° approximately 40-45 minutes. Cool. Cut into squares.

COCONUT BARS

1/2 c. soft butter	1 tsp. vanilla
1/2 c. brown sugar	2 T. flour
1 c. flour	1/2 tsp. baking powder
2 eggs	1 c. chopped nuts
1/8 tsp. salt	1 c. coconut
1 c. brown sugar	

Mix butter, 1/2 c. brown sugar and flour. Press into a 13x9-inch greased pan and bake at 350° for 15 minutes. Beat eggs, salt, 1 c. brown sugar, vanilla, flour and baking powder. Stir in nuts. Spread on partially baked crust. Sprinkle with coconut. Bake at 350° approximately 25 minutes longer.

DATE NUT BARS
"They are better than candy"

1 c. sugar	2 tsp. baking powder
3 eggs	1 lb. dates, cut fine
1 tsp. vanilla	1 c. chopped nuts
1 1/2 c. flour	powdered sugar

Combine sugar, eggs and vanilla, beating well. Mix in dry ingredients then add dates and nuts. Put in a greased 13x9-inch pan. Bake at 350° for 35-40 minutes. Cut immediately. When bars cool put in a bag with powdered sugar and shake gently.

FIG NEWTONS

1/2 c. butter	1/2 tsp. salt
1 1/2 c. sugar	3 c. flour
1 egg, well-beaten	3 tsp. baking powder
1 tsp. vanilla	1 c. chopped figs
1/2 c. milk	1 c. hot water

Cream butter and 1 c. sugar. Add eggs and beat until light. Add vanilla. Combine dry ingredients and add alternately with milk to creamed mixture. Blend well. Roll out on slightly-floured board to 1/8-inch thick rectangle. Put figs in a saucepan. Add remaining 1/2 c. of sugar and hot water. Boil 5 minutes. Cool. Spread cooked mixture over 1/2 of dough. Cover with other half. Cut into oblongs. Bake at 400° for 12-15 minutes.

"There is such a thing as being too neat and nice to take comfort in everyday life, and this is anything but cheerful. And then there is such a thing as being so disorderly and negligent that comfort and cheer are impossible."

HONEY ALMOND BARS

1 c. butter
1/2 c. sugar
1/2 c. honey
3 eggs, well-beaten
2 c. flour

2 tsp. baking powder
1/2 tsp. salt
1/2 c. chopped, almonds
1 tsp. vanilla
1/2 c. powdered milk

Cream butter and sugar. Add honey and eggs. Mix thoroughly. Combine dry ingredients and add. Add nuts and vanilla. Mix well. Pour into a greased 13x9-pan. Bake at 375° approximately 15 minutes. Cool. Cut into bars and roll in powdered sugar.

MOLASSES RAISIN BARS

1/4 c. butter
1/2 c. sugar
1 egg
1/2 c. molasses
2 c. flour

1 1/2 tsp. baking powder
1/2 tsp. salt
1/2 tsp. soda
1/2 c. milk or cream
1 c. chopped raisins or dates

Cream butter and sugar; add egg and beat until light. Add molasses. Combine dry ingredients and add alternately with milk to mixture. Add raisins. Spread in a greased 13x9-pan. Bake at 350° for 30 minutes.

PEANUT BUTTER OATMEAL BARS

1 c. shortening
1 c. sugar
1 c. brown sugar
2 eggs
2/3 c. peanut butter
1/2 c. sour milk

1 tsp. vanilla
2 c. flour
1 tsp. soda
1/2 tsp. salt
2 c. oatmeal

Cream shortening and sugar. Beat in eggs and peanut butter. Add sour milk and vanilla. Combine and add flour, soda and salt. Mix well. Stir in oatmeal. Spread on a greased 15x10-inch pan or on a baking sheet. Bake at 350° approximately 25 minutes.

ORANGE FROSTING

One orange, grate off the outside,
and mix with juice, and add sugar until
quite stiff.

FROSTING

Beat the whites of two eggs or more, according to the
quantity wanted, and add pulverized sugar till quite
thick; add a little powdered starch, and lay on the
cake, immediately after it is baked, with a broad
knife, returning to the oven for a moment.

FROSTING

Soak one teaspoonful of gelatine in one
tablespoonful of cold water half an hour;
dissolve in two tablespoonfuls of hot
water; add one cup of powdered
sugar and stir until smooth.

BUTTER ICING

Many of Grandma's recipes called powdered sugar pulverized sugar.

1/3 c. soft butter	1 tsp. vanilla
3 c. powdered sugar	1/8 tsp. salt
1/4 c. milk	

Cream butter and sugar. Add remaining ingredients and beat until smooth.

Variation for **COFFEE ICING:** Substitute 2 T. cold coffee for 2 T. of milk.

Variation for **LEMON BUTTER ICING:** Substitute lemon juice for milk.

BROWN BUTTER ICING

1/2 c. butter	3 1/2 c. powdered sugar
1/4 c. light cream or milk	1 tsp. vanilla

Brown butter in a saucepan, being careful not to burn it. Remove from heat and add cream. Beat in sugar and add vanilla.

BROWN SUGAR ICING

1/2 c. brown sugar	3 c. powdered sugar
1/3 c. milk	1 tsp. vanilla
2 T. butter	

Put brown sugar, milk and butter in a saucepan and bring to a boil, stirring constantly. Cool and add powdered sugar and vanilla. Beat until smooth.

CARAMEL ICING
No powdered sugar needed!

2 1/2 c. brown sugar
1 c. cream or milk
2 T. butter

1/8 tsp. salt
1 tsp. vanilla
1 T. cream

Combine sugar, cream or milk, butter and salt. Cook, stirring until sugar is dissolved. Then cook while stirring until mixture forms a soft ball when a little is dropped in cold water (234°). Remove from heat and cool to lukewarm (110°). Do not stir while cooling. When lukewarm beat until mixture starts to thicken. Add vanilla. Beat until spreading consistency. If icing thickens too rapidly add a tablespoon of milk.

Variation for **CARAMEL PECAN ICING:** Add 1/2 c. chopped pecans along with vanilla.

CHOCOLATE ICING

1/2 c. soft butter
1 lb. (3 1/2-4 c.) powdered
    sugar
1/4 c. cocoa

1/8 tsp. salt
1/4 c. milk
1 tsp. vanilla

Gradually add sugar, cocoa and salt to butter. Thin with milk as mixture becomes stiff. Add vanilla.

Variation for **CHOCOLATE NUT ICING:** Add 3/4 c. chopped nuts.

DARK CHOCOLATE ICING

2/3 c. cocoa
1/2 c. water
3 c. powdered sugar

1/4 c. butter, melted
1 tsp. vanilla
1/8 tsp. salt

Boil cocoa and water two minutes over low heat, stirring constantly. Add to sugar and beat until smooth. Add remaining ingredients and beat until smooth and thick.

CHOCOLATE ALMOND ICING

3 T. solid shortening
3 c. powdered sugar
1/3 c. cocoa
6 T. milk or cream

1/4 tsp. salt
1/2 tsp. vanilla
1/4 tsp. almond flavoring

Cream shortening, sugar and cocoa. Add milk, salt and flavoring. Beat thoroughly. Chopped almonds may be added.

CHOCOLATE FUDGE ICING

3 squares (3 oz.) unsweetened
    chocolate
1/4 c. butter
2 1/2 c. powdered sugar

1/8 tsp. salt
1/3 c. milk or cream
1 tsp. vanilla

Melt chocolate and butter in a heavy saucepan over low heat, stirring constantly. Combine remaining ingredients. Add chocolate; mix well.

GRANDMA HORST'S
SOFT CHOCOLATE ICING

1 c. sugar
4 tsp. cocoa
2 T. cornstarch

1 c. boiling water, scant
2 T. butter
1/2 tsp. vanilla

Combine sugar, cocoa and cornstarch. Stir into boiling water. Boil until thickened. Remove from heat. Add butter and vanilla.

CONFECTIONERS' ICING

1/4 c. solid shortening
3 c. powdered sugar
1/4 c. milk or cream

1/8 tsp. salt
1 tsp. vanilla

Cream shortening, adding sugar gradually. Beat thoroughly. Add milk, salt and vanilla.

CREAM CHEESE ICING
"This icing goes well on gingerbread, spice cake or nut cake."

3 oz. cream cheese
1/4 c. milk

2 1/2 c. powdered sugar
1 tsp. vanilla

Beat together cream cheese and milk. Add powdered sugar and vanilla. Beat until fluffy.

Variation for **ORANGE CREAM CHEESE ICING:** Use orange juice instead of milk. Add 1 tsp. grated orange rind.

JELLY ICING

fruit jelly

powdered sugar

Take fruit jelly that is not too hard and beat in enough powdered sugar to make it spreadable.

LEMON ICING

3 T. solid shortening
3 c. powdered sugar
1/4 c. lemon juice

2 tsp. lemon rind
1/8 tsp. salt

Cream shortening and sugar. Add remaining ingredients and beat until smooth.

Variation for **ORANGE ICING:** Substitute orange juice and rind for lemon juice and rind.

MAPLE BUTTER ICING

2/3 c. soft butter
2 c. powdered sugar

1/2 tsp. maple flavoring
2 T. milk

Cream butter and powdered sugar. Add flavoring and milk. Beat until light and fluffy. Spread on cooled cake.

MOCHA ICING

1/2 c. butter	1/4 c. cocoa
3 c. powdered sugar	3-4 T. cold coffee

Melt butter. Add powdered sugar and mix well. Add cocoa and enough cold coffee to make the right consistency to spread well. Spread on cold cake.

PEANUT BUTTER ICING

3 1/2 c. powdered sugar	1/2 tsp. cinnamon
1/4 c. peanut butter	1/8 tsp. nutmeg
1/3 c. milk	

Combine all ingredients and beat until smooth.

PINEAPPLE ICING

2 1/2 c. powdered sugar	1/4 c. pineapple juice
2 T. melted butter	1/4 c. crushed pineapple

Combine ingredients and beat until creamy. Add more powdered sugar if thicker icing is desired.

PLAIN ICING
Use for Hot Cross Buns and other rolls or on coffee cakes.

4 tsp. milk or warm water	1/4 tsp. vanilla
1 c. powdered sugar	

Add milk or water slowly to powdered sugar to make a smooth, fairly thick paste. Add vanilla. Water will make a more transparent icing than milk.

CHOCOLATE TOPPING

1 c. cream
1 tsp. vanilla
3/4 c. sugar

1/4 c. cocoa
1/4 tsp. salt

Mix well and whip until thick.

SPICED WHIPPED TOPPING

1 c. whipping cream
3 T. powdered sugar

1 tsp. cinnamon
1 tsp. ginger

Whip cream. Add sugar and spices. For plain whipped cream omit spices and add 1 tsp. vanilla.

ALMOND FILLING

2 c. powdered sugar
1/2 c. sour cream

1 T. vanilla
3/4 c. finely chopped almonds

Combine ingredients. Beat until smooth. Spread between layer cakes.

BANANA CREAM FILLING

1 c. whipping cream
3/4 c. powdered sugar
3/4 c. mashed banana

1 tsp. vanilla
1/8 tsp. salt

Whip cream until stiff. Mix in remaining ingredients. Spread on layer cake.

To decorate a cake covered with plain icing: "If the design is complicated outline it with a sharp-pointed knife."

CHOCOLATE FILLING

1 square (1 oz.) baking
   chocolate, melted
1/2 c. milk
1 T. corn syrup
1/8 tsp. salt

1/2 c. sugar
1 T. melted butter
1/2 tsp. vanilla
1/2 c. cream, whipped

Bring all but vanilla and cream to a boil, stirring frequently. Boil slowly, about 10 minutes, until very thick, stirring constantly. Cool thoroughly. Add vanilla and stir in whipped cream. Chill until ready to use. Three tablespoons cocoa may be used instead of chocolate. Mix in with sugar.

CREAM FILLING FOR CREAM PUFFS, ECLAIRS AND CAKES

2/3 c. sugar
1/4 c. cornstarch
1/8 tsp. salt

2 eggs, beaten
2 c. cream or milk
1 tsp. vanilla

Mix sugar, cornstarch and salt. Add beaten eggs. Add milk. Cook in a heavy saucepan, stirring constantly, until thick. Cool and add vanilla.

Variation for **CHOCOLATE CREAM FILLING:** Add 2 oz. of melted, unsweetened chocolate along with milk.

Variation for **COCONUT CREAM FILLING:** Add 1 c. cup coconut after removing from heat.

Variation for **PINEAPPLE CREAM FILLING:** Add 1/2 c. crushed pineapple along with milk.

LEMON FILLING

2 T. cornstarch	2 T. butter
1/2 c. sugar	2 T lemon juice
1/4 tsp. salt	1 tsp. grated lemon rind
3/4 c. water	

Mix cornstarch, sugar and salt in sauce pan. Add water and cook, stirring constantly until sauce boils and becomes clear. Cook 1-2 minutes longer, while stirring. Add butter, lemon juice and rind. Remove from heat and cool.

Variation for **ORANGE FILLING:** Substitute 3/4 c. orange juice for water.

PEACH FILLING

1/2 c. sugar	1 T. butter
3 T. cornstarch	3 T. lemon juice
1/4 tsp. salt	1 tsp. grated lemon rind
1 c. boiling water	1 c. crushed peaches

Combine sugar, cornstarch and salt in a heavy saucepan. Add boiling water and cook, stirring constantly, until thick and smooth. Add butter, lemon juice and rind. Mix thoroughly. Cool. Add peaches. Add food coloring if desired.

PINEAPPLE CHEESE AND NUT FILLING

1/4 c. milk	1/2 c. crushed pineapple
8 oz. soft cream cheese	1/4 c. finely-chopped nuts

Blend milk and cream cheese. Add well-drained pineapple and nuts. Mix well. Use as a spread for quick breads.

PRUNE FILLING

1 c. chopped, cooked prunes	2 T. butter
1 c. sugar	1/4 tsp. salt
2 eggs, well-beaten	1 tsp. vanilla
1/2 c. sour cream	

Combine all ingredients, except vanilla, in a heavy saucepan. Cook, stirring constantly, until thick. Add vanilla. Spread on layer cake.

RAISIN FILLING

1 c. raisins	2 T. flour
2/3 c. sugar	1 c. boiling water
1 T. lemon juice	

Combine all but water in a heavy saucepan. Add water. Cook, stirring constantly, until thick and smooth.

RASPBERRY CREAM FILLING

1/4 c. crushed raspberries	1 c. cream, whipped
1 T. powdered sugar	

Combine raspberries and sugar. Add sugared berries to half whipped cream. Continue to whip until cream is stiff. May be used on top of cake or as a filling. Other berries or peaches may be used in the same manner.

SOUR CREAM FILLING

1 c. sour cream	1 tsp. vanilla
3 T. powdered sugar	1/2 c. chopped nuts

Combine ingredients. Mix well. Use between layer cakes.

STRAWBERRY FILLING

1 c. crushed strawberries   1/2 c. whipping cream
3 T. sugar

Mix strawberries and sugar. Whip cream and fold into strawberries.

TEACH THE LITTLE ONES

*"There is scarcely a busy home mother in the land who has not at some
time or other felt how much easier it would be to do all the work herself
than to attempt to teach a child to assist her, whether it be in household
matters or in sewing. Now, we would speak particularly of the latter.
But it seems almost the right of every little girl to be taught to sew
neatly, even if it does cost the mother some self-sacrifice. Very few
grown women are wholly exempt from ever using a needle. On the
contrary, almost every woman must take more or less care of her own
wardrobe, even if she has no responsibility for that of any one's around
her. Machines cannot sew up rips in gloves, replace missing buttons, or
make or mend without any needlework by hand. Some stitches must be
taken, and how to sew neatly is an accomplishment quite as necessary, if
not more so, to the happiness of a majority of women than any other. If
a little girl be early taught how to use her needle, it very soon becomes a
sort of second nature to her, and very little ones can learn to thread the
needle and take simple stitches. Only the mother must be patient and
painstaking with them, not letting poor work receive praise or permitting
the child to slight what she undertakes. The stint can be a very short one
with very little children. It is usually best so, but frequent lessons should
be given."*

GRANDMA'S

NUT CANDY

Three cupfuls of sugar, one-half cupful
of vinegar, one-half cupful of water. Prepare
two cupfuls of any kind of nutmeats, spread
them on well-buttered plates, and pour the candy
over; when done, test it by dropping a little in cold
water; when it hardens into a little lump it is done.

CHOCOLATE CARAMELS

Three pounds of sugar (brown will do), half a
pound of butter, one teacupful of milk or cream—
the latter, of course, preferable, and two cupfuls
of chocolate. Boil rapidly until candied, when
it may be either cut into squares or
molded into small thin cakes.

CANDIES

CANDY MAKING TIPS

1. Make sure your saucepan is big enough to allow candy to boil. It should be heavy enough to minimize scorching.

2. Cook creamy candies rapidly and stir frequently until sugar is dissolved, then cook slowly, stirring as little as possible. Stir brittle and taffy just enough to keep from burning.

3. As candy cooks, wipe sides of saucepan with a clean damp cloth to remove sugar crystals.

4. Cool creamy candies before beating to prevent sugaring. Candy may be cooled by setting the pan in cold water. Do not stir. Candy is ready to beat when you can comfortably hold your hand on the bottom of the pan.

CANDY TEMPERATURES

Soft Ball	**234° -240°**
Firm Ball	**242° -248°**
Hard Ball	**250° -265°**
Soft Crack	**270° -290°**
Hard Crack	**295° -310°**

COLD WATER TEST

Use a thermometer if at all possible. If none is available use the cold water test. Remove boiling candy from heat while testing to prevent overcooking. Put about 1/2 tsp. of candy into a 1/2 c. of cold water. Press with fingers to note consistency. Soft ball looses its shape out of water. Firm ball retains its shape briefly then flattens out. Hard ball retains its shape. Soft crack makes a brittle thread when dropped in the water but softens out of water. Hard crack remains brittle after removing from water.

BUTTERSCOTCH PECAN PATTIES

2 c. sugar
1 c. brown sugar
2/3 c. white corn syrup
1 c. evaporated milk
1/4 tsp. salt

2/3 c. butter
1 tsp. vanilla or maple
   flavoring
1 1/2 c. broken pecans

Combine sugar, corn syrup, milk and salt in a saucepan. Boil and stir rapidly until sugar is dissolved. Reduce heat and boil to 236° or until a little dropped into cold water will just keep its shape. Remove from heat. Add butter and vanilla and let stand 10 minutes. Add nuts. Beat until thick and creamy. Drop by teaspoons on a waxed paper.

CANDIED APPLES

4 or 5 apples
2 c. sugar

1 c. hot water

Peel and quarter apples. Cut each quarter into three slices. Bring sugar and water to a boil. Cook apples a few slices at a time, until they look clear. Drain. Place on waxed paper. Dry 24 hours. Roll in sugar.

CANDIED ORANGE PEEL

peel of 3 oranges
1 c. sugar

2 T. corn syrup
1/2 c. water

Quarter each orange. Cover with water and boil 20 minutes. Drain. Repeat process. Cut peel into 1/4-inch strips. Combine remaining ingredients and bring to a boil. Add peel and cook slowly until peel is clear and tender. Cool in syrup several hours or overnight. Drain thoroughly. Roll in sugar. Dry in a 250° oven until surface is firm.

"A candy thermometer should not touch the pan at any point."

GRANDMA HOOVER'S
CANDY CRISPIES

1 c. sugar	1/2 pkg. rice crispies
1 c. dark corn syrup	1 c. coconut
1 c. thin cream	1 c. salted peanuts
1/2 pkg. corn flakes	

Rapidly cook and stir sugar, corn syrup and cream until sugar is dissolved. Reduce heat and cook until soft ball is formed in cold water (236°). Combine remaining ingredients. Pour syrup mixture over dry ingredients and mix well. Press into a buttered pan and cut into squares.

GRANDMA HORST'S
CARAMEL CORN

1 1/2 c. brown sugar	3/4 c. baking molasses
3/4 c. butter	6 qts. popped corn

Bring first three ingredients to a boil then pour over popped corn. Mix well. Heat in a 250° oven for one hour, stirring frequently.

CHOCOLATE NUT CARAMEL

1 1/2 c. broken nuts	2 c. cream or evaporated
4 oz. unsweetened chocolate	milk
2 c. sugar	1/2 c. butter
1 c. brown sugar	1/8 tsp. salt
1 c. corn syrup	1 tsp. vanilla

Spread nuts evenly in a well buttered 13x9inch pan. Cut chocolate in small pieces and put in a three quart heavy saucepan. Add all but vanilla. Bring to a boil, stirring constantly until sugar is dissolved. Reduce heat. Stir occasionally at the beginning, then constantly as mixture thickens. Cook until mixture forms a firm ball when a small amount is dropped into cold water (244°). Remove from heat and add vanilla. Pour over nuts or mix nuts into candy. Cut into squares.

VANILLA CARAMELS

2 c. sugar
2 c. light corn syrup
1/8 tsp. salt
1/2 c. butter

2 c. cream or evaporated
    milk
1 1/2 tsp. vanilla

In a three quart heavy saucepan, rapidly boil sugar, corn syrup and salt to 242°. Add butter and cream or milk, gradually so the mixture does not stop boiling at any time. Reduce heat and cook to the firm ball stage (244°). Stir frequently at the beginning and constantly as mixture thickens. After correct temperature is reached remove from heat and add vanilla. Pour into a well-buttered pan. Cool before cutting. Use heavy, sharp knife.

Variation for **VANILLA NUT CARAMELS:** Add one cup chopped nuts when vanilla is added.

CHERRY NUT DIVINITY

3 c. sugar
1 c. syrup
1 c. water
1/8 tsp. salt

2 egg whites
1 c. chopped candied cherries
1 c. chopped nuts
1 tsp. vanilla

Boil sugar, syrup, water and salt to firm ball stage (248°). Pour hot syrup over stiffly beaten egg whites. Beat until candy begins to stiffen. Add cherries, nuts and vanilla. Drop by spoonsful onto waxed paper or pour into well-buttered pan. Cool. Cut into squares.

COCONUT PATTIES

3 c. sugar
3/4 c. cream or evaporated
    milk
2 c. coconut

1/2 c. chopped nuts
1 T. butter
1 tsp. vanilla

Boil sugar and milk to soft ball stage (234°). Cool to lukewarm (110°). Add coconut, nuts, butter and vanilla. Beat. Drop by teaspoon onto waxed paper. For chocolate coconut patties add 3 T. cocoa with sugar.

COCONUT ROLL

2 c. sugar
1/2 c. cream or milk
2 T. butter
1/4 tsp. salt

1/2 c. chopped nuts
1/4 c. toasted coconut
1 tsp. vanilla

Boil sugar, cream, butter and salt to soft ball stage (234°). Cool until lukewarm (110°). Add nuts, coconut and vanilla. Beat until creamy. Turn onto powdered sugar covered board. Knead until smooth and creamy. Shape into a roll. Cover outside with more toasted coconut.

GRANDMA HORST'S
FRUIT CANDY

1 lb. dates, chopped
1 lb. raisins
1 lb. figs, chopped

1 lb. butter
2 lb. nuts, chopped

Mix well. Roll out and cut into squares or form into balls.

GRANDMA HOOVER'S
CHOCOLATE FRUIT CANDY
Grandma Hoover often made this candy at Christmas time.

1 lb. raisins
1 lb. figs or dates
8 oz. nuts

1 c. butter, warmed
1 lb. powdered sugar
1 1/2 lb. milk chocolate

Grind fruit and nuts. Mix in butter and sugar. Spread in a thin layer. Let set overnight. Melt chocolate and spread half of it on candy. After chocolate hardens, turn candy over and spread remaining chocolate on the other side.

CHOCOLATE FUDGE

2/3 c. cocoa <u>or</u>	2 T. corn syrup
4 oz. unsweetened	1 1/2 c. milk
chocolate	1/4 c. butter
3 c. sugar	1 tsp. vanilla
1/8 tsp. salt	

Combine cocoa, sugar, salt and syrup in a saucepan. If using chocolate cut into small pieces before adding. Stir in milk. Bring to a boil over high heat, stirring until sugar dissolves. Reduce to low heat and cook to 234° or to soft ball stage. Remove from heat and stir in butter. Set kettle in cold water. Cool to lukewarm (110°) without stirring. Add vanilla. Beat until mixture starts to thicken and lose its shiny appearance. Turn into a buttered 8x8-pan. Cool. Cut into squares. Store in tight container.

Variation for **CHOCOLATE NUT FUDGE:** Add 1 c. nuts along with vanilla.

Variation for **CHOCOLATE MARSHMALLOW FUDGE:** Fill the bottom of a buttered pan with a layer of marshmallows. Pour fudge over marshmallows. Cut with a sharp knife.

CHOCOLATE PEANUT BUTTER FUDGE

4 oz. unsweetened chocolate	2 c. evaporated milk
or 2/3 c. cocoa	1 c. peanut butter
4 c. sugar	1 T. vanilla

Cut chocolate in small pieces and place in heavy saucepan. Add sugar and milk. Cook and stir to dissolve sugar. Reduce heat. Cook to a soft ball stage (234°). Remove from heat. Add peanut butter and mix well. Add vanilla and mix well. Pour into a buttered pan.

VANILLA NUT FUDGE

3 c. sugar	2 T. butter
1 T. white corn syrup	1 T. vanilla
1 1/2 c. cream or evaporated milk	1 c. chopped nuts

Combine sugar, syrup and cream. Cook rapidly, stirring to dissolve sugar. When sugar is dissolved, boil slowly to 234°, or to soft ball stage. Cool to lukewarm without stirring. Add butter, vanilla and nuts. Beat until creamy. Pour into a well-buttered pan. Store in tight container.

Variation for **CHOCOLATE VANILLA FUDGE:** Make chocolate fudge and pour into a well-buttered 13x9-inch pan. Make vanilla fudge. Pour over chocolate fudge.

GUM DROPS

2 T. unflavored gelatin	3/4 c. boiling water
1/2 c. cold water	flavoring
2 c. sugar	food coloring

Soften gelatin in cold water. Boil sugar and water five minutes. Add gelatin. Stir until dissolved. Boil over low heat 15 minutes. Divide into three portions. Flavor and color each portion with different flavoring and coloring. Pour into small pans which have been dipped in cold water. Let stand overnight. Remove from pan and cut into squares. Roll in sugar. Let stand until firm.

"Children like to be useful, like to feel that they are a real help to older persons, and if a little praise and perhaps, too, a little money is given them, they will learn to enjoy the pleasure of helping mother and of earning something for themselves, and early taught the dignity of labor as well as save their mother a little time to keep herself in advance of them in study and thought, in general information, and in spiritual growth, so as to be always reverenced as their intellectual and spiritual guide and friend and counselor."

FONDANT

2 1/2 c. sugar
1 c. water

1/8 tsp. cream of tarter
flavoring

Heat all ingredients to boiling, stirring until sugar is dissolved. Boil to 236° or to soft ball stage. Wipe sugar crystals from sides of the pan with damp cloth. Pour in a shallow dish. When lukewarm (110°), stir until white and creamy. Add desired flavoring. Let set at least one day. Work in coconut, bits of candied cherries, mints or melted chocolate. Roll into balls and dip into chocolate. This can also be used as icing by warming slightly.

MAPLE CREAM CANDY

1 c. maple syrup
1 c. sugar

1/2 c. cream
1 T. butter

Combine and cook to soft ball stage (234°). Remove from heat. Beat until cool and creamy. Pour into a buttered 8x8-inch pan. Nuts may be added while beating.

MAPLE TOFFEE

1 c. chopped nuts
2 c. maple syrup
1 c. sugar

1/2 c. hot water
3 T. butter

Spread nuts in a buttered pan. Combine syrup, sugar, water and butter. Boil without stirring until mixture gets brittle quickly when dropped into cold water (290°). Pour candy over nuts. When cold break into pieces.

MOLASSES NUT TAFFY

1 c. finely chopped nuts
1 1/2 c. sugar
1/2 c. molasses
1 1/2 c. water
2 T. vinegar

1/2 tsp. cream of tarter
1/4 c. butter
1/8 tsp. salt
1/4 tsp. soda

Spread nuts into a well-buttered pan. Boil sugar, molasses, water, vinegar and cream of tarter to hard ball stage (265°). Add butter, salt and soda and pour over nuts. Cool. Pull until stiff and creamy. Cut into 1-inch pieces.

PECAN ROLL

2 c. sugar
1 c. brown sugar
1/2 c. corn syrup

1 c. cream or evaporated milk
1 1/2 c. pecans, chopped

Bring sugars, syrup and milk to a boil over high heat then boil slowly to 234°. Cool to lukewarm (110°). Beat until creamy. Turn out on a board covered with powdered sugar. Knead until firm then shape into a roll. Cover outside with pecans. Chill. Slice with a sharp knife.

PEANUT BRITTLE

2 c. sugar
1 c. white corn syrup
3/4 c. water
1/8 tsp. salt

2 T. butter
1 tsp. soda
2 c. peanuts

Cook sugar, syrup, water and salt, stirring only until sugar is dissolved. Add butter. Cook without stirring to 290° or to soft crack stage. Quickly stir in soda and nuts. Spread in a thin sheet on a well-buttered baking sheet. Do not scrape the bottom and sides of saucepan. Break into pieces when cool.

PENUCHE
A candy resembling fudge.

2 c. brown sugar
1/2 c. cream or evaporated
   milk
2 T. butter

1 tsp. vanilla
1/8 tsp. salt
1 c. chopped nuts

Combine sugar, cream and butter. Boil to soft ball stage (234°). Remove from heat. Cool to lukewarm. Add remaining ingredients and beat until creamy. Pour into a well-buttered pan. One half cup coconut may be substituted for 1/2 c. nuts. Store in tight container.

POPCORN SNOWMAN

This recipe was clipped from a newspaper dated December 3, 1949. It was found with Grandma Hoover's recipes. This can also be used as plain popcorn balls.

1 c. light brown sugar
1 c. white corn syrup
1/4 c. water
1/4 tsp. salt

3 T. butter
1 tsp. vanilla
4 qt. popped corn, unsalted

Mix brown sugar, corn syrup, water and salt in 3-quart saucepan. Cook over medium heat, stirring constantly, until mixture boils. Boil gently until a small amount of syrup forms a hard ball in cold water (265°). Remove from heat and add butter and vanilla. Stir thoroughly. Pour slowly over popped corn, mix with wooden spoon.

For snowman, shape candied corn while warm into 3 balls—one 3-inches in diameter (head), one 4-inches in diameter (body), and one 6-inches in diameter (base). Fashion arms into cylinder shapes about 4-inches long and 2-inches in diameter. Press into snowman form, using a portion of the candy mixture. Attach arms to the body after removing a portion of corn for the armholes. Use raisins or cranberries for eyes, nose and mouth. A red crepe hat will complete him.

GRANDMA'S

RASPBERRY JAM

Weigh equal quantities of fruit and
sugar. Put the former in a preserving pan,
boil and break it, stir constantly, and let it
boil very quickly. When most of the juice is
wasted, add the sugar, and simmer half an hour.
This way the jam is greatly superior in color and
flavor to that which is made by putting the
sugar in first.

MISCELLANEOUS

HOMEMADE CRACKERS

5 1/2 c. flour   1/2 c. lard or butter
1 tsp. salt   water
3/4 tsp. soda

Combine dry ingredients. Mix with lard or butter working in well as for pie crust. Add enough cold water to make a stiff dough. Beat with the rolling pin for 20 minutes, then roll out like pie crust. Cut into squares and prick with a fork. Bake at 350° until light brown.

Note: If beating with the rolling pin seems overwhelming, just knead the dough for awhile.

WHEAT CRACKERS

2 c. whole wheat flour   2 T. shortening
1/2 tsp. salt   cold water
1 tsp. sugar

Combine dry ingredients. Work in shortening. Add enough cold water to make a stiff dough. Roll very thin on a floured surface. Place on a buttered baking sheet and prick all over with a fork. Bake in a hot oven (400°) until a delicate brown.

GRAHAM CRACKERS

1 c. brown sugar   1 tsp. baking powder
1/2 c. shortening   1/2 tsp. soda
1 tsp. vanilla   1/4 tsp. salt
2 c. whole wheat flour   1/4 c. milk
1 c. flour

Cream sugar and shortening. Add vanilla. Combine dry ingredients and add alternately with milk. Chill overnight. Turn out on a floured board. Roll 1/8-inch thick. Cut into squares. Bake at 350° until crisp and golden brown, 10-12 minutes.

GRANDMA HORST'S
OATMEAL CRACKERS

1 1/2 c. oatmeal	1 1/2 tsp. baking powder
1 c. whole wheat flour	1/2 tsp. salt
1 T. sugar	1/3 c. cooking oil

Combine ingredients. Chill dough. Roll 1/8-inch thick. Cut into squares. Bake at 350° until crisp golden brown.

GRANDMA HORST'S
SOY CRACKERS

1 1/2 c. soy flour	1/2 c. water
1 1/2 c. cornmeal	1/4 c. oil
2 eggs	

Mix soy flour and cornmeal. Beat eggs and add water and oil. Stir until dough forms a ball. Pinch off pieces and shape into 1-inch balls. Place on a greased baking sheet and flatten. Bake at 325° for 10-12 minutes.

GRANDMA HORST'S
PICKLE RECIPE
This recipe was in grandma's handwritten cookbook, entitled "My own Pickle Recipe".

1 c. sugar	1 onion, chopped
1 c. vinegar	2 qt. sliced or chunked
1/2 tsp. salt	cucumbers
2 tsp. pickling spice	water

Combine first 4 ingredients. Pour over onions and cucumbers. Add enough water to cover cucumbers. Let stand several hours or over night. Heat to boiling very slowly. Pack into jars. Process in a boiling water canner for 10 minutes.

GRANDMA HORST'S
RHUBARB JAM

5 c. diced rhubarb
4 c. sugar

1/2 c. water
6 oz. box strawberry gelatin

Cook rhubarb, sugar and water five minutes. Stir in gelatin. Quickly fill jars and process in a boiling water canner for 5 minutes.

GRANDMA KULP'S
APPLE BUTTER

The aunt who gave this recipe mentioned they started making the apple butter at 5:00 a.m. They also had neighborhood "snitzings" the evening before to get the apples ready.

20 gal. apple cider
8 gal. quartered apples

15 lb. sugar
cinnamon

Use a large 30-40 gallon copper kettle. Heat cider to boiling and cook until half the starting volume. Add half of the apples and cook until soft. Add the remaining apples and cook until soft, stirring frequently. Add sugar and cinnamon and cook constantly to prevent burning. Cook until the cooled apple butter is a good spreading consistency. Butter may be added to prevent boiling over.

GRANDMA HORST'S
MUENSTER CHEESE

2 gal. milk
1 c. buttermilk
1 1/2 T. salt

3 junket (rennet) tablets
1/4 c. cold water

Heat milk and buttermilk to 86°. Dissolve rennet in cold water and add to milk. Let stand one hour. Cut into 1/2-inch squares and drain off whey. Add salt to the curds and put in cheese press for 24 hours. Eat fresh or refrigerate two weeks.

GRANDMA MARTINS
MINCE MEAT PIE FILLING

3 qt. ground or finely chopped, roasted and cooled chuck roast	6 oranges ground (use peeling and all)
	1 qt. apple juice or cider
3 qt. raisins	2 tsp. cinnamon
7 qt. shredded apples	2 tsp. cloves
3 qt. brown sugar	1 tsp. ginger

Mix all ingredients. Heat to boiling then simmer until apples and raisins are soft. Finished filling can be canned or frozen.

CANNED BEEF AND CHICKEN

Pack uniform pieces of raw meat loosely into jars, leaving 11/4 inch headspace. Do not add liquid. Add 1 tsp. salt to each quart. Process quarts of beef in a pressure cooker for 90 minutes at 10 pounds of pressure and pints 75 minutes at 10 pounds. Process raw chicken pieces in quarts for 75 minutes and pints for 65 minutes at 10 pounds of pressure. Altitudes above 1000 feet should process meat at 15 pounds.

GRANDMA HORST'S
HOMEMADE SOAP

10 c. warm water	3 T. borax
9 c. melted lard, tallow or cooking oil	1 T. citronella oil
	8 oz. lye
1/2 c. ammonia	

Put warm water in a large container. Add melted fat, ammonia, borax, and citronella oil. Cautiously add lye to the mixture. Let stand for 10-15 minutes. For granular soap begin stirring and stir often until the mixture forms granules. For bar soap pour into flat containers and cut into squares before soap gets too hard. Recipe can also be made without citronella oil.

GRANDMA'S

MARY MARTIN
1892-1963

AMANDA KULP
1900-1985

MYRTLE HOOVER
1903-1992

LYDIA ZIMMERMAN
1908-

HISTORY

Mary (Shaum) Martin
November 11, 1892 - March 2, 1963

Joseph and Elizabeth Shaum were married almost thirty-one years when Elizabeth died in 1890, leaving eight children, ages thirteen to thirty. Her youngest daughter preceded her in death in 1886 at the age of six. In 1891 Joseph remarried, this time to Barbara Berkey Markley, a widow with three children ages two, five and eight. On November 11 of the following year Joseph and Barbara had the only child born to their union. They named her Mary.

At the age of twenty, on June 1, 1913, Mary married twenty-four year old Joseph Eberly Martin, the son of John W. and Susannah Martin. Joseph and Mary moved onto a farm near Wakarusa, Indiana during the era of corduroy roads. Over the years they lived on three farms but always in the same general area. They moved onto their last farm on December 23, 1936 and lived there for 27 years until Mary's death. Joseph and Mary had milk cows, laying hens and raised potatoes. One of Joseph and Mary's daughters remembers her father saying people who lived on a farm should never go hungry.

In 1918 Mary's mother Barbara went to Ohio to visit her sons, Mary's half brothers. While there she became quite ill so Mary, with her small baby took the train to help care for her. Joseph came later with their three preschool daughters. As mother Barbara lay dying she spoke of angels singing. Mary and those with her said they too heard and saw angels.

Mary, like her mother, moved quickly. When she went to the cellar, out to the garden, or even from room to room, the children remember her going fast, nearly running.

During the first eleven years of their married life Joseph and Mary had eight children, seven girls and one boy. In those early years when Mary had so many girls to braid for church or school she lined up the girls that knew how to braid hair in order of age. Mary combed and braided the oldest girl while that girl in turn combed the one in front of her and so on down the line. They later had five more boys and four more girls making a total of seventeen children. With such a large family they did some things a bit different. Instead of putting a cup with every plate when setting the table they put a cup between every other plate with two children sharing a cup. Because their seventeen children spanned twenty-four years the entire family only sat around the table once - on Christmas day in 1942.

In 1924 Joseph, like his father before him, was ordained as a minister, then later as a bishop, in the Old Order Mennonite church. This added to his responsibilities and, no doubt, to Mary's as well.

Mary had a community-wide reputation as a good cook. One of her sons writes, "she taught her daughters the art of cooking. In contrast to her husband she was a motivator and organizer. The household generally ran smoothly and she never raised her voice nor became angry, at least not visibly." Mary apparently taught her sons some basic cooking skills as well. A son recalls his mother telling him how to make pancakes. "Watch the bubbles, when they burst and the holes stay open, turn them." He still makes the pancakes in his home. One of Mary's daughters writes, "I have no doubt Mother was an outstanding cook. One thing that stands out to me is how fascinating it was to watch her make pies. They were artistic." She remembers her mother telling her how to make pies. "Use one cup flour per crust, add a little salt..." She had no recipe. Mary told her daughters it usually takes about a cup of sugar to make most pies good. Delicious pies remembered by family and friends include sour cream raisin pies, vanilla pies and open faced apple pies. Because of her large family Mary usually made ten to twelve pies at once. When finished, her daughters carried the pies to the cool basement and set them on the hanging pie shelf. Joseph and Mary didn't have a refrigerator until sometime in the early fifties, after they had electricity in their home. In a room off the kitchen called "es kicha eck" they had a tank with spring water flowing into to it from a hydraulic ram. They put bricks into the water tank to set pots and pans on to keep cool. Later, but before they had the refrigerator, they had an ice box. It looked like a refrigerator but had a compartment at the top on one side large enough to put a hundred pound block of ice into it.

A common Saturday noon meal was pot pie, made with their home canned beef, and green beans and fruit. Saturday supper many times consisted of tomato soup and sugar milk pie. Sunday dinner often included baked beans. On Saturday afternoon or evening one of the children went up to the attic storeroom and got a bowl full of beans out of the one hundred pound bag of beans. Then they poured the beans out on the kitchen table to sort out the bad ones. After washing the beans they soaked them over night. Mary didn't have a written recipe for baked beans. In the morning she either made the beans or told one of the girls how much tomato juice, sorghum molasses, brown sugar, salt and bacon to add to the beans.

A common supper dish was corn pone (corn bread) eaten with fruit, sugar, and milk. Winter evenings they often had cornmeal mush. Sometimes they made a big batch of cornmeal mush and let the leftovers set in bread pans until firm. In the morning they sliced the firm mush and fried it. They ate it with syrup or with sweetened oatmeal thinned with milk. Other breakfast foods included eggs, cooked oatmeal, and graham mush. Sometimes they combined leftover potatoes with chopped onion, bread cubes and eggs and baked it.

In Spring dandelion and rhubarb started the canning season. Mary's children gathered dandelion by the bushel. They also picked mulberries to can with the rhubarb for added flavor. One of Mary's specialties was her delicious hominy. Once when Joseph and Mary and their youngest son went on a trip they stayed with friends in Virginia. Their son had slept late and while eating by himself later on he told the hostess that her hominy wasn't as good as his mother's. In later years Mary sold jars of her hominy at the South Bend Farmer's Market. Sometimes she made hominy cakes for breakfast that the family ate with syrup. In fall when they butchered they also made and canned mincemeat. Thanksgiving dinner usually included roasted chicken and mincemeat pies.

Joseph grew up the eighth child in a family of ten children. When Joseph was five years old his mother died, at thirty-five years of age, giving birth to her stillborn son. Joseph's oldest sister was fifteen and the youngest of the ten children was twenty-one months old. John Martin remarried almost two years later. After the hectic household's succession of hired girls the family no doubt looked forward to good meals again. Unfortunately it didn't happen. The new stepmother was a poor cook. Joseph never allowed his children to complain about their food. He told the children, "if you would have had a mother [his stepmother] like I did, you would not complain about this good food".

The younger children don't remember Mary helping with farm chores, but one of the older girls remembers staying home from school to watch the preschoolers so her mother could help husk corn. As time went on and her health declined she did a lot of cooking, sewing, mending and darning socks while the children did the more active work like cleaning and gardening.

Mary suffered from a heart condition. In 1963 she was admitted to the hospital where she died a short time later. Mary was seventy years old. When she died Mary had 117 living grandchildren. Sixteen more were born after her death. Joseph died in 1974 at 85 years of age.

Ray's
Grandma and Grandpa Martin
Grandma Martin's Family

Joseph Shaum born Jan. 7, 1837 married Elizabeth Gable on Nov. 10, 1859. They had nine children before she died May 22, 1890.

1. Amanda	Sept. 27, 1860	6. Elizabeth	Dec. 18, 1871
2. Annetta	Feb. 28, 1863	7. Emma	Sept. 29, 1874
3. Lydia Ann	Feb. 9, 1865	8. Harvey	Mar. 16, 1877
4. William Henry	Oct. 30, 1867	9. Ida b. Sept. 19, 1879 d. July 28,
5. Isaiah	Feb. 4, 1890	1886

In 1891 Joseph married Barbara Berkey Markley, a widow with three living children.

1. Ephriam Markley	1883	3. Lizzie Markley	1886
2. Maria Markley	1885-1887	4. Isaac Markley	1889

Joseph and Barbara had one child.
1. Mary   **Nov.11, 1892**

Grandpa Martin's Family

John Martin married Susannah Eberly on Dec. 7, 1876. Susannah died during child birth on Dec. 11, 1893.

1. Fannie	Jan. 14, 1878	7. Infant son b. and d. Sept. 28, 1887
2. Elias	Aug. 19, 1879	**8. Joseph**	**Oct. 28, 1888**
3. Levi	Aug. 31, 1881	9. Amanda	Aug. 29, 1890
4. Anna	Jan. 29, 1883	10. William	Mar. 24, 1892
5. Henry	Jan. 23, 1885	11. Stillborn son	Dec. 11, 1893
6. Magdalena	Feb. 25, 1886		

Grandpa and Grandma Martin's Family

Joseph Martin married **Mary Shaum** on June 1, 1913. They had 17 children.

1. Barbara	June 21, 1914	10. Jason	Jan. 23, 1927
2. Susannah	Dec. 14, 1915	11. Edna	Aug. 14, 1928
3. Ida	Feb. 27, 1917	12. Allen	June 2, 1930
4. Emma	July 19, 1918	**13. Miriam**	**Nov. 24, 1931**
5. Daniel	Jan. 18, 1920	14. Rufus	Aug. 14, 1933
6. Bertha	July 6, 1921	15. Rhoda	Apr. 3, 1935
7. Grace	Nov. 19, 1922	16. Suetta	Sept. 15, 1936
8. Ruth	Feb. 24, 1924	17. Benjamin	Aug. 19, 1938
9. Naaman	July 30, 1925		

ONE OF GRANDMA MARTIN'S
HANDWRITTEN RECIPES

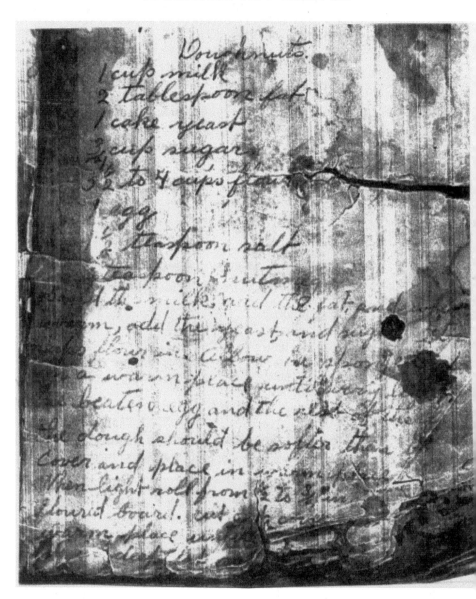

Amanda (Eby) Kulp
February 5, 1900 - June 25, 1985

In 1830 Samuel Eby married an Irish orphan girl. The young couple started a pottery business in Perth County, Ontario called The Eby Pottery. In 1847 Samuel, also known as Potter Sam, died suddenly. He was only 42 years old. Samuel's oldest son William eventually took over the business, moved it to a new location in Canada, and called it Conestogo Pottery. The family worked together and had a thriving business.

In 1890 Cyrus, William's fourth son, married Elizabeth Brubacher. Eight years later Cyrus, Elizabeth and their three young children left Canada and moved to a farm near Brutus, Michigan. Two years after arriving in Michigan their fourth child, Amanda, was born. Amanda remained the baby of the family for six years until she had a sister. Five years later a little boy completed the family of three boys and three girls.

Tragedy struck when Amanda was thirteen years old. One June morning her father Cyrus woke Amanda and her siblings and told them mother died during the night. About four years later Amanda's father married Susannah Martin, a widow from Canada. Susannah had a son that also came to live in Amanda's home. The new mother and son fit well into the Cyrus Eby home.

At age 24 Amanda married Mannasseh Brubacher Kulp, a 22 year old from the Old Order Mennonite church Amanda attended. Mannasseh's mother had also died when he was thirteen but his stepmother didn't mesh as well as Amanda's had. She did not want Mannasseh to live with them so, according to custom in such cases, they sent him to live wherever they needed a farmhand. One of the families Mannasseh liked to stay with boarded two other children also ousted by new spouses.

Over the next sixteen years Mannasseh and Amanda had five boys and four girls, however, with one son stillborn they raised only eight children to maturity. In 1936 Amanda, expecting their sixth child, became very ill and lapsed into a coma for a week. Not long afterward, she gave birth to twin daughters. She gradually recovered but was never quite the same after that. Amanda's oldest daughter, though only seven, fell heir to much of the housework after the twins joined the family. Amanda just did what had to be done. All the girls learned to take a lot of responsibility at a young age.

Mannasseh and Amanda had ten to twelve dairy cows and grew navy beans as a cash crop. They raised produce which they took by horse and wagon to Harbor Springs, MI. They also tapped their maple trees, cooking sap in a big pan in the sugar shanty in the sugar bush. One day when the school children came to watch, Amanda made maple syrup taffy, then dribbled it over a dish pan full of snow. The children took turns winding the delicious treat around their forks.

In January of 1942, after the church they attended disbanded, Mannasseh and Amanda moved their family to a dairy farm in the Old Order Mennonite community in northern Indiana. Their last child was born about a year and a half after the move.

While still living in Michigan, Amanda's stepmother, Susannah, lived with them until she died in 1934. Her father Cyrus spent the last two months of his life with them in Indiana. He died in their home in 1951.

Mannasseh's father, a double amputee, lived in a very small house at the end of Mannasseh and Amanda's lane in Michigan. He had a shoe repair business and sold shoe laces, candy and gum. They strung a wire with a bell between the two houses so he could ring for help if needed. Several months after Mannasseh and Amanda moved to Indiana he came to live with them. They built a wooden ramp so they could get him in and out of the house on his wheel chair. He lived in their home almost a year before his death in April of 1943.

Amanda didn't help with the milking after they moved to Indiana, or even do much household cleaning, but fed her chickens and cleaned and packed the eggs. During the winter she warmed five-gallon pails of mash by her stove for the chickens. She used sandpaper wrapped around a block of wood to clean the eggs. One daughter said they tried not to get between mother and her light source because, "here comes the sander, fast!"

Her older children don't remember her working in the garden much but she did some in her later years. One of the younger sons remembers his mother putting a rhubarb leaf under her sunbonnet to keep her head cool as she worked in the garden.

Amanda Kulp was a very basic cook. A daughter said of her, "she wasn't the best cook. She cooked so we could eat and be filled". Another daughter wrote, "mother cooked more or less as a matter of survival, but did it willingly. It was something she could do while we did other things."

Amanda and the girls often made rivel soup, navy bean soup, or cooked navy beans that they ate with graham gems (whole wheat muffins). They grew their own wheat, roasted it in the oven then had it ground at a local mill. Another staple was corn pone (corn bread) often eaten with milk and sugar. The family ate a wide variety of vegetables including red beets, parsnips and salsify. In Spring they made dandelion salad and also canned dandelion. Raw fried potatoes were served with tomato gravy or applesauce. They made cottage cheese and, like most other farm women, churned their own butter. Amanda had a glass butter churn set on a platform that the children took turns cranking. When they tired she cheered them on by telling them the butter is saying, "bol butta, bol butta, bol butta", (almost butter, almost butter.). In later years one of the younger daughters remembers taking a two quart jar with cream in it out under the pear tree and shaking the jar until the cream turned into butter.

Desserts were basic too. Common desserts included baked custard, baked apples, baked rice pudding, applesauce cake and fruit. In the spring they thickened sweetened cooked rhubarb with tapioca. They didn't have pies often, but had rhubarb pies in spring and apple, elderberry, grape and pumpkin pies in fall. For a special treat the children put brown sugar on a piece of bread then soaked it with cream. Sometimes on winter Sunday mornings or on Christmas morning they had hot cocoa. " On holidays", writes one of the daughters, "we did nothing special, except for a devotional period from dad."

A memory the children have of home is going to sleep hearing their parents singing together. One song they often sang was "Build it Well", a song about building character pleasing to God.

In 1964 Mannesseh and Amanda moved into a small house built near the farmhouse. They lived there for thirteen years. Then in the summer of 1977 they had their house jacked up, set on a moving dolly, and pulled 7 miles northwest to a daughter and son-in-law's farm. They connected the little house to the big farmhouse for easy access.

Mannaseh died in July of 1982 at the age of 80. Amanda died three years later in June of 1985. She was 85 years old.

Elsie's
Grandma and Grandpa Kulp

Grandma Kulp's Family

Cyrus Eby married Elizabeth Brubacher in 1890. They had six children before Elizabeth died June 11, 1913.

1. Jeremiah	Aug. 2, 1891	**4. Amanda**	**Feb. 5, 1900**
2. Susannah	Sept. 10, 1895	5. Lydia Ann	Sept. 27, 1906
3. Israel	July 3, 1897	6. William	May 1, 1911

Cyrus married Susannah Martin, a widow from Canada in 1917. She had a son.

1. Mahlon Martin   Mar. 18, 1912

Grandpa Kulp's Family

In April of 1900 Isaac Kulp married Barbara Brubacher. They had two children.

Infant daughter
Mannasseh   **May 5, 1902**

Grandpa and Grandma Kulp's family

Mannasseh Kulp married Amanda Eby on Nov. 4, 1924. They had nine children.

1. Paul	Aug. 1, 1927	6. Lydia Ann(twin)	Mar. 11, 1936
2. Rachel	Jan. 30, 1929	7. Lena Ann (twin)	Mar. 11, 1936
3.Titus (stillborn)	Nov. 1, 1930	8. Cyrus	June 28, 1941
4. Mary Ann	July 31, 1932	9. Reuben	June 13. 1943
5.Isaac	**Nov. 8, 1934**		

ONE OF GRANDMA KULP'S
HANDWRITTEN RECIPES

Fork Cookies:

2 cups brown sugar
1¼ cups shortening
2 eggs
1 teaspoon soda,
1 teaspoon cream tartar
1 teaspoon vanilla.
4 cups flour.
Roll in tiny balls and
put on cookie tray and
press with fork.

Myrtle (Good) Hoover
November 7, 1903 - July 22, 1992

Two days before Christmas in 1902, Benjamin Good married May Rohrer. They moved onto a farm near Dalton, OH. On November 7 of the following year their first child, Myrtle, arrived. A month before Myrtle's second birthday her mother May had a set of twins; a boy and a girl. The little boy died the same day. Shortly before Myrtle turned four her father Benjamin was chosen by lot and ordained as a minister in the Mennonite church. More excitement and more responsibility entered their lives when, two weeks after Myrtle's fifth birthday, May gave birth to another set of twins. Both were boys and both survived. During the next eight years three more boys joined the family. Then, on November 20, 1918, almost sixteen years after her marriage to Benjamin, at the age of forty-one, May died giving birth to another little boy. The baby also died.

Fifteen year old Myrtle and her thirteen year old sister now found themselves the primary caretakers of five younger brothers ages two to ten. Two years after the death of her mother, Myrtle's father married a twenty-eight year old single lady, Martha Hoover. Myrtle's father and Martha had three girls, the last of which was born after Myrtle had already left home.

After her father's second marriage the family got better acquainted with their stepmother's parents as well as her five brothers. Eventually Myrtle and Paul, one of her stepmother's younger brothers, started writing letters. On the sixth of November of 1929, one day before Myrtle's twenty-sixth birthday and two weeks before Paul's twenty-fifth birthday, Myrtle married her "uncle" and her father became her brother-in-law. Shortly before their wedding Paul bought a new Chevy Touring car. They not only used it for their wedding trip to Pennsylvania, but also used it as a family car for the next eleven years.

Some time, probably when Myrtle got married, her stepmother wrote some recipes into a maroon colored hard cover 1928 diary. The recipes have lists of ingredients but few instructions. Later Myrtle added recipes of her own to the small book.

After their wedding trip they went to Five Points, Indiana and moved in with Paul's parents, William and Emma Hoover. They made some changes in the big farmhouse, making another kitchen for his parents and his two brothers that still lived at home. The downstairs bedroom, because of its proximity to the new kitchen, became his parents' dining room and the parlor became their bedroom. Paul and Myrtle had the main kitchen, living room, large entry way, a storage room and some of the upstairs bedrooms. They shared the bathroom with his parents and brothers.

Paul and Myrtle had a dairy farm with Guernsey cows. In the early forties they started a herd of registered cows. They also raised potatoes to sell for close to thirty years and consquently named their farm Spudridge Farm. In the early years, as a supplemental income, they did some butchering, selling pork and chicken in Goshen and Elkhart.

About a year after Paul and Myrtle's marriage they had their first child. When the baby, a boy, was eight months old Paul, like Myrtle's father, was also chosen by lot and ordained as a minister in the Mennonite Church. Paul and Myrtle had four more boys but their third son lived only one day. When, in 1942, Myrtle finally had a daughter she named the baby May, in remembrance of her mother, who had died almost twenty-four years earlier. Another little girl, born three years later, completed the family.

Four months after the birth of their last child Paul's father, William, died. Along with the care of her own children Myrtle increasingly helped her mother-in-law Emma, until Emma died in 1951, six years after her husband. Paul's youngest brother lived with them almost seven years before getting married in 1935. Lewis, one of Paul's older brothers, lived with them until his death in 1970. Lewis had polio as a young child and as a result had a paralyzed shoulder and arm. He had minimal use of his left hand.

Not only did Paul and Myrtle have extended family living with them the first forty years of their married life, they also, over a twenty-five year period, had one hundred and twenty Oaklawn patients stay at their place. Oaklawn, a mental health care facility, would bus patients out to participating community homes for supper, the night and breakfast with some patients staying over the weekend. Myrtle too, over the many years they raised potatoes, made dinner, six days a week, for ten to twenty people that helped pick up potatoes. This lasted about a month each Fall. Other extra people in their home included Goshen College students who stayed with them on two separate occasions. They also had several out-of-state 1W boys stay at their place while doing alternate service at the Elkhart Hospital. As a minister's wife Myrtle often had out-of-state visitors coming. Spur of the moment company didn't surprise Myrtle. It was not unusual for Paul to invite to dinner the milkman, a salesman, or whoever happened to come to the door around mealtime. Despite all the cooking she did a daughter writes, " I think she liked to cook. I can't ever remember her saying, 'Oh dear, what shall we have for supper.' "

According to her children Myrtle was a good cook, but a basic one; also health conscious. She served a lot of vegetables and if they had meat for dinner that was it for the day. Myrtle didn't make ham or pork other than a little bacon used for seasoning. She often used less sugar than recipes called for if it didn't alter the end result. She made her pies without crumbs or crusts on top.

Myrtle baked her own bread and, especially in later years, made a lot of yogurt. For Thanksgiving or Christmas she often served a delicious stuffing with roasted chicken or turkey. Christmas treats included fruit candy with chocolate on both sides, as well as corn flake candy. Common company desserts were pumpkin custard with graham cracker crumbs and whipped cream, and graham cracker fluff.

Myrtle had a big garden and loved to work in it. She always planted both red and yellow tomatoes. If visitors came during the summer they found a dish of red and yellow tomatoes on the table. Grandchildren enjoyed her fresh strawberries and raspberries. One of the daughters wrote, "we always ate what was in season. Strawberries three times a day for three weeks - apples, peaches, watermelon, muskmelon. We never opened a canned jar of anything until winter." In the fall they left the carrots in the garden and covered them with a thick layer of leaves. All winter long, whenever they wanted carrots, someone went out and dug some.

Paul and Myrtle had a number of apple trees. They used windfall apples to make cider which they sold to friends and neighbors. In their earlier years they made apple butter outside in big copper kettles.

In 1972 Paul and Myrtle moved into a house an eighth of a mile down the road. Their youngest son and his wife moved onto the home farm. For the next ten or so years she walked to the farm whenever she could to help with chores. She kept this up until, in her late seventies, she fell and broke a rib. Even then she didn't mention the pain until one of her sons noticed she didn't act right. When asked why she didn't say anything about it she said Paul (who wasn't feeling well just then) had enough trouble and she didn't want to add to it.

In 1983 Myrtle was hospitalized and seriously ill with congestive heart failure. She recovered. Five years later she was hospitalized again but soon discharged. The doctor said he couldn't do much for such a weak and worn out heart. He sent her home with several medications and told her to take it easy. Myrtle loved flowers and actually improved enough to work in her flower beds again, even pushing a heavy wheelbarrow around.

Myrtle died on July 22, 1992 at eighty-nine. She and Paul had been married for sixty-three years. Shortly after Myrtle's death Paul wrote the following poem. He died in August of 1997.

Alone

Oh, the house, it seems so silent.
There's the old familiar chair,
But the presence of a loved one
I can see no longer there.

When I need to run an errand
To the bank or Family Fare,
The familiar voice is silent
That would go with me there.

And when the day is over,
And I kneel in silent prayer,
As I reach my hand beside me,
A loved one is no longer there.

But there is a home in Glory
For which we all should prepare,
And it seems I hear her singing
With the angels over there.

W. Paul Hoover

Ray's
Grandma and Grandpa Hoover

Grandma Hoover's Family

Benjamin Good married May Rohrer on Dec. 23, 1902. They had nine children before she died on Nov. 20, 1918.

1. Myrtle	**Nov. 7, 1903**	6. Henry Jason	Mar. 21, 1911
2. Bertha (twin)	Oct. 7, 1905	7. Heber	Jan. 13, 1914
3.Infant son(twin)	Oct. 8, 1905	8. Elmer	Jun. 9, 1916
4. Willis (twin)	Nov. 23, 1908	9. Alvin	b. and d. Nov. 20, 1918
5. Willard (twin)	Nov. 23, 1908		

On Nov. 25, 1920 Benjamin married Martha Hoover. They had three children.

1. Emma Ruth	May 16, 1925	3. Anna Miriam	Apr. 27, 1931
2. Mary Catherine	May 13, 1927		

Grandpa Hoover's Family

William Hoover married Emma Shaum on Aug. 27, 1889. They had six children.

1. Warren Dennis	June 5, 1890	4. John Maynard	July 16, 1900
2. Martha Edna	Sept. 5, 1892	**5. William Paul**	**Nov. 20, 1904**
3. Lewis Ruskin	May 4, 1895	6. George Edward	July 26, 1906

Grandma and Grandpa Hoover's Family

Myrtle Good married W. Paul Hoover on Nov. 6, 1929. They had seven children.

1. David	**Sept. 19, 1930**	4. Marion Paul	Nov. 19, 1937
2. Elvin	Feb. 1, 1933	5. Clarence	June 11, 1940
3. James -died the next day-		6. May Elizabeth	Oct. 15, 1942
	Mar. 7, 1935	7. Rhoda Arlene	July 28, 1945

ONE OF GRANDMA HOOVER'S
HANDWRITTEN RECIPES

mothers Brown

sugar Cookies

FEBRUARY 10   **FRIDAY**

2 cups Brown sugar
1 egg
1 cup sour milk
1 " shortening
1 teaspoon soda
1 " " baking powder
1 teaspoon nutmeg (optional)
Flour to make soft dough

FEBRUARY 11   **SATURDAY**

Butterscotch cookies
1 lb dark brown sugar
3 eggs
2 teaspoons vanilla
1 cup soft butter or margarine
2½ cups unsifted allpurpose flour
2 ² cups nuts raisins May be
substituted

February 10—1899—President McKinley signed the peace treaty with Spain.
1916—Demand for an eight-hour day law made by representatives of 400,000 railway employees meeting at Cleveland.
February 11—1889—Bill creating U. S. Department of Agriculture approved.
1892—United States millers contributed 4,500,000 pounds of flour to Russian peasants.

25

NOTES

Lydia (Zimmerman) Horst
October 19, 1908 -

In November of 1907 Abram Zimmerman married Lizzie Shirk, the granddaughter of Joseph Shirk, the inventor/surveyor. Abram and Lizzie had six sons and five daughters. One son died in early childhood. As the oldest of this large family my grandmother, Lydia, learned to work early in life. Along with their work the family also had fun times.

One of Lydia's not-so-fun early childhood memories is lying on the kitchen table while the doctor stood over her with shiny tools. The doctor anesthetized her with ether. She still carries a scar on her ribcage where the doctor made an incision to drain an abscess. He also removed a piece of rib.

Lydia's childhood home bordered the town of Terre Hill, PA. A trolley car came out almost to their farm. Lydia and her family would sometimes take the trolley to surrounding towns. If still in town by evening they would see the lamplighter going from street lamp to street lamp with a can of kerosene. By morning the lamps burned out; in the evening the lamplighter started his rounds again.

Lydia enjoyed school. She liked history and geography best.

The winter after Lydia turned 21 she worked in a garment factory in Terre Hill. They lived close enough that she could walk to work. The following winter, on December 2, 1930, she married 22 year old Barton Martin Horst, the son of Henry and Barbara Horst. Barton's father, Henry was a minister in the Old Order Mennonite Church where both Barton and Lydia had their membership.

After their marriage they moved into a second house on Barton's parents' farm. Their three oldest children were born while living on this farm. A few years later Barton's youngest brother married and took over the home farm so they had to move on.

They found a farm on the edge of Terre Hill, close to Lydia's childhood home. Seven of their thirteen children were born while they lived here. Though Barton and Lydia spent almost the first decade of their marriage living during the Great Depression they didn't feel the effects very much because they lived simply, thriftily, and raised their own food.

When their two oldest children were in sixth and eighth grade Lydia's father had a farm available close to Akron, a town about ten miles away. Barton and Lydia decided to take it. One reason for the move was that the childrens' town friends spent so much time on the farm after school that it kept their children from house and farm chores.

Barton and Lydia and their family spent only a year or so on the Akron farm before moving onto a farm close to Bowmansville. They bought the eighty six acre farm from Barton's father for twelve thousand dollars.

Barton and Lydia lived on this farm close to twenty years. They raised steers and pigs to sell, and grew cash crops, mostly tobacco. They had horses for work and transportation and always kept a cow or two and some chickens. Avid trappers, hunters and fishermen Barton and Lydia's boys enjoyed the woods and the big creek that ran through their land. They also enjoyed collecting arrow heads from the fields.

Barton and Lydia weren't wealthy but they always had enough and willingly shared with the less fortunate. Bums, as they were called then, always felt welcome. Barton would make straw beds for them in the barn. As a fire precaution he asked for their matches in the evening then returned them in the morning. The homeless wanderers offered to sharpen scissors or chop wood in return for lodging, supper and breakfast. Barton and Lydia's children remember their mother calling upstairs on various occasions, "time to get up, there's someone here that wants to eat".

The big farmhouse on their farm was made of red sandstone. Down a hill, but close to the house, stood a smaller two story sandstone structure called a springhouse. The lowest story of the springhouse had a large cement trough at one end. From a pipe protruding from one end came a constant flow of cold spring water. Lydia and her girls covered dishes of food they wanted to keep cool and floated them on the water. During the winter, instead of running to the springhouse, they kept food cold by setting it in their unheated enclosed porch. They didn't get an ice box until years later when they moved off the farm and didn't have a springhouse.

Lydia liked to cook. A daughter says, "Mom was a good cook, putting a pinch of salt in fruit desserts, pies and drinks to bring out the flavor. She also used lemon juice to perk up different dishes."

Always health conscious, Lydia made whole grain bread instead of white and served a lot of vegetables. She did, however, use plenty of butter and cream in cooking and baking. Lydia baked pies and cookies more often than cakes. Though a good cook she wasn't elaborate. One daughter wrote, "cooking was mostly based on what could be raised on the farm and what was nutritious and not expensive".

With milk and cream from their cows Lydia and the girls churned butter and made cottage cheese, soda cheese and rolls of cheese. They made the rolls of cheese with rennet or cheese enzymes then aged them six weeks in a glass show case in the cellar. Buttermilk and cream that soured went into baked goods. Pigs got the extra skimmed milk and the whey left from draining curds.

Along with canning fruits and vegetables Lydia and her daughters also dried corn and beans. They cooked the corn and beans then spread them on framed screens and laid the full screens out on a hot metal roof to hasten drying. When they wanted to eat the dried vegetables they soaked them in the morning then cooked them for supper, sometimes adding bacon to the beans. They also dried apple slices.

The family ate a lot of potatoes, usually cooked in skins or baked. Lydia would tell her children, "the vitamins are right under the skin, if you peel them you don't get the nutrition you do otherwise". Another common dish was noodles served with browned butter and saffron. Homemade ice cream was a treat they all enjoyed. The ice truck passed their lane once a week. Whenever they wanted the truck to stop they hung a red cloth on their mailbox. The iceman carried the large blocks of ice on his leather protected shoulder. If not ready to make ice cream the day the ice block came they put it in the barn; covering it with feed bags and packing hay around it, so it wouldn't melt before they used it. Pretzels too were a treat. Lydia occasionally bought a five gallon tin of pretzels when the pretzel man came around. She placed the tin beside the cookstove to keep the pretzels crisp.

In the early years, after wheat harvest they emptied straw ticks and refilled them with fresh straw. The children enjoyed their high fluffy beds before the mattresses gradually flattened again.

In Fall Lydia told the younger girls to gather hickory nuts and black walnuts from the trees along the field lane for her yearly baking needs. They gathered nuts as they walked home from school. Lydia made delicious cakes with the nut pieces. They saved the halves to press on top of cookies.

Each year when cold weather set in they butchered a steer. Because Barton and Lydia never had a freezer (they never had electricity) they had to can their meat. Occasionally they made dried beef. Fresh roasts were available only at butchering time; but since they gave the neighbors fresh roasts and the neighbors then returned the favor when they butchered, each family enjoyed roast beef more often.

When the young chickens started laying, their old hens made hearty winter evening eating. Lydia and the girls generally boiled or roasted the hens. They canned chicken as well. Another winter evening meal was cornmeal mush eaten with sugar and milk. To make the cornmeal they roasted ears of corn in their wood cooking stove. After shelling it they took it to a neighbor to have it ground.

Gardening was Lydia's favorite work. She had grapes and a large blueberry patch. She liked working with trees too. Another hobby Lydia enjoyed after she didn't have little children was beekeeping. She often served comb honey with her whole wheat bread. Lydia also did some woodworking. Using a hand saw, hammer and nails she made a table and a corner cupboard.

In 1964 when their youngest son got married Barton and Lydia moved into a small house they built at the end of their farm lane. They lived there until Barton died in June of 1989. Lydia stayed alone until September of 1991 when she had a disbursement sale and moved in briefly with one of her sisters. Since then she lived with her children, staying two or three month with each, sometimes longer. Lydia is 94. Time has taken its toll on both her mind and body, but she is in relatively good health.

In speaking of her parents one daughter said, "they were not what we'd call well-to-do in our days and they worked hard to make a living off the farm. Their main goal in life, I believe, was not an aim to gain a lot of earthly possessions, but to bring their family up in the fear of the Lord in concern for their never dying souls".

Elsie's
Grandma and Grandpa Horst

Grandma Horst's Family

Abram Zimmerman married Lizzie Shirk on Nov. 28, 1907. They had eleven children.

1. Lydia	**Oct. 19,1908**	6. John	Jul. 22, 1918
2. Lena	Jan. 25, 1910	7. Lizzie	Jun. 22, 1920
3. Weaver	Oct. 25, 1911	8. Joseph	Dec. 13, 1921
4. Aaron	Jul. 22, 1913	9. Mary Anna	May 20, 1924
5. Abram b. Dec. 8, 1915 d. Jun. 27, 1916		10. Mabel	Oct. 20, 1926
		11. Harvey	Nov. 11, 1929

Grandpa Horst's Family

Henry Horst married Barbara Martin. They had twelve children.

1. Rufus	Sept. 20, 1893	7. Barbara	Dec. 16, 1902
2. Harvey	Oct. 1, 1894	8. Mahlon (twin)	Jun. 30, 1904
3. Martha	Dec. 27, 1895	9. Milton (twin)	Jun. 30, 1904
4. Lea	Aug. 6, 1897	10. Anna	Jan. 20, 1906
5. Henry	Feb. 10, 1899	**11.Barton**	**Dec. 23, 1907**
6. Phares	Jun. 16, 1900	12. Adam	May 25, 1910

Grandma and Grandpa Horst's Family

Barton Horst married Lydia Zimmerman on Dec. 2, 1930. They had thirteen children.

1. Amos	Oct. 14, 1931	8. Ella	Jan. 11, 1942
2. Florence	**Aug. 18, 1933**	9. James	Apr. 16, 1943
3. Melvin	Sept. 10, 1934	10. Elsie	Aug. 11, 1944
4. Sarah	Sept. 24, 1935	11. Laura	May 9, 1946
5. Edwin	Apr. 7, 1937	12. Lydia Ann	Nov. 15, 1948
6. Vera	Jan. 21, 1939	13. Miriam	Feb. 12, 1952
7. Ida	May 22, 1940		

SOME OF GRANDMA HORST"S HANDWRITTEN RECIPES

Jelly Roll

4 eggs seperated   beat yolks till thick
1 cup sugar   with 1/4 cup water
1 .. c flour   fold in beaten egg
1 tesp. baking powder   whites last.
   salt flavor (for chocolate add 1/4 cup
     cocoa to flour

White Cake

2 3/4 cup four   2/3 cup lard
4 tesp baking powd: 1 1/4 " milk
1 .. salt   4 egg whites unbeaten
1 1/2 cup sugar   2 tesp vanilla 1/2 almond

Carmel Cake

Cream 2 cup brown sugar with 1/2
cup butter. add add 2 eggs 2 cup flour
vanilla put 1 tesp. cocoa in cup add
2 tesp. hot water and fill cup with
sour milk 1 tesp soda stir mix
with ~~dry~~ other ingredients.

NOTES

INDEX

INDEX

Other cookbooks available by Ray and Elsie Hoover:

The Basics and More Cookbook

The Practical Produce Cookbook

Order Form

Shipping Address:

name _____

street address _____

city, state zip code _____

TITLE	AMOUNT	QUANTITY	TOTAL
Grandma's Recipes	$11.95		
The Basics and More Cookbook	$12.95		
The Practical Produce Cookbook	$12.95		
		Subtotal	
	Shipping and Handling $2.50 per book		
		Subtotal	
	Wisconsin Residents add 5.5% tax		
		order total	

Send order to: Ray and Elsie Hoover
EP 4230 March Rapids Ave.
Stratford, WI   54484

Phone   715-687-4558

Or order on line: BasicCookbooks.com
toll free   1-866-385-0242